T0386719

A

Sir Frederick Roberts.

THE AFGHAN WARS

1839-42 AND 1878-80

BY

ARCHIBALD FORBES

With Portraits and Plans

DARF PUBLISHERS LTD
London
1987

First Published 1892

New Impression 1987

ISBN 1 85077 902 3

Printed by LR Printing Services Ltd, Crawley, England.

CONTENTS

PART I.—THE FIRST AFGHAN WAR

PART II.—THE SECOND AFGHAN WAR

LIST OF ILLUSTRATIONS AND PLANS

*⁎⁎⁎ The Portraits of Sir G. Pollock and Sir F. Roberts are engraved by permission
of Messrs Henry Graves & Co.*

The First Afghan War

THE AFGHAN WARS

PART I

THE FIRST AFGHAN WAR

CHAPTER I

PRELIMINARY

SINCE it was the British complications with Persia which mainly furnished what pretext there was for the invasion of Afghanistan by an Anglo-Indian army in 1839, some brief recital is necessary of the relations between Great Britain and Persia prior to that aggression.

By a treaty, concluded between England and Persia in 1814, the former state bound itself, in case of the invasion of Persia by any European nation, to aid the Shah either with troops from India or by the payment of an annual subsidy in support of his war expenses. It was a dangerous engagement, even with the *caveat* rendering the undertaking inoperative if such invasion should be provoked by Persia.   During the fierce struggle of 1825-7, between Abbas Meerza and the Russian General Paskevitch, England refrained from supporting Persia either with men or with money, and when prostrate Persia was in financial extremities because of the war indemnity which the treaty of Turkmanchai imposed upon her,

England took advantage of her needs by purchasing the cancellation of the inconvenient obligation at the cheap cost of about £300,000. It was the natural result of this transaction that English influence with the Persian Court should sensibly decline, and it was not less natural that in conscious weakness Persia should fall under the domination of Russian influence.

Futteh Ali, the old Shah of Persia, died in 1834, and was succeeded by his grandson Prince Mahomed Meerza, a young man who inherited much of the ambition of his gallant father Abbas Meerza. His especial aspiration, industriously stimulated by his Russian advisers, urged him to the enterprise of conquering the independent principality of Herat, on the western border of Afghanistan. Herat was the only remnant of Afghan territory that still remained to a member of the legitimate royal house. Its ruler was Shah Kamran, son of that Mahmoud Shah who, after ousting his brother Shah Soojah from the throne of Cabul, had himself been driven from that elevation, and had retired to the minor principality of Herat. The young Shah of Persia was not destitute of justification for his designs on Herat. That this was so was frankly admitted by Mr Ellis, the British envoy to his Court, who wrote to his Government that the Shah had fair claim to the sovereignty of Afghanistan as far as Ghuznee, and that Kamran's conduct in occupying part of the Persian province of Seistan had given the Shah 'a full justification for commencing hostilities against Herat.'

The serious phase of the situation for England and India was that Russian influence was behind Persia in this hostile action against Herat. Mr Ellis pointed out that in the then existing state of relations between Persia and Russia, the progress of the former in Afghanistan was tantamount to the advancement of the latter. But unfortunately there remained valid an article in the treaty of 1814 to the effect that, in case of war between the Afghans and the Persians, the English Government should not interfere with either party unless when called on by both to mediate. In vain did Ellis and his successor M'Neill remonstrate with the Persian monarch against the Herat expedition. An appeal to St Petersburg, on the part of Great Britain, produced merely an evasive reply. How diplomatic disquietude had become intensified may be inferred from this, that whereas in April 1836 Ellis wrote of Persia as a Russian first parallel of attack against India, Lord Auckland, then Governor-General of India, directed M'Neill, in the early part of 1837, to urge the Shah to abandon his enterprise, on the ground that he (the Governor-General) 'must view with umbrage and displeasure schemes of interference and conquest on our western frontier.'

The Shah, unmoved by the representations of the British envoy, marched on Herat, and the siege was opened on November 23d, 1837. Durand, a capable critic, declares that the strength of the place, the resolution of the besiegers, the skill of their Russian military advisers, and the gallantry of the besieged, were alike objects of much exaggeration. 'The siege was from first to last thoroughly ill-conducted, and the defence, in reality not better managed, owed its *éclat* to Persian ignorance, timidity and supineness. The advice of Pottinger, the gallant English officer who assisted the defence, was seldom asked, and still more seldom taken; and no one spoke more plainly of the conduct of both besieged and besiegers than did Pottinger himself.' M'Neill effected nothing definite during a long stay in the Persian camp before Herat, the counteracting influence of the Russian envoy being too strong with the Shah; and the British representative, weary of continual slights, at length quitted the Persian camp completely foiled. After six days' bombardment, the Persians and their Russian auxiliaries delivered an assault in force on June 23d, 1838. It failed, with heavy loss, and the dispirited Shah determined on raising the siege. His resolution was quickened by the arrival of Colonel Stoddart in his camp, with the information that a military force from Bombay, supported by ships of war, had landed on the island of Karrack in the Persian Gulf, and with the peremptory ultimatum to the Shah that he must retire from Herat at once. Lord Palmerston, in ordering this diversion in the Gulf, had thought himself justified by circumstances in overriding the clear and precise terms of an article in a treaty to which England had on several occasions engaged to adhere. As for the Shah, he appears to have been relieved by the ultimatum. On the 9th September he mounted his horse and rode away from Herat. The siege had lasted nine and a half months. To-day, half a century after Simonich the Russian envoy followed Mahomed Shah from battered but unconquered Herat, that city is still an Afghan place of arms.

Shah Soojah-ool Moolk, a grandson of the illustrious Ahmed Shah, reigned in Afghanistan from 1803 till 1809. His youth had been full of trouble and vicissitude. He had been a wanderer, on the verge of starvation, a pedlar and a bandit, who raised money by plundering caravans. His courage was lightly reputed, and it was as a mere creature of circumstance that he reached the throne. His reign was perturbed, and in 1809 he was a fugitive and an exile. Runjeet Singh, the Sikh ruler of the Punjaub, defrauded him of the famous Koh-i-noor, which is now the most precious of the crown jewels of England, and plundered and imprisoned the fallen man. Shah Soojah at length escaped from Lahore. After further misfortunes he at length reached the British frontier station of Loodianah, and in 1816 became a pensioner of the East India Company.

After the downfall of Shah Soojah, Afghanistan for many years was a prey to anarchy. At length in 1826, Dost Mahomed succeeded in making himself supreme at Cabul, and this masterful man thenceforward held sway until his death in 1863, uninterruptedly save during the three years of the British occupation. Dost Mahomed was neither kith nor kin to the legitimate dynasty which he displaced. His father Poyndah Khan was an able statesman and gallant soldier. He left twenty-one sons, of whom Futteh Khan was the eldest, and Dost Mahomed one of the youngest. Futteh Khan was the Warwick of Afghanistan, but the Afghan ' Kingmaker' had no Barnet as the closing scene of his chequered life. Falling into hostile hands, he was blinded and scalped. Refusing to betray his brothers, he was leisurely cut to pieces by the order and in the presence of the monarch whom he had made. His young brother Dost Mahomed undertook to avenge his death. After years of varied fortunes the

Dost had worsted all his enemies, and in 1826 he became the ruler of Cabul.   Throughout his long reign
Dost Mahomed was a strong and wise ruler.   His youth
had been neglected and dissolute.   His education was
defective, and he had been addicted to wine.   Once seated
on the throne, the reformation of our Henry Fifth was
not more thorough than was that of Dost Mahomed.
He taught himself to read and write, studied the Koran,
became scrupulously abstemious, assiduous in affairs, no
longer truculent but courteous.   He is said to have made
a public acknowledgment of the errors of his previous
life, and a firm profession of reformation ; nor did his after
life belie the pledges to which he committed himself.
There was a fine rugged honesty in his nature, and a
streak of genuine chivalry; notwithstanding the despite
he suffered at our hands, he had a real regard for the
English, and his loyalty to us was broken only by his
armed support of the Sikhs in the second Punjaub war.

The fallen Shah Soojah, from his asylum in Loodianah,
was continually intriguing for his restoration.   His schemes
were long inoperative, and it was not until 1832 that
certain arrangements were entered into between him and
the Maharaja Runjeet Singh.   To an application on
Shah Soojah's part for countenance and pecuniary aid,
the Anglo-Indian Government replied that to afford him
assistance would be inconsistent with the policy of
neutrality which the Government had imposed on itself ;
but it unwisely contributed financially toward his undertaking by granting him four months' pension in advance.
Sixteen thousand rupees formed a scant war fund with
which to attempt the recovery of a throne, but the Shah

started on his errand in February 1833. After a successful contest with the Ameers of Scinde, he marched on Candahar, and besieged that fortress. Candahar was in extremity when Dost Mahomed, hurrying from Cabul, relieved it, and joining forces with its defenders, he defeated and routed Shah Soojah, who fled precipitately, leaving behind him his artillery and camp equipage. During the Dost's absence in the south, Runjeet Singh's troops crossed the Attock, occupied the Afghan province of Peshawur, and drove the Afghans into the Khyber Pass. No subsequent efforts on Dost Mahomed's part availed to expel the Sikhs from Peshawur, and suspicious of British connivance with Runjeet Singh's successful aggression, he took into consideration the policy of fortifying himself by a counter alliance with Persia. As for Shah Soojah, he had crept back to his refuge at Loodianah.

Lord Auckland succeeded Lord William Bentinck as Governor-General of India in March 1836. In reply to Dost Mahomed's letter of congratulation, his lordship wrote: 'You are aware that it is not the practice of the British Government to interfere with the affairs of other independent states;' an abstention which Lord Auckland was soon to violate. He had brought from England the feeling of disquietude in regard to the designs of Persia and Russia which the communications of our envoy in Persia had fostered in the Home Government, but it would appear that he was wholly undecided what line of action to pursue. 'Swayed,' says Durand, 'by the vague apprehensions of a remote danger entertained by others rather than himself,' he despatched to Afghanistan Captain

Burnes on a nominally commercial mission, which, in fact, was one of political discovery, but without definite instructions. Burnes, an able but rash and ambitious man, reached Cabul in September 1837, two months before the Persian army began the siege of Herat. He had a strong prepossession in favour of the Dost, whose guest he had already been in 1832, and the policy he favoured was not the revival of the legitimate dynasty in the person of Shah Soojah, but the attachment of Dost Mahomed to British interests by strengthening his throne and affording him British countenance.

Burnes sanguinely believed that he had arrived at Cabul in the nick of time, for an envoy from the Shah of Persia was already at Candahar, bearing presents and assurances of support. The Dost made no concealment to Burnes of his approaches to Persia and Russia, in despair of British good offices, and being hungry for assistance from any source to meet the encroachments of the Sikhs, he professed himself ready to abandon his negotiations with the western powers if he were given reason to expect countenance and assistance at the hands of the Anglo-Indian Government. Burnes communicated to his Government those friendly proposals, supporting them by his own strong representations, and meanwhile, carried away by enthusiasm, he exceeded his powers by making efforts to dissuade the Candahar chiefs from the Persian alliance, and by offering to support them with money to enable them to make head against the offensive, by which Persia would probably seek to revenge the rejection of her overtures. For this unauthorised excess of zeal Burnes was severely reprimanded by his Government, and was directed to retract his offers to the Candahar chiefs. The situation of Burnes in relation to the Dost was presently complicated by the arrival at Cabul of a Russian officer claiming to be an envoy from the Czar, whose credentials, however, were regarded as dubious, and who, if that circumstance has the least weight, was on his return to Russia utterly repudiated by Count Nesselrode. The Dost took small account of this emissary, continuing to assure Burnes that he cared for no connection except with the English, and Burnes professed to his Government his fullest confidences in the sincerity of those declarations. But the tone of Lord Auckland's reply, addressed to the Dost, was so dictatorial and supercilious as to indicate the writer's intention that it should give offence. It had that effect, and Burnes' mission at once became hopeless. Yet, as a last resort, Dost Mahomed lowered his pride so far as to write to the Governor-General imploring him 'to remedy the grievances of the Afghans, and afford them some little encouragement and power.' The pathetic representation had no effect. The Russian envoy, who was profuse in his promises of everything which the Dost was most anxious to obtain, was received into favour and treated with distinction, and on his return journey he effected a treaty with the Candahar chiefs, which was presently ratified by the Russian minister at the Persian Court. Burnes, fallen into discredit at Cabul, quitted that place in August 1838. He had not been discreet, but it was not his indiscretion that brought about the failure of his mission. A nefarious transaction, which Kaye denounces with the passion of a just indignation, connects itself with Burnes' negotiations with the Dost;

his official correspondence was unscrupulously mutilated and garbled in the published Blue Book with deliberate purpose to deceive the British public.

Burnes had failed because, since he had quitted India for Cabul, Lord Auckland's policy had gradually altered. Lord Auckland had landed in India in the character of a man of peace. That, so late as April 1837, he had no design of obstructing the existing situation in Afghanistan is proved by his written statement of that date, that 'the British Government had resolved decidedly to discourage the prosecution by the ex-king Shah Soojah-ool-Moolk, so long as he may remain under our protection, of further schemes of hostility against the chiefs now in power in Cabul and Candahar.' Yet, in the following June, he concluded a treaty which sent Shah Soojah to Cabul, escorted by British bayonets. Of this inconsistency no explanation presents itself. It was a far cry from our frontier on the Sutlej to Herat in the confines of Central Asia—a distance of more than 1200 miles, over some of the most arduous marching ground in the known world. No doubt the Anglo-Indian Government was justified in being somewhat concerned by the facts that a Persian army, backed by Russian volunteers and Russian roubles, was besieging Herat, and that Persian and Russian emissaries were at work in Afghanistan. Both phenomena were rather of the 'bogey' character; how much so to-day shows when the Afghan frontier is still beyond Herat, and when a descendant of Dost Mahomed still sits in the Cabul *musnid*. But neither England nor India scrupled to make the Karrack counter-threat which arrested the siege of Herat; and the obvious

policy as regarded Afghanistan was to watch the results
of the intrigues which were on foot, to ignore them should
they come to nothing, as was probable, to counteract
them by familiar methods if serious consequences should
seem impending. Our alliance with Runjeet Singh was
solid, and the quarrel between Dost Mahomed and him
concerning the Peshawur province was notoriously easy
of arrangement.

On whose memory rests the dark shadow of responsibility for the first Afghan war? The late Lord
Broughton, who, when Sir John Cam Hobhouse, was
President of the Board of Control from 1835 to 1841,
declared before a House of Commons Committee, in
1851, 'The Afghan war was done by myself; entirely
without the privity of the Board of Directors.' The
meaning of that declaration, of course, was that it was
the British Government of the day which was responsible, acting through its member charged with the control of Indian affairs; and further, that the directorate
of the East India Company was accorded no voice in
the matter. But this utterance was materially qualified
by Sir J. C. Hobhouse's statement in the House of
Commons in 1842, that his despatch indicating the
policy to be adopted, and that written by Lord Auckland, informing him that the expedition had already been
undertaken, had crossed each other on the way.

It would be tedious to detail how Lord Auckland,
under evil counsel, gradually boxed the compass from
peace to war. The scheme of action embodied in the
treaty which, in the early summer of 1838, was concluded
between the Anglo-Indian Government, Runjeet Singh,

and Shah Soojah, was that Shah Soojah, with a force
officered from an Indian army, and paid by British
money, possessing also the goodwill and support of the
Maharaja of the Punjaub, should attempt the recovery
of his throne without any stiffening of British bayonets at
his back. Then it was urged, and the representation was
indeed accepted, that the Shah would need the buttress
afforded by English troops, and that a couple of regiments only would suffice to afford this prestige. But
Sir Harry Fane, the Commander-in-Chief, judiciously
interposed his veto on the despatch of a handful of British
soldiers on so distant and hazardous an expedition.
Finally, the Governor-General, committed already to a
mistaken line of policy, and urged forward by those
about him, took the unfortunate resolution to gather
together an Anglo-Indian army, and to send it, with the
ill-omened Shah Soojah on its shoulders, into the unknown and distant wilds of Afghanistan. This action
determined on, it was in accordance with the Anglo-
Indian fitness of things that the Governor-General should
promulgate a justificatory manifesto. Of this composi-
tion it is unnecessary to say more than to quote Durand's
observation that in it ' the words "justice and necessity"
were applied in a manner for which there is fortunately
no precedent in the English language,' and Sir Henry
Edwardes' not less trenchant comment that ' the views
and conduct of Dost Mahomed were misrepresented with a
hardihood which a Russian statesman might have envied.'

All men whose experience gave weight to their words
opposed this ' preposterous enterprise.' Mr Elphinstone,
who had been the head of a mission to Cabul thirty years

earlier, held that ' if an army was sent up the passes, and if we could feed it, no doubt we might take Cabul and set up Shah Soojah ; but it was hopeless to maintain him in a poor, cold, strong and remote country, among so turbulent a people.' Lord William Bentinck, Lord Auckland's predecessor, denounced the project as an act of incredible folly. Marquis Wellesley regarded ' this wild expedition into a distant region of rocks and deserts, of sands and ice and snow,' as an act of infatuation. The Duke of Wellington pronounced with prophetic sagacity, that the consequence of once crossing the Indus to settle a government in Afghanistan would be a perennial march into that country.

CHAPTER II

THE MARCH TO CABUL

THE two main objects of the venturesome offensive movement to which Lord Auckland had committed himself were, first, the raising of the Persian siege of Herat if the place should hold out until reached—the recapture of it if it should have fallen; and, secondly, the establishment of Shah Soojah on the Afghan throne. The former object was the more pressing, and time was very precious; but the distances in India are great, the means of communication in 1838 did not admit of celerity, and the seasons control the safe prosecution of military operations. Nevertheless, the concentration of the army at the frontier station of Ferozepore was fully accomplished toward the end of November. Sir Harry Fane was to be the military head of the expedition, and he had just right to be proud of the 14,000 carefully selected and well-seasoned troops who constituted his Bengal contingent. The force consisted of two infantry divisions, of which the first, commanded by Major-General Sir Willoughby Cotton, contained three brigades, commanded respectively by Colonels Sale, Nott, and Dennis, of whom the two former were to attain high distinction within the borders of Afghanistan. Major-General Duncan commanded the second infantry division of the two brigades, of which one was commanded by Colonel Roberts, the gallant father of a gallant son, the other by Colonel Worsley. The 6000 troops raised for Shah Soojah, who were under Fane's orders, and were officered from our army in India, had been recently and hurriedly recruited, and although rapidly improving, were not yet in a state of high efficiency. The contingent which the Bombay Presidency was to furnish to the 'Army of the Indus,' and which landed about the close of the year near the mouth of the Indus, was under the command of General Sir John Keane, the Commander-in-Chief of the Bombay army. The Bombay force was about 5000 strong.

Before the concentration at Ferozepore had been completed, Lord Auckland received official intimation of the retreat of the Persians from before Herat. With their departure had gone, also, the sole legitimate object of the expedition; there remained but a project of wanton aggression and usurpation. The Russo-Persian failure at Herat was scarcely calculated to maintain in the astute and practical Afghans any hope of fulfilment of the promises which the western powers had thrown about so lavishly, while it made clear that, for some time at least to come, the Persians would not be found dancing again to Russian fiddling. The abandonment of the siege of Herat rendered the invasion of Afghanistan an aggression destitute even of pretext. The Governor-General endeavoured to justify his resolution to persevere in it by putting forth the argument that its prosecution was

required, 'alike in observation of the treaties entered into
with Runjeet Singh and Shah Soojah as by paramount
considerations of defensive policy.' A remarkable illus-
tration of 'defensive policy' to take the offensive against
a remote country from whose further confines had faded
away foiled aggression, leaving behind nothing but a
bitter consciousness of broken promises! As for the
other plea, the tripartite treaty contained no covenant that
we should send a corporal's guard across our frontier.
If Shah Soojah had a powerful following in Afghanistan,
he could regain his throne without our assistance; if he
had no holding there, it was for us a truly discreditable
enterprise to foist him on a recalcitrant people at the
point of the bayonet.

One result of the tidings from Herat was to reduce by
a division the strength of the expeditionary force. Fane,
who had never taken kindly to the project, declined to
associate himself with the diminished array that remained.
The command of the Bengal column fell to Sir Willoughby
Cotton, with whom as his aide-de-camp rode that Henry
Havelock whose name twenty years later was to ring
through India and England. Duncan's division was to
stand fast at Ferozepore as a support, by which disposition
the strength of the Bengal marching force was cut down
to about 9500 fighting men. After its junction with the
Bombay column, the army would be 14,500 strong, without reckoning the Shah's contingent. There was an in-
terlude at Ferozepore of reviews and high jinks with the
shrewd, debauched old Runjeet Singh; of which proceedings Havelock in his narrative of the expedition gives
a detailed account, dwelling with extreme disapprobation

on Runjeet's addiction to a 'pet tipple' strong enough
to lay out the hardest drinker in the British camp, but
which the old reprobate quaffed freely without turning a
hair.

At length, on December 10th, 1838, Cotton began the
long march which was not to terminate at Cabul until
August 6th of the following year. The most direct route
was across the Punjaub, and up the passes from Peshawur,
but the Governor-General had shrunk from proposing to
Runjeet Singh that the force should march through his
territories, thinking it enough that the Maharaja had.per-
mitted Shah Soojah's heir, Prince Timour, to go by Peshawur to Cabul, had engaged to support him with a Sikh
force, and had agreed to maintain an army of reserve at
Peshawur. The chosen route was by the left bank of the
Sutlej to its junction with the Indus, down the left bank
of the Indus to the crossing point at Roree, and from
Sukkur across the Scinde and northern Belooch provinces
by the Bolan and Kojuk passes to Candahar, thence by
Khelat-i-Ghilzai and Ghuznee to Cabul. This was a line
excessively circuitous, immensely long, full of difficulties,
and equally disadvantageous as to supplies and communications. On the way the column would have to
effect a junction with the Bombay force, which at Vikkur
was distant 800 miles from Ferozepore. Of the distance
of 850 miles from the latter post to Candahar the first half
to the crossing of the Indus presented no serious difficulties, but from Sukkur beyond the country was inhos-
pitable and cruelly rugged. It needed little military
knowledge to realise how more and yet more precarious
would become the communications as the chain lengthened,

to discern that from Ferozepore to the Indus they would be at the mercy of the Sikhs, and to comprehend this also, that a single serious check, in or beyond the passes, would involve all but inevitable ruin.

Shah Soojah and his levies moved independently some marches in advance of Cotton. The Dooranee monarch-elect had already crossed the Indus, and was encamped at Shikarpore, when he was joined by Mr William Hay Macnaghten, of the Company's Civil Service, the high functionary who had been gazetted as 'Envoy and Minister on the part of the Government of India at the Court of Shah Soojah-ool-Moolk.' Durand pronounces the selection an unhappy one, 'for Macnaghten, long accustomed to irresponsible office, inexperienced in men, and ignorant of the country and people of Afghanistan, was, though an erudite Arabic scholar, neither practised in the field of Asiatic intrigue nor a man of action. His ambition was, however, great, and the expedition, holding out the promise of distinction and honours, had met with his strenuous advocacy.' Macnaghten was one of the three men who chiefly inspired Lord Auckland with the policy to which he had committed himself. He was the negotiator of the tripartite treaty. He was now on his way toward a region wherein he was to concern himself in strange adventures, the outcome of which was to darken his reputation, consign him to a sudden cruel death, bring awful ruin on the enterprise he had fostered, and inflict incalculable damage on British prestige in India.

Marching through Bhawulpore and Northern Scinde, without noteworthy incident save heavy losses of draught cattle, Cotton's army reached Roree, the point at which the Indus was to be crossed, in the third week of January 1839. Here a delay was encountered. The Scinde Ameers were, with reason, angered by the unjust and exacting terms which Pottinger had been instructed to enforce on them. They had been virtually independent of Afghanistan for nearly half a century; there was now masterfully demanded of them quarter of a million sterling in name of back tribute, and this in the face of the fact that they held a solemn release by Shah Soojah of all past and future claims. When they demurred to this, and to other exactions, they were peremptorily told that 'neither the ready power to crush and annihilate them, nor the will to call it into action, was wanting if it appeared requisite, however remotely, for the safety and integrity of the Anglo-Indian empire and frontier.'

It was little wonder that the Ameers were reluctant to fall in with terms advanced so arrogantly. Keane marched up the right bank of the Indus to within a couple of marches of Hyderabad, and having heard of the rejection by the Ameers of Pottinger's terms, and of the gathering of some 20,000 armed Belooches about the capital, he called for the co-operation of part of the Bengal column in a movement on Hyderabad. Cotton started on his march down the left bank, on January 30th, with 5600 men. Under menaces so ominous the unfortunate Ameers succumbed. Cotton returned to Roree; the Bengal column crossed the Indus, and on February 20th its headquarters reached Shikarpore. Ten days later, Cotton, leading the advance, was in Dadur, at the foot of the Bolan Pass, having suffered heavily in trans-

port animals almost from the start. Supplies were scarce
in a region so barren, but with a month's partial food on
his beasts of burden he quitted Dadur March 10th, got
safely, if toilsomely, through the Bolan, and on 26th
reached Quetta, where he was to halt for orders. Shah
Soojah and Keane followed, their troops suffering not a
little from scarcity of supplies and loss of animals.

Keane's error in detaining Cotton at Quetta until he
should arrive proved itself in the semi-starvation to which
the troops of the Bengal column were reduced. The
Khan of Khelat, whether from disaffection or inability,
left unfulfilled his promise to supply grain, and the
result of the quarrel which Burnes picked with him was
that he shunned coming in and paying homage to Shah
Soojah, for which default he was to suffer cruel and
unjustifiable ruin. The sepoys were put on half, the
camp followers on quarter rations, and the force for
eleven days had been idly consuming the waning supplies,
when at length, on April 6th, Keane came into camp,
having already formally assumed the command of the
whole army, and made certain alterations in its organisation and subsidiary commands. There still remained to
be traversed 147 miles before Candahar should be reached,
and the dreaded Kojuk Pass had still to be penetrated.

Keane was a soldier who had gained a reputation for
courage in Egypt and the Peninsula. He was indebted
to the acuteness of his engineer and the valour of his
troops, for the peerage conferred on him for Ghuznee, and
it cannot be said that during his command in Afghanistan
he disclosed any marked military aptitude. But he had
sufficient perception to recognise that he had brought the

Bengal column to the verge of starvation in Quetta, and sufficient common sense to discern that, since if it remained there it would soon starve outright, the best thing to be done was to push it forward with all possible speed into a region where food should be procurable. Acting on this reasoning, he marched the day after his arrival. Cotton, while lying in Quetta, had not taken the trouble to reconnoitre the passes in advance, far less to make a practicable road through the Kojuk defile if that should prove the best route. The resolution taken to march through it, two days were spent in making the pass possible for wheels; and from the 13th to the 21st the column was engaged in overcoming the obstacles it presented, losing in the task, besides, much baggage, supplies, transport and ordnance stores. Further back in the Bolan Willshire with the Bombay column was faring worse; he was plundered severely by tribal marauders.

By May 4th the main body of the army was encamped in the plain of Candahar. From the Kojuk, Shah Soojah and his contingent had led the advance toward the southern capital of the dominions from the throne of which he had been cast down thirty years before. The Candahar chiefs had meditated a night attack on his raw troops, but Macnaghten's intrigues and bribes had wrought defection in their camp; and while Kohun-dil-Khan and his brothers were in flight to Girishk on the Helmund, the infamous Hadji Khan Kakur led the venal herd of turncoat sycophants to the feet of the claimant who came backed by the British gold, which Macnaghten was scattering abroad with lavish hand. Shah Soojah recovered from his trepidation, hurried forward in advance

of his troops, and entered Candahar on April 24th. His
reception was cold. The influential chiefs stood aloof,
abiding the signs of the times; the populace of Candahar
stood silent and lowering. Nor did the sullenness abate
when the presence of a large army with its followers
promptly raised the price of grain, to the great distress
of the poor. The ceremony of the solemn recognition of
the Shah, held close to the scene of his defeat in 1834,
Havelock describes as an imposing pageant, with homag-
ings and royal salutes, parade of troops and presentation
of *nuzzurs;* but the arena set apart for the inhabitants
was empty, spite of Eastern love for a *tamasha*, and the
display of enthusiasm was confined to the immediate
retainers of His Majesty.

The Shah was eager for the pursuit of the fugitive
chiefs; but the troops were jaded and sickly, the cavalry
were partially dismounted, and what horses remained were
feeble skeletons. The transport animals needed grazing
and rest, and their loss of numbers to be made good. The
crops were not yet ripe, and provisions were scant and
dear. When, on May 9th, Sale marched toward Girishk,
his detachment carried half rations, and his handful of
regular cavalry was all that two regiments could furnish.
Reaching Girishk, he found that the chiefs had fled toward
Seistan, and leaving a regiment of the Shah's contingent
in occupation, he returned to Candahar.

Macnaghten professed the belief, and perhaps may
have deluded himself into it, that Candahar had received
the Shah with enthusiasm. He was sanguine that the
march to Cabul would be unopposed, and he urged on
Keane, who was wholly dependent on the Envoy for

political information, to move forward at once, lighten-
ing the difficulties of the march by leaving the Bombay
troops at Candahar. But Keane declined, on the advice
of Thomson, his chief engineer, who asked significantly
whether he had found the information given him by the
political department in any single instance correct. Food
prospects, however, did not improve at Candahar, and
leaving a strong garrison there as well, curious to say,
as the siege train which with arduous labour had been
brought up the passes, Keane began the march to Cabul
on June 27th. He had supplies only sufficient to carry
his army thither on half rations. Macnaghten had
lavished money so freely that the treasury chest was all
but empty. How the Afghans regarded the invasion was
evinced by condign slaughter of our stragglers.

As the army advanced up the valley of the Turnuk,
the climate became more temperate, the harvest was
later, and the troops improved in health and spirit. Con-
centrating his forces, Keane reached Ghuznee on July
21st. The reconnaissance he made proved that fortress
occupied in force. The outposts driven in, and a close
inspection made, the works were found stronger than
had been represented, and its regular reduction was out
of the question without the battering train which Keane
had allowed himself to be persuaded into leaving behind. A wall some 70 feet high and a wet ditch in its
front made mining and escalade alike impracticable.
Thomson, however, noticed that the road and bridge to
the Cabul gate were intact. He obtained trustworthy
information that up to a recent date, while all the other
gates had been built up, the Cabul gate had not been so

dealt with. As he watched, a horseman was seen to enter by it. This was conclusive. The ground within 400 yards of the gate offered good artillery positions. Thomson therefore reported that although the operation was full of risk, and success if attained must cost dear, yet in the absence of a less hazardous method of reduction there offered a fair chance of success in an attempt to blow open the Cabul gate, and then carry the place by a *coup de main*. Keane was precluded from the alternative of masking the place and continuing his advance by the all but total exhaustion of his supplies, which the capture of Ghuznee would replenish, and he therefore resolved on an assault by the Cabul gate.

During the 21st July the army circled round the place, and camped to the north of it on the Cabul road. The following day was spent in preparations, and in defeating an attack made on the Shah's contingent by several thousand Ghilzai tribesmen of the adjacent hill country. In the gusty darkness of the early morning of the 23d the field artillery was placed in battery on the heights opposite the northern face of the fortress. The 13th regiment was extended in skirmishing order in the gardens under the wall of this face, and a detachment of sepoys was detailed to make a false. attack on the eastern face. Near the centre of the northern face was the Cabul gate, in front of which lay waiting for the signal, a storming party consisting of the light companies of the four European regiments, under command of Colonel Dennie of the 13th. The main column consisted of two European regiments and the support of a third, the whole commanded by Brigadier Sale ; the native regiments constituted the reserve. All those dispositions were completed by three A.M., and, favoured by the noise of the wind and the darkness, without alarming the garrison.

Punctually at this hour the little party of engineers charged with the task of blowing in the gate started forward on the hazardous errand. Captain Peat of the Bombay Engineers was in command. Durand, a young lieutenant of Bengal Engineers, who was later to attain high distinction, was entrusted with the service of heading the explosion party. The latter, leading the party, had advanced unmolested to within 150 yards of the works, when a challenge, a shot and a shout gave intimation of his detection. A musketry fire was promptly opened by the garrison from the battlements, and blue lights illuminated the approach to the gate, but in the fortunate absence of fire from the lower works the bridge was safely crossed, and Peat with his handful of linesmen halted in a sally-port to cover the explosion operation. Durand advanced to the gate, his sappers piled their powder bags against it and withdrew; Durand and his sergeant uncoiled the hose, ignited the quick-match under a rain from the battlements of bullets and miscellaneous missiles, and then retired to cover out of reach of the explosion.

At the sound of the first shot from the battlements, Keane's cannon had opened their fire. The skirmishers in the gardens engaged in a brisk fusillade. The rattle of Hay's musketry was heard from the east. The garrison was alert in its reply. The northern ramparts became a sheet of flame, and everywhere the cannonade and musketry fire waxed in noise and volume. Suddenly, as the day was beginning to dawn, a dull, heavy sound was heard by

B

the head of the waiting column, scarce audible elsewhere because of the boisterous wind and the din of the firing. A pillar of black smoke shot up from where had been the Afghan gate, now shattered by the 300 pounds of gun-powder which Durand had exploded against it. The signal to the storming party was to be the 'advance' sounded by the bugler who accompanied Peat. But the bugler had been shot through the head. Durand could not find Peat. Going back through the bullets to the nearest party of infantry, he experienced some delay, but at last the column was apprised that all was right, the 'advance' was sounded, Dennie and his stormers sped forward, and Sale followed at the head of the main column.

After a temporary check to the latter, because of a misconception, it pushed on in close support of Dennie. That gallant soldier and his gallant followers had rushed into the smoking and gloomy archway to find themselves met hand to hand by the Afghan defenders, who had re-covered from their surprise. Nothing could be distinctly seen in the narrow gorge, but the clash of sword blade against bayonet was heard on every side. The stormers had to grope their way between the yet standing walls in a dusk which the glimmer of the blue light only made more perplexing. But some elbow room was gradually gained, and then, since there was neither time nor space for methodic street fighting, each loaded section gave its volley and then made way for the next, which, crowding to the front, poured a deadly discharge at half pistol-shot into the densely crowded defenders. Thus the storming party won steadily its way, till at length Dennie and his leading files discerned over the heads of their opponents a patch of blue sky and a twinkling star or two, and with a final charge found themselves within the place.

A body of fierce Afghan swordsmen projected themselves into the interval between the storming party and the main column. Sale, at the head of the latter, was cut down by a tulwar stroke in the face; in the effort of his blow the assailant fell with the assailed, and they rolled together among the shattered timbers of the gate. Sale, wounded again on the ground, and faint with loss of blood, called to one of his officers for assistance. Kershaw ran the Afghan through the body with his sword ; but he still struggled with the Brigadier. At length in the grapple Sale got uppermost, and then he dealt his adversary a sabre cut which cleft him from crown to eyebrows. There was much confused fighting within the place, for the Afghan garrison made furious rallies again and again ; but the citadel was found open and undefended, and by sunrise British banners were waving above its battlements Hyder Khan, the Governor of Ghuznee, one of the sons of Dost Mahomed, was found concealed in a house in the town and taken prisoner. The British loss amounted to about 200 killed and wounded, that of the garrison, which was estimated at from 3000 to 4000 strong, was over 500 killed. The number of wounded was not ascertained ; of prisoners taken in arms there were about 1600. The booty consisted of numerous horses, camels and mules, ordnance and military weapons of various descriptions, and a vast quantity of supplies of all kinds.

Keane, having garrisoned Ghuznee, and left there his sick and wounded, resumed on July 30th his march on

Cabul. Within twenty-four hours after the event Dost Mahomed heard of the fall of Ghuznee. Possessed of the adverse intelligence, the Dost gathered his chiefs, received their facile assurances of fidelity, sent his brother the Nawaub Jubbar Khan to ask what terms Shah Soojah and his British allies were prepared to offer him, and recalled from Jellalabad his son Akbar Khan, with all the force he could muster there. The Dost's emissary to the allied camp was informed that 'an honourable asylum' in British India was at the service of his brother; an offer which Jubbar Khan declined in his name without thanks. Before he left to share the fortunes of the Dost, the Sirdar is reported to have asked Macnaghten, ' If Shah Soojah is really our king, what need has he of your army and name? You have brought him here,' he continued, 'with your money and arms. Well, leave him now with us Afghans, and let him rule us if he can.' When Jubbar Khan returned to Cabul with his sombre message, the Dost, having been joined by Akbar Khan, concentrated his army, and found himself at the head of 13,000 men, with thirty guns; but he mournfully realised that he could lean no reliance on the constancy and courage of his adherents. Nevertheless, he marched out along the Ghuznee road, and drew up his force at Urgundeh, where he commanded the most direct line of retreat toward the western hill country of Bamian, in case his people would not fight, or should they fight, if they were beaten.

There was no fight in his following; scarcely, indeed, was there a loyal supporter among all those who had eaten his salt for years. There was true manhood in this chief whom we were replacing by an effete puppet. The

Dost, Koran in hand, rode among his perfidious troops, and conjured them in the name of God and the Prophet not to dishonour themselves by transferring their allegiance to one who had filled Afghanistan with infidels and blasphemers. 'If,' he continued, 'you are resolved to be traitors to me, at least enable me to die with honour. Support the brother of Futteh Khan in one last charge against these Feringhee dogs. In that charge he will fall; then go and make your own terms with Shah Soojah.' The high-souled appeal inspired no worthy response; but one is loth to credit the testimony of the soldier-of-fortune Harlan that his guards forsook the Dost, and that the rabble of troops plundered his pavilion, snatched from under him the pillows of his divan, seized his prayer carpet, and finally hacked into pieces the tent and its appurtenances. On the evening of August 2d the hapless man shook the dust of the camp of traitors from his feet, and rode away toward Bamian, his son Akbar Khan, with a handful of resolute men, covering the retreat of his father and his family. Tidings of the flight of Dost Mahomed reached Keane on the 3d, at Sheikabad, where he had halted to concentrate; and Outram volunteered to head a pursuing party, to consist of some British officers as volunteers, some cavalry and some Afghan horse. Hadji Khan Kakur, the earliest traitor of his race, undertook to act as guide. This man's devices of delay defeated Outram's fiery energy, perhaps in deceit, perhaps because he regarded it as lacking discretion. For Akbar Khan made a long halt on the crown of the pass, waiting to check any endeavour to press closely on his fugitive father, and it would have gone hard with

Outram, with a few fagged horsemen at his back, if Hadji
Khan had allowed him to overtake the resolute young
Afghan chief. As Keane moved forward, there fell to
him the guns which the Dost had left in the Urgundeh
position. On August 6th he encamped close to Cabul;
and on the following day Shah Soojah made his public
entry into the capital which he had last seen thirty years
previously. After so many years of vicissitude, adventure
and intrigue, he was again on the throne of his ancestors,
but placed there by the bayonets of the Government
whose creature he was, an insult to the nation whom he
had the insolence to call his people.

The entry, nevertheless, was a goodly spectacle enough.
Shah Soojah, dazzling in coronet, jewelled girdle and
bracelets, but with no Koh-i-noor now glittering on his
forehead, bestrode a white charger, whose equipments
gleamed with gold. By his side rode Macnaghten and
Burnes; in the pageant were the principal officers of the
British army. Sabres flashed in front of the procession,
bayonets sparkled in its rear, as it wended its way
through the great bazaar which Pollock was to destroy
three years later, and along the tortuous street to the
gate of the Balla Hissar. But neither the monarch nor
his pageant kindled the enthusiasm in the Cabulees.
There was no voice of welcome; the citizens did not
care to trouble themselves so much as to make him a
salaam, and they stared at the European strangers harder
than at his restored majesty. There was a touch of pathos
in the burst of eagerness to which the old man gave
way as he reached the palace, ran through the gardens,
visited the apartments, and commented on the neglect

everywhere apparent. Shah Soojah was rather a poor
creature, but he was by no means altogether destitute of
good points, and far worse men than he were actors in
the strange historical episode of which he was the figurehead. He was humane for an Afghan ; he never was
proved to have been untrue to us; he must have had
some courage of a kind else he would never have remained in Cabul when our people left it, in the all but
full assurance of the fate which presently overtook him as
a matter of course. Havelock thus portrays him : ' A stout
person of the middle height, his chin covered with
a long thick and neatly trimmed beard, dyed black to
conceal the encroachments of time. His manner toward
the English is gentle, calm and dignified, without haughti-
ness, but his own subjects have invariably complained of
his reception of them as cold and repulsive, even to rude-
ness. His complexion is darker than that of the generality
of Afghans, and his features, if not decidedly handsome,
are not the reverse of pleasing ; but the expression of his
countenance would betray to a skilful physiognomist that
mixture of timidity and duplicity so often observable in
the character of the higher order of men in Southern
Asia.'

CHAPTER III

THE FIRST YEAR OF OCCUPATION

SIR JOHN KAYE, in his picturesque if diffuse history of the first Afghan war, lays it down that, in seating Shah Soojah on the Cabul throne, 'the British Government had done all that it had undertaken to do,' and Durand argues that, having accomplished this, 'the British army could have then been withdrawn with the honour and fame of entire success.' The facts apparently do not justify the reasoning of either writer. In the Simla manifesto, in which Lord Auckland embodied the rationale of his policy, he expressed the confident hope 'that the Shah will be speedily replaced on his throne by his own subjects and adherents, and when once he shall be received in power, and the independence and integrity of Afghanistan established, the British army will be withdrawn.' The Shah had been indeed restored to his throne, but by British bayonets, not by 'his own subjects and adherents.' It could not seriously be maintained that he was secure in power, or that the independence and integrity of Afghanistan were established when British troops were holding Candahar, Ghuznee and Cabul, the only three positions where the Shah was nominally paramount, when the fugitive Dost was still within its borders, when intrigue and disaffection were seething in every valley and on every hill-side, and when the principality of Herat maintained a contemptuous independence. Macnaghten might avow himself convinced of the popularity of the Shah, and believe or strive to believe that the Afghans had received the puppet king 'with feelings nearly amounting to adoration,' but he did not venture to support the conviction he avowed by advocating that the Shah should be abandoned to his adoring subjects. Lord Auckland's policy was gravely and radically erroneous, but it had a definite object, and that object certainly was not a futile march to Cabul and back, dropping incidentally by the wayside the aspirant to a throne whom he had himself put forward, and leaving him to take his chance among a truculent and adverse population. Thus early, in all probability, Lord Auckland was disillusioned of the expectation that the effective restoration of Shah Soojah would be of light and easy accomplishment, but at least he could not afford to have the enterprise a *coup manqué* when as yet it was little beyond its inception.

The cost of the expedition was already, however, a strain, and the troops engaged in it were needed in India. Lord Auckland intimated to Macnaghten his expectation that a strong brigade would suffice to hold Afghanistan in conjunction with the Shah's contingent, and his desire that the rest of the army of the Indus should at once return to India. Macnaghten, on the other hand, in spite of his avowal of the Shah's popularity, was anxious to retain in Afghanistan a large body of troops. He meditated strange enterprises, and proposed that Keane should support his

project of sending a force toward Bokhara to give check
to a Russian column which Pottinger at Herat had heard
was assembling at Orenburg, with Khiva for its objective.
Keane derided the proposal, and Macnaghten reluctantly
abandoned it, but he demanded of Lord Auckland with
success, the retention in Afghanistan of the Bengal division
of the army.   In the middle of September General Willshire marched with the Bombay column, with orders, on
his way to the Indus to pay a hostile visit to Khelat, and
punish its khan for the 'disloyalty' with which he had
been charged, a commission which the British officer fulfilled with a skill and thoroughness that could be admired
with less reservation had the aggression on the gallant
Mehrab been less wanton.   A month later Keane started
for India by the Khyber route, which Wade had opened
without serious resistance when in August and September
he escorted through the passes Prince Timour, Shah
Soojah's heir-apparent.   During the temporary absence
of Cotton, who accompanied Keane, Nott had the command at Candahar, Sale at and about Cabul, and the
troops were quartered in those capitals, and in Jellalabad, Ghuznee, Charikar and Bamian.   The Shah and
the Envoy wintered in the milder climate of Jellalabad,
and Burnes was in political charge of the capital and its
vicinity.

It was a prophetic utterance that the accomplishment
of our military succession would mark but the commencement of our real difficulties in Afghanistan.   In theory
and in name Shah Soojah was an independent monarch;
it was, indeed, only in virtue of his proving himself able
to rule independently that he could justify his claim to

rule at all. But that he was independent was a con-
tradiction in terms while British troops studded the
country, and while the real powers of sovereignty were
exercised by Macnaghten. Certain functions, it is true,
the latter did permit the nominal monarch to exercise.
While debarred from a voice in measures of external
policy, and not allowed to sway the lines of conduct to be
adopted toward independent or revolting tribes, the Shah
was allowed to concern himself with the administration of
justice, and in his hands were the settlement, collection
and appropriation of the revenue of those portions of the
kingdom from which any revenue could be exacted. He
was allowed to appoint as his minister of state, the com-
panion of his exile, old Moolla Shikore, who had lost
both his memory and his ears, but who had sufficient
faculty left to hate the English, to oppress the people, to
be corrupt and venal beyond all conception, and to appoint
subordinates as flagitious as himself. 'Bad ministers,'
wrote Burnes, 'are in every government solid ground
for unpopularity; and I doubt if ever a king had a worse
set than has Shah Soojah.' The oppressed people ap-
pealed to the British functionaries, who remonstrated with
the minister, and the minister punished the people for ap-
pealing to the British functionaries. The Shah was free to
confer grants of land on his creatures, but when the holders
resisted, he was unable to enforce his will since he was not
allowed to employ soldiers; and the odium of the forcible
confiscation ultimately fell on Macnaghten, who alone had
the ordering of expeditions, and who could not see the
Shah belittled by non-fulfilment of his requisitions.

Justice sold by venal judges, oppression and corruption

rampant in every department of internal administration,
it was no wonder that nobles and people alike resented
the inflictions under whose sting they writhed. They
were accustomed to a certain amount of oppression; Dost
Mahomed had chastised them with whips, but Shah
Soojah, whom the English had brought, was chastising
them with scorpions. And they felt his yoke the more
bitterly because, with the shrewd acuteness of the race,
they recognised the really servile condition of this new
king. They fretted, too, under the sharp bit of the British
political agents who were strewn about the country, in
the execution of a miserable and futile policy, and whose
lives, in a few instances, did not maintain the good name
of their country. Dost Mahomed had maintained his
sway by politic management of the chiefs, and through
them of the tribes. Macnaghten would have done well
to impress on Shah Soojah the wisdom of pursuing the
same tactics. There was, it is true, the alternative of
destroying the power of the barons, but that policy involved a stubborn and doubtful struggle, and prolonged
occupation of the country by British troops in great
strength. Macnaghten professed our occupation of
Afghanistan to be temporary; yet he was clearly ad-
venturing on the rash experiment of weakening the nobles
when he set about the enlistment of local tribal levies,
who, paid from the Royal treasury and commanded by
British officers, were expected to be staunch to the
Shah, and useful in curbing the powers of the chiefs.
The latter, of course, were alienated and resentful, and
the levies, imbued with the Afghan attribute of fickle-
ness, proved for the most part undisciplined and faithless.

The winter of 1839-40 passed without much note-worthy incident. The winter climate of Afghanistan is severe, and the Afghan, in ordinary circumstances, is among the hibernating animals. But down in the Khyber, in October, the tribes gave some trouble. They were dis-satisfied with the amount of annual black-mail paid them for the right of way through their passes. When the Shah was a fugitive thirty years previously, they had con-cealed and protected him ; and mindful of their kindly services, he had promised them, unknown to Macnaghten, the augmentation of their subsidy to the old scale from which it had gradually dwindled. Wade, returning from Cabul, did not bring them the assurances they expected, whereupon they rose and concentrated and invested Ali Musjid, a fort which they regarded as the key of their gloomy defile. Mackeson, the Peshawur political officer, threw provisions and ammunition into Ali Musjid, but the force, on its return march, was attacked by the hillmen, the Sikhs being routed, and the sepoys incurring loss of men and transport. The emboldened Khyberees now turned on Ali Musjid in earnest ; but the garrison was strengthened, and the place was held until a couple of regiments marched down from Jellalabad, and were pre-paring to attack the hillmen, when it was announced that Mackeson had made a compact with the chiefs for the pay-ment of an annual subsidy which they considered adequate.

Afghanistan fifty years ago, and the same is in a measure true of it to-day, was rather a bundle of provinces, some of which owned scarcely a nominal allegiance to the ruler in Cabul, than a concrete state. Herat and Canda-har were wholly independent, the Ghilzai tribes inhabiting the wide tracts from the Suliman ranges westward beyond the road through Ghuznee, between Candahar and Cabul, and northward into the rugged country between Cabul and Jellalabad, acknowledged no other authority than that of their own chiefs. The Ghilzais are agriculturists, shepherds, and robbers ; they are constantly engaged in internal feuds ; they are jealous of their wild independence, and through the centuries have abated little of their untamed ferocity. They had rejected Macnaghten's advances, and had attacked Shah Soojah's camp on the day before the fall of Ghuznee. Outram, in reprisal, had promptly raided part of their country. Later, the winter had restrained them from activity, but they broke out again in the spring. In May Captain Anderson, marching from Candahar with a mixed force about 1200 strong, was offered battle near Jazee, in the Turnuk, by some 2000 Ghilzai horse and foot. Anderson's guns told heavily among the Ghilzai horsemen, who, impatient of the fire, made a spirited dash on his left flank. Grape and musketry checked them ; but they rallied, and twice charged home on the bayonets before they withdrew, leaving 200 of their number dead on the ground. Nott sent a detachment to occupy the fortress of Khelat-i-Ghilzai, between Candahar and Ghuznee, thus rendering the communications more secure ; and later, Macnaghten bribed the chiefs by an annual subsidy of £600 to abstain from infesting the highways. The terms were cheap, for the Ghilzai tribes mustered some 40,000 fighting men.

Shah Soojah and the Envoy returned from Jellalabad to Cabul in April 1840. A couple of regiments had

wintered not uncomfortably in the Balla Hissar. That
fortress was then the key of Cabul, and while our troops
remained in Afghanistan it should not have been left
ungarrisoned a single hour. The soldiers did their best
to impress on Macnaghten the all-importance of the
position. But the Shah objected to its continued occupation, and Macnaghten weakly yielded. Cotton, who had
returned to the chief military command in Afghanistan,
made no remonstrance ; the Balla Hissar was evacuated,
and the troops were quartered in cantonments built in an
utterly defenceless position on the plain north of Cabul,
a position whose environs were cumbered with walled
gardens, and commanded by adjacent high ground, and by
native forts which were neither demolished nor occupied.
The troops, now in permanent and regularly constructed
quarters, ceased to be an expeditionary force, and became
substantially an army of occupation. The officers sent
for their wives to inhabit with them the bungalows in
which they had settled down. Lady Macnaghten, in the
spacious mission residence which stood apart in its own
grounds, presided over the society of the cantonments,
which had all the cheery surroundings of the half-settled,
half-nomadic life of our military people in the East.
There were the 'coffee house' after the morning ride, the
gathering round the bandstand in the evening, the
impromptu dance, and the *burra khana* occasionally in
the larger houses. A racecourse had been laid out, and
there were 'sky' races and more formal meetings. And
so 'as in the days that were before the flood, they were eat-
ing and drinking, and marrying and giving in marriage, and
knew not until the flood came, and took them all away.'

Macnaghten engaged himself in a welter of internal and external intrigue, his mood swinging from singular complacency to a disquietude that sometimes approached despondency. It had come to be forced on him, in spite of his intermittent optimism, that the Government was a government of sentry-boxes, and that Afghanistan was not governed so much as garrisoned. The utter failure of the winter march attempted by Peroffski's Russian column across the frozen steppes on Khiva was a relief to him ; but the state of affairs in Herat was a constant trouble and anxiety. Major Todd had been sent there as political agent, to make a treaty with Shah Kamran, and to superintend the repair and improvement of the fortifications of the city. Kamran was plenteously subsidised ; he took Macnaghten's lakhs, but furtively maintained close relations with Persia. Detecting the double-dealing, Macnaghten urged on Lord Auckland the annexation of Herat to Shah Soojah's dominions, but was instructed to condone Kamran's duplicity, and try to bribe him higher. Kamran by no means objected to this policy, and, while continuing his intrigues with Persia, cheerfully accepted the money, arms and ammunition which Macnaghten supplied him with so profusely as to cause remonstrance on the part of the financial authorities in Calcutta. The Commander-in-Chief was strong enough to counteract the pressure which Macnaghten brought to bear on Lord Auckland in favour of an expedition against Herat, which his lordship at length finally negatived, to the great disgust of the Envoy, who wrote of the conduct of his chief as 'drivelling beyond contempt,' and 'sighed for a Wellesley or a Hastings.' The ultimate result of Mac-

naghten's negotiations with Shah Kamran was Major
Todd's withdrawal from Herat. Todd had suspended the
monthly subsidy, to the great wrath of Kamran's rapacious
and treacherous minister Yar Mahomed, who made a
peremptory demand for increased advances, and refused
Todd's stipulation that a British force should be admitted
into Herat. Todd's action in quitting Herat was severely
censured by his superiors, and he was relegated to regi-
mental duty. Perhaps he acted somewhat rashly, but he
had not been kept well informed ; for instance, he had
been unaware that Persia had become our friend, and had
engaged to cease relations with Shah Kamran—an important arrangement of which he certainly should have
been cognisant. Macnaghten had squandered more gold
on Herat than the fee-simple of the principality was worth,
and to no purpose ; he left that state just as he found it,
treacherous, insolent, greedy and independent.

The precariousness of the long lines of communications
between British India and the army in Afghanistan—a
source of danger which from the first had disquieted
cautious soldiers—was making itself seriously felt, and
constituted for Macnaghten another cause of solicitude.
Old Runjeet Singh, a faithful if not disinterested ally,
had died on June 27th, 1839, the day on which Keane
marched out from Candahar. The breath was scarcely
out of the old reprobate when the Punjaub began to drift
into anarchy. So far as the Sikh share in it was concerned, the tripartite treaty threatened to become a dead
letter. The Lahore Durbar had not adequately fulfilled
the undertaking to support Prince Timour's advance by the
Khyber, nor was it duly regarding the obligation to main-

tain a force on the Peshawur frontier of the Punjaub. But those things were trivial in comparison with the growing reluctance manifested freely, to accord to our troops and convoys permission to traverse the Punjaub on the march to and from Cabul. The Anglo-Indian Government sent Mr Clerk to Lahore to settle the question as to the thoroughfare. He had instructions to be firm, and the Sikhs did not challenge Mr Clerk's stipulation that the Anglo-Indian Government must have unmolested right of way through the Punjaub, while he undertook to restrict the use of it as much as possible. This arrangement by no means satisfied the exacting Macnaghten, and he continued to worry himself by foreseeing all sorts of troublous contingencies unless measures were adopted for 'macadamising' the road through the Punjaub.

The summer of 1840 did not pass without serious interruptions to the British communications between Candahar and the Indus; nor without unexpected and ominous disasters before they were restored. General Willshire, with the returning Bombay column, had in the previous November stormed Mehrab Khan's ill-manned and worse armed fort of Khelat, and the Khan, disdaining to yield, had fallen in the hopeless struggle. His son Nusseer Khan had been put aside in favour of a collateral pretender, and became an active and dangerous malcontent. All Northern Beloochistan fell into a state of anarchy. A detachment of sepoys escorting supplies was cut to pieces in one of the passes. Quetta was attacked with great resolution by Nusseer Khan, but was opportunely relieved by a force sent from another post. Nusseer made himself master of Khelat, and there fell into his cruel hands

Lieutenant Loveday, the British political officer stationed there, whom he treated with great barbarity, and finally murdered. A British detachment under Colonel Clibborn, was defeated by the Beloochees with heavy loss, and compelled to retreat. Nusseer Khan, descending into the low country of Cutch, assaulted the important post of Dadur, but was repulsed, and taking refuge in the hills, was routed by Colonel Marshall with a force from Kotree, whereupon he became a skulking fugitive. Nott marched down from Candahar with a strong force, occupied Khelat, and fully re-established communications with the line of the Indus, while fresh troops moved forward into Upper Scinde, and thence gradually advancing to Quetta and Candahar, materially strengthened the British position in Southern Afghanistan.

Dost Mahomed, after his flight from Cabul in 1839, had soon left the hospitable refuge afforded him in Khooloom, a territory west of the Hindoo Koosh beyond Bamian, and had gone to Bokhara on the treacherous invitation of its Ameer, who threw him into captivity. The Dost's family remained at Khooloom, in the charge of his brother Jubbar Khan. The advance of British forces beyond Bamian to Syghan and Bajgah, induced that Sirdar to commit himself and the ladies to British protection. Dr Lord, Macnaghten's political officer in the Bamian district, was a rash although well-meaning man. The errors he had committed since the opening of spring had occasioned disasters to the troops whose dispositions he controlled, and had incited the neighbouring hill tribes to active disaffection. In July Dost Mahomed made his escape from Bokhara, hurried to Khooloom, found its ruler and the tribes full of

zeal for his cause, and rapidly grew in strength. Lord
found it was time to call in his advance posts and concentrate at Bamian, losing in the operation an Afghan
regiment which deserted to the Dost. Macnaghten reinforced Bamian, and sent Colonel Dennie to command
there. On September 18th Dennie moved out with two
guns and 800 men against the Dost's advance parties raid-
ing in an adjacent valley. Those detachments driven back,
Dennie suddenly found himself opposed to the irregular
mass of Oosbeg horse and foot which constituted the army
of the Dost. Mackenzie's cannon fire shook the undisciplined horde, the infantry pressed in to close quarters,
and soon the nondescript host of the Dost was in panic
flight, with Dennie's cavalry in eager pursuit. The Dost
escaped with difficulty, with the loss of his entire personal
equipment. He was once more a fugitive, and the Wali of
Khooloom promptly submitted himself to the victors, and
pledged himself to aid and harbour the broken chief no
more. Macnaghten had been a prey to apprehension
while the Dost's attitude was threatening; he was now in
a glow of joy and hope.

But the Envoy's elation was short-lived. Dost Mahomed was yet to cause him much solicitude. Defeated in
Bamian, he was ready for another attempt in the Kohistan
country to the north of Cabul. Disaffection was rife everywhere throughout the kingdom, but it was perhaps most
rife in the Kohistan, which was seething with intrigues
in favour of Dost Mahomed, while the local chiefs were
intensely exasperated by the exactions of the Shah's
revenue collectors. Macnaghten summoned the chiefs to
Cabul. They came, they did homage to the Shah and

swore allegiance to him ; they went away from the capital pledging each other to his overthrow, and jeering at the scantiness of the force they had seen at Cabul. Intercepted letters disclosed their schemes, and in the end of September Sale, with a considerable force, marched out to chastise the disaffected Kohistanees. The fort of Tootundurrah fell without resistance. Julgah, however, the next fort assailed, stubbornly held out, and officers and men fell in the unsuccessful attempt to storm it. In three weeks Sale marched to and fro through the Kohistan, pursuing will-o'-the-wisp rumours as to the whereabouts of the Dost, destroying forts on the course of his weary pilgrimage, and subjected occasionally to night attacks.

Meanwhile, in the belief that Dost Mahomed was close to Cabul, and mournfully conscious that the capital and surrounding country were ripe for a rising, Macnaghten had relapsed into nervousness, and was a prey to gloomy forebodings. The troops at Bamian were urgently recalled. Cannon were mounted on the Balla Hissar to overawe the city, the concentration of the troops in the fortress was under consideration, and men were talking of preparing for a siege. How Macnaghten's English nature was undergoing deterioration under the strain of events is shown by his writing of the Dost : 'Would it be justifiable to set a price on this fellow's head ? ' How his perceptions were warped was further evinced by his talking of 'showing no mercy to the man who has been the author of all the evil now distracting the country,' and by his complaining of Sale and Burnes that, 'with 2000 good infantry, they are sitting down before a fortified place, and are afraid to attack it.'

Learning that for certain the Dost had crossed the Hindoo Koosh from Nijrao into the Kohistan, Sale, who had been reinforced, sent out reconnaissances which ascertained that he was in the Purwan Durrah valley, stretching down from the Hindoo Koosh to the Gorebund river; and the British force marched thither on 2d November. As the village was neared, the Dost's people were seen evacuating it and the adjacent forts, and making for the hills. Sale's cavalry was some distance in advance of the infantry of the advance guard, but time was precious. Anderson's horse went to the left, to cut off retreat down the Gorebund valley. Fraser took his two squadrons of Bengal cavalry to the right, advanced along the foothills, and gained the head of the valley. He was too late to intercept a small body of Afghan horsemen, who were already climbing the upland; but badly mounted as the latter were, he could pursue them with effect. But it seemed that the Afghans preferred to fight rather than be pursued. The Dost himself was in command of the little party, and the Dost was a man whose nature was to fight, not to run. He wheeled his handful so that his horsemen faced Fraser's troop down there below them. Then the Dost pointed to his banner, bared his head, called on his supporters in the name of God and the Prophet to follow him against the unbelievers, and led them down the slope.

Fraser had formed up his troopers when recall orders reached him. Joyous that the situation entitled him to disobey them, he gave instead the word to charge. As the Afghans came down at no great pace, they fired occasionally; either because of the bullets, or because of an

access of pusillanimity, Fraser's troopers broke and fled
ignominiously. The British gentlemen charged home unsupported. Broadfoot, Crispin and Lord were slain; Pon-
sonby, severely wounded and his reins cut, was carried
out of the *mêlée* by his charger ; Fraser, covered with
blood and wounds, broke through his assailants, and
brought to Sale his report of the disgrace of his troopers.
After a sharp pursuit of the poltroons, the Dost and his
followers leisurely quitted the field.

Burnes wrote to the Envoy—he was a soldier, but he
was also a 'political,' and political employ seemed often
in Afghanistan to deteriorate the attribute of soldierhood
—that there was no alternative for the force but to fall
back on Cabul, and entreated Macnaghten to order immediate concentration of all the troops. This letter Macnaghten received the day after the disaster in the Kohistan,
when he was taking his afternoon ride in the Cabul plain.
His heart must have been very heavy as he rode, when
suddenly a horseman galloped up to him and announced
that the Ameer was approaching. 'What Ameer?' asked
Macnaghten. 'Dost Mahomed Khan,' was the reply, and
sure enough there was the Dost close at hand. Dis-
mounting, this Afghan prince and gentleman saluted the
Envoy, and offered him his sword, which Macnaghten
declined to take. Dost and Envoy rode into Cabul together, and such was the impression the former made on
the latter that Macnaghten, who a month before had permitted himself to think of putting a price on 'the fellow's'
head, begged now of the Governor-General 'that the Dost
be treated more handsomely than was Shah Soojah, who
had no claim on us.' And then followed a strange con-

fession for the man to make who made the tripartite treaty, and approved the Simla manifesto : ' We had no hand in depriving the Shah of his kingdom, *whereas we ejected the Dost, who never offended us, in support of our policy, of which he was the victim.'*

Durand regards Dost Mahomed's surrender as ' evincing a strange pusillanimity.' This opprobrious judgment appears unjustified. No doubt he was weary of the fugitive life he had been leading, but to pronounce him afraid that the Kohistanees or any other Afghans would betray him is to ignore the fact that he had been for months among people who might, any hour of any day, have betrayed him if they had chosen. Nobler motives than those ascribed to him by Durand may be supposed to have actuated a man of his simple and lofty nature. He had given the arbitrament of war a trial, and had realised that in that way he could make no head against us. He might, indeed, have continued the futile struggle, but he was the sort of man to recognise the selfishness of that persistency which would involve ruin and death to the devoted people who would not desert his cause while he claimed to have a cause. When historians write of Afghan treachery and guile, it seems to have escaped their perception that Afghan treachery was but a phase of Afghan patriotism, of an unscrupulous character, doubtless, according to our notions, but nevertheless practical in its methods, and not wholly unsuccessful in its results. It may have been a higher and purer patriotism that moved Dost Mahomed to cease, by his surrender, from being an obstacle to the tranquillisation of the country of which he had been the ruler.

CHAPTER IV

DOST MAHOMED remained for a few days in the British cantonments on the Cabul plain, an honoured guest rather than a prisoner. His soldierly frankness, his bearing at once manly and courteous, his honest liking for and trust in our race, notwithstanding the experiencs which he had undergone, won universal respect and cordiality. Officers who stood aloof from Shah Soojah vied with each other in evincing to Dost Mahomed their sympathy with him in his fallen fortunes. Shah Soojah would not see the man whom he had ingloriously supplanted, on the pretext that he 'could not bring himself to show common civility to such a villain.' How Macnaghten's feeling in regard to the two men had altered is disclosed by his comment on this refusal. 'It is well,' he wrote, 'as the Dost must have suffered much humiliation in being subjected to such an ordeal.'

In the middle of November 1840 the Dost began his journey toward British India, accompanied by Sir Willoughby Cotton, who was finally quitting Afghanistan, and under the escort of a considerable British force which had completed its tour of duty in Afghanistan. Sale suc-

ceeded Cotton in temporary divisional command pending
the arrival of the latter's successor. About the middle of
December Shah Soojah and his Court, accompanied by
the British Envoy, arrived at Jellalabad for the winter,
Burnes remaining at Cabul in political charge.

Macnaghten was mentally so constituted as to be continually alternating between high elation and the depths
of despondency; discerning to-day ominous indications of
ruin in an incident of no account, and to-morrow scorning
imperiously to recognise danger in the fierce rising of a
province. It may almost be said that each letter of his to
Lord Auckland was of a different tone from the one which
had preceded it. Burnes, who was nominally Macnaghten's
chief lieutenant, with more self-restraint, had much the same
temperament. Kaye writes of him: 'Sometimes sanguine,
sometimes despondent, sometimes confident, sometimes
credulous, Burnes gave to fleeting impressions all the importance and seeming permanency of settled convictions,
and imbued surrounding objects with the colours of his
own varying mind.' But if Burnes had been a discreet and
steadfast man, he could have exercised no influence on the
autocratic Macnaghten, since between the two men there
was neither sympathy nor confidence. Burnes had, indeed,
no specific duties of any kind ; in his own words, he was in
'the most nondescript situation.' Macnaghten gave him
no responsibility, and while Burnes waited for the promised reversion of the office of envoy, he chiefly employed
himself in writing long memorials on the situation and
prospects of affairs, on which Macnaghten's marginal comments were brusque, and occasionally contemptuous. The
resolute and clear-headed Pottinger, who, if the oppor-

tunity had been given him, might have buttressed and steadied Macnaghten, was relegated to provincial service. Throughout his career in Afghanistan the Envoy could not look for much advice from the successive commanders of the Cabul force, even if he had cared to commune with them. Keane, indeed, did save him from the perpetration of one folly. But Cotton appears to have been a respectable nonentity. Sale was a stout, honest soldier, who was not fortunate on the only occasion which called him outside of his restricted *métier*. Poor Elphinstone was an object for pity rather than for censure.

It happened fortunately, in the impending misfortunes, that two men of stable temperament and lucid perception were in authority at Candahar. General Nott was a grand old Indian officer, in whom there was no guile, but a good deal of temper. He was not supple, and he had the habit of speaking his mind with great directness, a propensity which accounted, perhaps, for the repeated supersessions he had undergone. A clear-headed, shrewd man, he was disgusted with very many things which he recognised as unworthy in the conduct of the affairs of Afghanistan, and he was not the man to choose mild phrases in giving vent to his convictions. He had in full measure that chronic dislike which the Indian commander in the field nourishes to the political officer who is imposed on him by the authorities, and who controls his measures and trammels his actions. Nott's 'political,' who, the sole survivor of the men who were prominent during this unhappy period, still lives among us esteemed and revered, was certainly the ablest officer of the unpopular department to which he belonged ; and how cool was Henry Rawlinson's temper is evinced in his ability to live in amity with the rugged and outspoken chief who addressed him in such a philippic as the following—words all the more trenchant because he to whom they were addressed must have realised how intrinsically true they were :—

'I have no right to interfere with the affairs of this country, and I never do so. But in reference to that part of your note where you speak of political influence, I will candidly tell you that these are not times for mere ceremony, and that under present circumstances, and at a distance of 2000 miles from the seat of the supreme Government, I throw responsibility to the wind, and tell you that in my opinion you have not had for some time past, nor have you at present, one particle of political influence in this country.'

Nott steadily laboured to maintain the *morale* and discipline of his troops, and thus watching the flowing tide of misrule and embroilment, he calmly made the best preparations in his power to meet the storm the sure and early outbreak of which his clear discernment prognosticated.

Shah Soojah's viceroy at Candahar was his heir-apparent Prince Timour. The Dooranee chiefs of Western Afghanistan had not unnaturally expected favours and influence under the rule of the Dooranee monarch ; and while in Candahar before proceeding to Cabul, and still uncertain of what might occur there, Shah Soojah had been lavish of his promises. The chiefs had anticipated that they would be called around the vice-throne of Prince Timour ; but Shah Soojah made the same error as that into which Louis XVIII. fell on his restoration. He constituted his Court of the men who had shared his Loodianah exile. The counsellors who went to Candahar with Timour were returned *émigrés*, in whom fitness for duty counted less than the qualification of companionship in exile. Those people had come back to Afghanistan poor; now they made haste to be rich by acts of oppressive injustice, in the exaction of revenue from the people, and by intercepting from the Dooranee chiefs the flow of royal bounty to which they had looked forward.

Uktar Khan was prominent among the Dooranee noblemen, and he had the double grievance of having been disappointed of the headship of the Zemindawar province on the western bank of the Helmund, and having been evilly entreated by the minions of Prince Timour. He had raised his clan and routed a force under a royalist follower, when Nott sent a detachment against him. Uktar Khan had crossed the Helmund into Zemindawar, when Farrington attacked him, and, after a brisk fight, routed and pursued him. The action was fought on January 3, 1841, in the very dead of winter; the intensity of the cold dispersed Uktar's levies, and Farrington returned to Candahar.

In reply to Macnaghten's demand for information regarding the origin of this outbreak, Rawlinson wrote him some home truths which were very distasteful. Rawlinson warned his chief earnestly of the danger which threatened the false position of the British in Afghanistan. He pointed out how cruel must be the revenue exactions which enabled Prince Timour's courtiers to absorb great sums. He expressed his suspicion that

Shah Soojah had countenanced Uktar Khan's rising, and
spoke of intrigues of dark and dangerous character. Macnaghten scouted Rawlinson's warning, and instructed him
that 'it will make the consideration of all questions more
simple if you will hereafter take for granted that as
regards us "the king can do no wrong."' However, he
and the Shah did remove from Candahar the Vakeel and
his clique of obnoxious persons, who had been grinding
the faces of the people; and the Envoy allowed himself
to hope that this measure would restore order to the
province of Candahar.

The hope was vain, the evil lay deeper; disaffection
to the Shah and hatred to the British power were becoming intensified from day to day, and the aspiration for
relief was swelling into a passion. In the days before our
advent there had been venality and corruption in public
places—occasionally, likely enough, as Macnaghten as-
serted, to an extent all but incredible. But exaction so
sweeping could have occurred only in regions under complete domination; and in Afghanistan, even to this day,
there are few regions wholly in this condition. When the
yoke became over-weighty, a people of a nature so intractable knew how to resent oppression and oppose exaction.
But now the tax gatherer swaggered over the land, and the
people had to endure him, for at his back were the soldiers
of the Feringhees and the levies of the Shah. The latter
were paid by assignments on the revenues of specified
districts; as the levies constituted a standing army of
some size, the contributions demanded were heavier and
more permanent than in bygone times. Macnaghten,
aware of the discontent engendered by the system of

assignments, desired to alter it. But the Shah's needs were pressing; the Anglo-Indian treasury was strained already by the expenditure in Afghanistan; and it was not easy in a period of turmoil and rebellion to carry out the amendment of a fiscal system. That, since the surrender of the Dost, there had been no serious rising in Northern or Eastern Afghanistan, sufficed to make Macnaghten an optimist of the moment. He had come by this time to a reluctant admission of the fact against which he had set his face so long, that Shah Soojah was unpopular. ' He has incurred,' he wrote, ' the odium that attaches to him from his alliance with us '; but the Envoy would not admit that our position in Afghanistan was a false one, in that we were maintaining by our bayonets, against the will of the Afghans, a sovereign whom they detested. ' It would,' he pleaded, ' be an act of downright dishonesty to desert His Majesty before he has found the means of taking root in the soil to which we have transplanted him.' While he wrote, Macnaghten must have experienced a sudden thrill of optimism or of self-delusion, for he continued: 'All things considered, the present tranquillity of this country is to my mind perfectly miraculous. Already our presence has been infinitely beneficial in allaying animosities and in pointing out abuses.' If it had been the case that the country was tranquil, his adjective would have been singularly appropriate, but not precisely in the sense he meant to convey.

But there was no tranquillity, miraculous or otherwise. While Macnaghten was writing the letter which has just been quoted, Brigadier Shelton, who, about the New Year, had reached Jellalabad with a brigade from British

India in relief of the force which was withdrawing with
Cotton, was contending with an outbreak of the wild
and lawless clans of the Khyber.   When Macnaghten
wrote, he had already received intelligence of the collapse
of his projects in Herat, and that Major Todd, who had
been his representative there, judging it imperative to
break up the mission of which he was the head, had
abruptly quitted that city, and was on his way to Candahar.   Mischief was simmering in the Zemindawar country.
The Ghilzai tribes of the region between Candahar and
Ghuznee had accepted a subsidy to remain quiet, but the
indomitable independence of this wild and fierce race was
not to be tamed by bribes, and the spirit of hostility was
manifesting itself so truculently that a British garrison
had been placed in Khelat-i-Ghilzai, right in the heart
of the disturbed territory.   This warning and defensive
measure the tribes had regarded with angry jealousy ; but
it was not until a rash 'political' had directed the unprovoked assault and capture of a Ghilzai fort that the tribes
passionately flew to arms, bent on contesting the occupation of their rugged country.   Colonel Wymer was sent
from Candahar with a force, escorting a convoy of stores
intended for the equipment of Khelat-i-Ghilzai.   The tribes
who had been loosely beleaguering that place marched
down the Turnuk upon Wymer, and on May 19th attacked him with great impetuosity, under the command
of a principal chief who was known as the 'Gooroo.'
Wymer, in the protection of his convoy, had to stand on
the defensive.   The Ghilzais, regardless of the grape which
tore through their masses, fell on sword in hand, and with
an intuitive tactical perception struck Wymer simultane-

ously in front and flank. His sepoys had to change their
dispositions, and the Ghilzais took the opportunity of their
momentary dislocation to charge right home. They were
met firmly by the bayonet, but again and again the hillmen renewed their attacks; and it was not till after five
hours of hard fighting which cost them heavy loss, that
at length, in the darkness, they suddenly drew off. Had
they been Swiss peasants defending their mountains, or
Poles struggling against the ferocious tyranny of Russia,
their gallant effort might have excited praise and sympathy. Had they been Soudanese, a statesman might
have spoken of them as a people 'rightly struggling to be
free'; as it was, the Envoy vituperated them as 'a parcel
of ragamuffins,' and Wymer's sepoys were held to have
'covered themselves with glory.' Macnaghten proceeded
to encourage a sense of honour among the tribes by proposing the transfer to another chief, on condition of his
seizing and delivering over the inconvenient 'Gooroo,' of
the share of subsidy of which the latter had been in receipt.

While this creditable transaction was under consideration, Uktar Khan was again making himself very unpleasant; so much so that Macnaghten was authorising
Rawlinson to offer a reward of 10,000 rupees for his
capture, which accomplished, Rawlinson was instructed
to 'hang the villain as high as Haman.' The gallows
was not built, however, on which Uktar was to hang,
although that chief sustained two severe defeats at the
hands of troops sent from Candahar, and had to become
a fugitive. The Ghilzais, who had gathered again after
their defeat under the 'Gooroo,' had made little stand
against the detachment which Colonel Chambers led out

from Candahar, and they were again temporarily dispersed. The 'Gooroo' himself was in our hands. If the
disaffection was in no degree diminished, the active ebullitions of it were assuredly quelled for the time. It was
true, to be sure, that Akbar Khan, the fierce and resolute
son of Dost Mahomed, had refused the Envoy's overtures
to come in, and was wandering and plotting in Khooloom,
quite ready to fulfil Macnaghten's prophetic apprehension
that 'the fellow will be after some mischief should the
opportunity present itself'; that the Dooranees were still
defiant; that an insurgent force was out in the Dehra-
wat; and that the tameless chief Akram Khan was being
blown from a gun by the cruel and feeble Timour. But
unquestionably there was a comparative although short-
lived lull in the overt hostility of the Afghan peoples
against Shah Soojah and his foreign supporters; and Macnaghten characteristically announced that 'the country
was quiet from Dan to Beersheba.' To one of his corre-
spondents he wrote: 'From Mookoor to the Khyber Pass,
all is content and tranquillity; and wherever we Europeans
go, we are received with respect, attention and welcome.
I think our prospects are most cheering; and with the
materials we have there ought to be little or no difficulty
in the management of the country. The people are perfect children, and they should be treated as such. If
we put one naughty boy in the corner, the rest will be
terrified.'

General Nott at Candahar, who 'never interfered in the
government of the country,' but regarded the situation
with shrewd, clear-headed common sense, differed utterly
from the Envoy's view. The stout old soldier did not

squander his fire ; it was a close volley he discharged in the following words : ' The conduct of the thousand and one politicals has ruined our cause, and bared the throat of every European in this country to the sword and knife of the revengeful Afghan and bloody Belooch ; and unless several regiments be quickly sent, not a man will be left to describe the fate of his comrades. Nothing will ever make the Afghans submit to the hated Shah Soojah, who is most certainly as great a scoundrel as ever lived.'

Nott's conclusions were in the main justified by after events; but the correctness of his premiss may be questioned. That the conduct of some of the political officers intensified the rancour of the Afghans is unhappily true, but the hate of our domination, and of the puppet thrust upon them by us, seems to have found its origin in a deeper feeling. The patriotism of a savage race is marked by features repulsive to civilised communities, but through the ruthless cruelty of the indiscriminate massacre, the treachery of the stealthy stab, and the lightly broken pledges, there may shine out the noblest virtue that a virile people can possess. A semi-barbarian nation whose manhood pours out its blood like water in stubborn resistance against an alien yoke, may be pardoned for many acts shocking to civilised communities which have not known the bitterness of stern and masterful subjugation.

CHAPTER V

THE BEGINNING OF THE END

THE deceptive quietude of Afghanistan which followed the sharp lessons administered to the Dooranees and the Ghilzais was not seriously disturbed during the month of September 1841, and Macnaghten was in a full glow of cheerfulness. His services had been recognised by his appointment to the dignified and lucrative post of Governor of the Bombay Presidency, and he was looking forward to an early departure for a less harassing and tumultuous sphere of action than that in which he had been labouring for two troubled years. The belief that he would leave behind him a quiescent Afghanistan, and Shah Soojah firmly established on its throne, was the complement, to a proud and zealous man, of the satisfaction which his promotion afforded.

One distasteful task he had to perform before he should go. The Home Government had become seriously disquieted by the condition of affairs in Afghanistan. The Secret Committee of the Court of Directors, the channel through which the ministry communicated with the Governor-General, had expressed great concern at the heavy burden imposed on the Indian finances by the cost of the maintenance of the British force in Afghanistan,

and by the lavish expenditure of the administration which
Macnaghten directed. The Anglo-Indian Government
was urgently required to review with great earnestness
the question of its future policy in regard to Afghanistan,
and to consider gravely whether an enterprise at once so
costly and so unsatisfactory in results should not be
frankly abandoned. Lord Auckland was alive to the
difficulties and embarrassments which encompassed the
position beyond the Indus, but he was loth to admit that
the policy of which he had been the author, and in which
the Home Government had abetted him so eagerly, was
an utter failure. He and his advisers finally decided in
favour of the continued occupation of Afghanistan ; and
since the Indian treasury was empty, and the annual
charge of that occupation was not less than a million and
a quarter sterling, recourse was had to a loan. Macnaghten
was pressed to effect economies in the administration,
and he was specially enjoined to cut down the subsidies
which were paid to Afghan chiefs as bribes to keep them
quiet. Macnaghten had objected to this retrenchment,
pointing out that the stipends to the chiefs were simply
compensation for the abandonment by them of their
immemorial practice of highway robbery, but he yielded
to pressure, called to Cabul the chiefs in its vicinity, and
informed them that thenceforth their subsidies would be
reduced. The chiefs strongly remonstrated, but without
effect, and they then formed a confederacy of rebellion.
The Ghilzai chiefs were the first to act. Quitting Cabul,
they occupied the passes between the capital and
Jellalabad, and entirely intercepted the communications
with India by the Khyber route.

Macnaghten did not take alarm at this significant demonstration, regarding the outbreak merely as ' provoking,'
and writing to Rawlinson. that ' the rascals would be well
trounced for their pains.' Yet warnings of gathering
danger were rife, which but for his mood of optimism
should have struck home to his apprehension. Pottinger
had come down from the Kohistan, where he was acting
as political officer, bent on impressing on him that a
general rising of that region was certain unless strong
measures of prevention were resorted to. For some time
before the actual outbreak of the Ghilzais, the Afghan
hatred to our people had been showing itself with exceptional openness and bitterness. Europeans and camp
followers had been murdered, but the sinister evidences of
growing danger had been regarded merely as ebullitions
of private rancour. Akbar Khan, Dost Mahomed's son,
had moved forward from Khooloom into the Bamian
country, and there was little doubt that he was fomenting
the disaffection of the Ghilzai chiefs, with some of whom
this indomitable man, who in his intense hatred of the
English intruders had resolutely rejected all offers of
accommodation, and preferred the life of a homeless exile
to the forfeiture of his independence, was closely con-
nected by marriage.

The time was approaching when Sale's brigade was to
quit Cabul on its return journey to India. Macnaghten
seems to have originally intended to accompany this
force, for he wrote that he ' hoped to settle the hash of
the Ghilzais on the way down, if not before.' The rising,
however, spread so widely and so rapidly that immediate
action was judged necessary, and on October 9th Colonel

Monteath marched towards the passes with his own regiment, the 35th Native Infantry, some artillery and cavalry details, and a detachment of Broadfoot's sappers.

How able, resolute, and high-souled a man was George Broadfoot, the course of this narrative will later disclose. He was one of three gallant brothers, all of whom died sword in hand. The corps of sappers which he commanded was a remarkable body — a strange medley of Hindustanees, Goorkhas, and Afghan tribesmen of divers regions. Many were desperate and intractable characters, but Broadfoot, with mingled strength and kindness, moulded his heterogeneous recruits into skilful, obedient and disciplined soldiers. Broadfoot's description of his endeavours to learn something of the nature of the duties expected of him in the expedition for which he had been detailed, and to obtain such equipment as those duties might require, throws a melancholy light on the deteriorated state of affairs among our people at this period, and on the relations between the military and civilian authorities.

Broadfoot went for information, in the first instance, to Colonel Monteath, who could give him no orders, having received none himself. Monteath declined to apply for details as to the expedition, as he knew 'these people' (the authorities) too well; he was quite aware of the danger of going on service in the dark, but explained that it was not the custom of the military authorities at Cabul to consult or even instruct the commanders of expeditions. Broadfoot then went to the General. Cotton's successor in the chief military command in Afghanistan was poor General Elphinstone, a most gallant soldier, but with no experience of Indian warfare, and utterly ignorant of the Afghans and of Afghanistan. Wrecked in body and impaired in mind by physical ailments and infirmities, he had lost all faculty of energy, and such mind as remained to him was swayed by the opinion of the person with whom he had last spoken. The poor gentleman was so exhausted by the exertion of getting out of bed, and being helped into his visiting-room, that it was not for half-an-hour, and after several ineffectual efforts, that he could attend to business. He knew nothing of the nature of the service on which Monteath was ordered, could give Broadfoot no orders, and was unwilling to refer to the Envoy on a matter which should have been left to him to arrange. He complained bitterly of the way in which he was reduced to a cypher—'degraded from a general to the "Lord-Lieutenant's head constable."' Broadfoot went from the General to the Envoy, who 'was peevish,' and denounced the General as fidgety. He declared the enemy to be contemptible, and that as for Broadfoot and his sappers, twenty men with pickaxes were enough ; all they were wanted for was to pick stones from under the gun wheels. When Broadfoot represented the inconvenience with which imperfect information as to the objects of the expedition was fraught, Macnaghten lost his temper, and told Broadfoot that, if he thought Monteath's movement likely to bring on an attack, ' he need not go, he was not wanted'; whereupon Broadfoot declined to listen to such language, and made his bow. Returning to the General, whom he found 'lost and perplexed,' he was told to follow his own judgment as to what quantity of tools he should take.   The Adjutant-

General came in, and 'this officer, after abusing the
Envoy, spoke to the General with an imperiousness and
disrespect, and to me, a stranger, with an insolence it
was painful to see the influence of on the General. His
advice to his chief was to have nothing to say to Macnaghten, to me, or to the sappers, saying Monteath had
men enough, and needed neither sappers nor tools.' At
parting the poor old man said to Broadfoot : ' If you go
out, for God's sake clear the passes quickly, that I may
get away; for if anything were to turn up, I am unfit for
it, done up in body and mind.' This was the man whom
Lord Auckland had appointed to the most responsible
and arduous command at his disposal, and this not in
ignorance of General Elphinstone's disqualifications for
active service, but in the fullest knowledge of them !

Monteath's camp at Bootkhak, the first halting-place
on the Jellalabad road, was sharply attacked on the
night of the 9th, and the assailants, many of whom
were the armed retainers of chiefs living in Cabul sent
out specially to take part in the attack, although unsuccessful, inflicted on Monteath considerable loss. Next
day Sale, with H.M.'s 13th, joined Monteath, and on
the 13th he forced the long and dangerous ravine of the
Khoord Cabul with sharp fighting, but no very serious
loss, although Sale himself was wounded, and had to re-
linquish the active command to Colonel Dennie. Monteath encamped in the valley beyond the pass, and Sale,
with the 13th, returned without opposition to Bootkhak,
there to await reinforcements and transports. In his
isolated position Monteath remained unmolested until the
night of the 17th, when he repulsed a Ghilzai attack made

in considerable strength, and aided by the treachery of
'friendly' Afghans who had been admitted into his camp;
but he had many casualties, and lost a number of camels.
On the 20th Sale, reinforced by troops returned from the
Zurmut expedition, moved forward on Monteath, and on
the 22d pushed on to the Tezeen valley, meeting with
no opposition either on the steep summit of the Huft
Kotul or in the deep narrow ravine opening into the
valley.   The Ghilzais were in force around the mouth of
the defile, but a few cannon-shots broke them up.   The
advance guard pursued with over-rashness ; the Ghilzais
rallied, in the skirmish which ensued an officer and several
men were killed, and the retirement of our people unfortunately degenerated into precipitate flight, with the
Ghilzais in hot pursuit.   The 13th, to which the fugitive
detachment mainly belonged, now consisted mainly of
young soldiers, whose constancy was impaired by this
untoward occurrence.

Macnaghten had furnished Sale with a force which,
in good heart and vigorously commanded, was strong
enough to have effected great things.   The Ghilzai chief
of Tezeen possessed a strong fort full of supplies, which
Dennie was about to attack, when the wily Afghan sent
to Major Macgregor, the political officer accompanying
Sale, a tender of submission.   Macgregor fell into the
snare, desired Sale to countermand the attack, and
entered into negotiations.   In doing so he committed a
fatal error, and he exceeded his instructions in the concessions which he made.   Macnaghten, it was true, had left
matters greatly to Macgregor's discretion ; and if 'the
rebels were very humble,' the Envoy was not disposed to

be too hard upon them. But one of his firm stipulations
was that the defences of Khoda Buxsh's fort must be
demolished, and that Gool Mahomed Khan 'should have
nothing but war.' Both injunctions were disregarded by
Macgregor, who, with unimportant exceptions, surrendered
all along the line. The Ghilzais claimed and obtained
the restoration of their original subsidies ; a sum was
handed to them to enable them to raise the tribes in order
to keep clear the passes ; Khoda Buxsh held his fort, and
sold the supplies it contained to Sale's commissary at a
fine price. Every item of the arrangement was dead in
favour of the Ghilzais, and contributory to their devices.
Sale, continuing his march, would be separated further and
further from the now diminished force in Cabul, and by
the feigned submission the chiefs had made they had
escaped the permanent establishment of a strong detachment in their midst at Tezeen.

Macnaghten, discontented though he was with the
sweeping concessions which Macgregor had granted to
the Ghilzais, put the best face he could on the completed
transaction, and allowed himself to believe that a stable
settlement had been effected. On the 26th Sale continued his march, having made up his baggage animals at
the expense of the 37th Native Infantry, which, with half
of the sappers and three guns of the mountain train,
he sent back to Kubbar-i-Jubbar, there to halt in a
dangerously helpless situation until transport should be
sent down from Cabul. His march as far as Kutti
Sung was unmolested. Mistrusting the good faith of his
new-made allies, he shunned the usual route through the
Purwan Durrah by taking the mountain road to the south

of that defile, and thus reached the Jugdulluk valley with little opposition, baulking the dispositions of the Ghilzais, who, expecting him to traverse the Purwan Durrah, were massed about the southern end of the defile, ready to fall on the column when committed to the tortuous gorge.

From the Jugdulluk camping ground there is a steep and winding ascent of three miles, commanded until near the summit by heights on either side. Sale's main body had attained the crest with trivial loss, having detached parties by the way to ascend to suitable flanking positions, and hold those until the long train of slow-moving baggage should have passed, when they were to fall in and come on with the rear-guard. The dispositions would have been successful but that on reaching the crest the main body, instead of halting there for the rear to close up, hurried down the reverse slope, leaving baggage, detachments, and rear-guard to endure the attacks which the Ghilzais promptly delivered, pressing fiercely on the rear, and firing down from either side on the confused mass in the trough below. The flanking detachments had relinquished their posts in panic, and hurried forward in confusion to get out of the pass. The rear-guard was in disorder, when Broadfoot, with a few officers and some of his sappers, valiantly checked the onslaught, but the crest was not crossed until upwards of 120 men had fallen, the wounded among whom had to be abandoned with the dead. On October 30th Sale's force reached Gundamuk without further molestation, and halted there temporarily to await orders. During the halt melancholy rumours filtered down the passes from the capital, and later came

confirmation of the evil tidings from the Envoy, and
orders from Elphinstone directing the immediate return
of the brigade to Cabul, if the safety of its sick and
wounded could be assured. Sale called a council of war,
which pronounced, although not unanimously, against a
return to Cabul; and it was resolved instead to march
on to Jellalabad, which was regarded as an eligible
point d'appui on which a relieving force might move up
and a retiring force might move down. Accordingly
on November 11th the brigade quitted Gundamuk, and
hurried down rather precipitately, and with some fighting by the way, to Jellalabad, which was occupied on
the 14th.

Some members of the Gundamuk council of war, fore-
most among whom was Broadfoot, argued vigorously in
favour of the return march to Cabul. Havelock, who
was with Sale as a staff-officer, strongly urged the further
retreat into Jellalabad. Others, again, advocated the
middle course of continuing to hold Gundamuk. It may
be said that a daring general would have fought his way
back to Cabul, that a prudent general would have remained at Gundamuk, and that the occupation of Jellalabad was the expedient of a weak general. That a well-
led march on Cabul was feasible, although it might have
been difficult and bloody, cannot be questioned, and the
advent of such men as Broadfoot and Havelock would
have done much toward rekindling confidence and stimulating the restoration of soldierly virtue, alike in the military authorities and in the rank and file of the Cabul force.
At Gundamuk, again, the brigade, well able to maintain
its position there, would have made its influence felt all

through the Ghilzai country and as far as Cabul. The evacuation of that capital decided on, it would have been in a position to give the hand to the retiring army, and so to avert at least the worst disasters of the retreat. The retirement on Jellalabad, in the terse language of Durand, 'served no conceivable purpose except to betray weakness, and still further to encourage revolt.'

While Sale was struggling through the passes on his way to Gundamuk, our people at Cabul were enjoying unwonted quietude. Casual entries in Lady Sale's journal, during the later days of October, afford clear evidence how utterly unconscious were they of the close gathering of the storm that so soon was to break upon them. Her husband had written to her from Tezeen that his wound was fast healing, and that the chiefs were extremely polite. She complains of the interruption of the mails owing to the Ghilzai outbreak, but comforts herself with the anticipation of their arrival in a day or two. She was to leave Cabul for India in a few days, along with the Macnaghtens and General Elphinstone, and her diary expresses an undernote of regret at having to leave the snug house in the cantonments which Sale had built on his own plan, the excellent kitchen garden in which her warrior husband, in the intervals of his soldiering duties, grew fine crops of peas, potatoes, cauliflowers and artichokes, and the parterres of flowers which she herself cultivated, and which were the admiration of the Afghan gentlemen who came to pay their morning calls.

The defencelessness of the position at Cabul had long engaged the solicitude of men who were no alarmists. Engineer officer after engineer officer had unavailingly

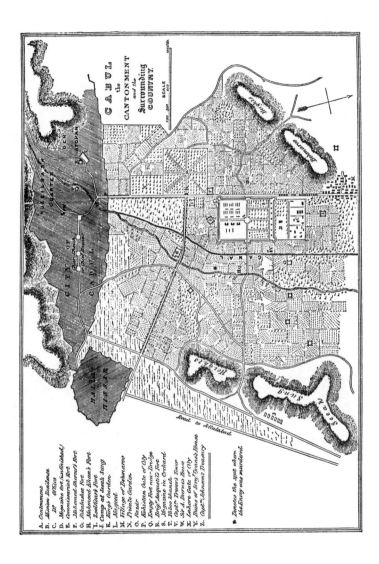

CABUL
the
CANTONMENT
and the
Surrounding
COUNTRY.

SCALE

Road to Killalabad

A. Cantonment
B. Mission Residence
C. D° Offices
D. Magazine Fort (unfinished)
E. Commissariat Fort
F. Mahomed Shereef's Fort
G. Rikabashee Fort
H. Mahmood Khan's Fort
I. Zoolficar's Fort
J. Camp at small Sung
K. King's Garden
L. Shopgeed
M. Village of Behmaroo
N. Private Garden
O. Hazir
P. Kohistan Gate of City
Q. Empty Fort near Bridge
R. Brig' Anquetil's Fort
S. Magazine in Orchard
T. Rhika Mirards
U. Capt" Trevor's Tower
V. Sir A. Burnes' House
W. Lahore Gate of City
X. Ruins of Sir" Dennis's House
Y. Capt" Johnson's Treasury

* Denotes the spot where
the Envoy was murdered

urged the construction of barracks in the Balla Hissar, the repair and improvement of the defences of that strong-hold, and the occupation of it by our troops. The canton-ments on the plain northward of the city would have served their purpose fairly as residential quarters in peace time if the Balla Hissar, which in case of need could have accommodated all our people, had been repaired and adequately garrisoned. But the fateful errors were made of yielding to the Shah Soojah's objections to the British occupation of the Balla Hissar, and of making a pretence of rendering the cantonments defensible by sur-rounding the great parallelogram with the caricature of an obstacle in the shape of a shallow ditch and feeble earthwork over which an active cow could scramble. The enclosed area was commanded on all sides by Afghan forts, which were neither occupied nor destroyed. The commissariat stores were actually located in a fort out-side the cantonments altogether, the communication with which was commanded by a fort held by the Afghans. In all essentials of a defensive position the Cabul canton-ments, at the beginning of the outbreak, were simply contemptible.

Sir William Macnaghten and his political staff occupied the Mission compound, an annexe of the cantonments. General Elphinstone had his quarters in the cantonments; Sir Alexander Burnes lived in a house in the city opposite to the Treasury, which was in charge of Captain Johnson, and several other officers resided in the suburbs. Brigadier Shelton, a brave and experienced soldier, but of curiously impracticable and ill-conditioned nature, was in camp with a considerable force on the Seah Sung hills, about a mile and a half from the cantonments, with the Cabul river intervening. With Shelton's troops and those in the cantonments General Elphinstone had at his disposition, apart from the Shah's contingent, four infantry regiments, two batteries of artillery, three companies of sappers, a regiment of cavalry, and some irregular horse—a force fully equipped and in good order. In the Balla Hissar Shah Soojah had a considerable, if rather mixed, body of military and several guns.

The rising of the 2d November may not have been the result of a fully organised plan. There are indications that it was premature, and that the revolt in force would have been postponed until after the expected departure of the Envoy and the General with all the troops except Shelton's brigade, but for an irrepressible burst of personal rancour against Burnes. Durand holds, however, that the malcontents acted on the belief that to kill Burnes and sack the Treasury was to inaugurate the insurrection with an imposing success. Be this as it may, a truculent mob early in the morning of November 2d assailed Burnes' house. He at first regarded the outbreak as a casual riot, and wrote to Macnaghten to that effect. Having harangued the throng without effect, he and his brother, along with William Broadfoot his secretary, prepared for defence. Broadfoot was soon killed, and a little later Burnes and his brother were hacked to pieces in the garden behind the house. The Treasury was sacked; the sepoys who had guarded it and Burnes' house were massacred, and both buildings were fired ; the armed mob swelled in numbers, and soon the whole city was in a roar of tumult.

Prompt and vigorous military action would no doubt have crushed the insurrection, at least for the time. But the indifference, vacillation and delay of the British authorities greatly encouraged its rapid development. Macnaghten at first 'did not think much of it.' Shelton was ordered into the Balla Hissar, countermanded, a second time ordered, and again instructed to halt for orders. At last the Envoy himself despatched him, with the loose order to act on his own judgment in communication with the Shah. Shelton marched into the Balla Hissar with part of his force, and the rest of it was moved into the cantonments. When the Brigadier went to the Shah, that potentate demanded to know who sent him, and what he had come for. But the Shah, to do him justice, had himself taken action. Informed that Burnes was attacked and the city in revolt, he had ordered Campbell's regiment of his own levies and a couple of guns to march to his assistance. Campbell recklessly attempted to push his way through the heart of the city, instead of reaching Burnes' house by a circuitous but opener route, and after some sharp street fighting in which he lost heavily, he was driven back, unable to penetrate to the scene of plunder and butchery. Shelton remained inactive in the Balla Hissar until Campbell was reported beaten and retreating, when he took some feeble measures to cover the retreat of the fugitives, who, however, abandoned their guns outside the fortress. The day was allowed to pass without anything further being done, except the despatch of an urgent recall to Major Griffiths, whom Sale had left at Kubbar-i-Jubbar, and that good soldier, having fought every step of the way through the passes, brought in his detachment in unbroken order and without loss of baggage, notwithstanding his weakness in transport. Shelton, reinforced in the Balla Hissar, maintained an intermittent and ineffectual fire on the city. Urgent orders were despatched to Sale, recalling him and his brigade—orders with which, as has been mentioned, Sale did not comply— and also to Nott, at Candahar, begging him to send a brigade to Cabul. In compliance with this requisition, Maclaren's brigade immediately started from Candahar, but soon returned owing to the inclemency of the weather.

Captain Mackenzie was in charge of a fort containing the Shah's commissariat stores; this fort was on the outskirts of a suburb of Cabul, and was fiercely attacked on the 2d. For two days Mackenzie maintained his post with unwearying constancy. His garrison was short of water and of ammunition, and the fort was crowded with women and children, but he held on resolutely until the night of the 3d. No assistance was sent, no notice, indeed, of any kind was taken of him; his garrison was discouraged by heavy loss, and by the mines which the enemy were pushing forward. At length, when the gate of the fort had been fired, and his wounded were dying for lack of medical aid, he evacuated the fort, and fought his way gallantly into cantonments, bringing in his wounded and the women and children. With this solitary exception the Afghans had nowhere encountered resistance, and the strange passiveness of our people encouraged them to act with vigour. From the enclosed space of the Shah Bagh, and the adjacent forts of Mahmood Khan and Mahomed Shereef, they were threatening the Commissariat fort, hindering access to it, and be-

setting the south-western flank of the cantonments. A
young officer commanded the hundred sepoys garrisoning
the Commissariat fort; he reported himself in danger of
being cut off, and Elphinstone gave orders that he and
his garrison should be brought off, and the fort and its
contents abandoned. Several efforts to accomplish the
withdrawal were thwarted by the Afghan flanking fire,
with the loss of several officers and many men. The
commissary officer urged on the General the disastrous
consequences which the abandonment of the fort would
entail, containing as it did all the stores, adding that
in cantonments there were only two days' supplies, without prospect of procuring any more. Orders were then
sent to Warren to hold out to the last extremity; which
instructions he denied having received. Early in the
morning of the 5th troops were preparing to attack the
Afghan fort and reinforce the Commissariat fort, when
Warren and his garrison reached the cantonments. The
gate of the Commissariat fort had been fired, but the
enemy had not effected an entrance, yet Warren and his
people had evacuated the fort through a hole cut in its
wall. Thus, with scarcely a struggle to save it, was this
vital fort allowed to fall into the enemy's hands, and
thenceforward our unfortunate people were to be reduced
to precarious and scanty sources for their food.

From the 5th to the 9th November there was a good
deal of desultory fighting, in the course of which, after one
failure, Mahomed Shereef's fort was stormed by a detachment of our people, under the command of Major Griffiths;
but this success had little influence on the threatening
attitude maintained by the Afghans. On the 9th, owing

to the mental and physical weakness of poor General Elphinstone, Brigadier Shelton was summoned into cantonments from the Balla Hissar, bringing with him part of the garrison with which he had been holding the latter post. The hopes entertained that Shelton would display vigour, and restore the confidence of the troops, were not realised. He from the first had no belief in the ability of the occupants of the cantonment to maintain their position, and he never ceased to urge prompt retreat on Jellalabad.   From the purely military point of view he was probably right ; the Duke of Wellington shared his opinion when he said in the House of Lords : 'After the first few days, particularly after the negotiations at Cabul had commenced, it became hopeless for General Elphinstone to maintain his position.' Shelton's situation was unquestionably a very uncomfortable one, for Elphinstone, broken as he was, yet allowed his second in command no freedom of action, and was testily pertinacious of his prerogative of command.   If in Shelton, who after his manner was a strong man, there had been combined with his resolution some tact and temper, he might have exercised a beneficial influence.   As it was he became sullen and despondent, and retired behind an ' uncommunicative and disheartening reserve.'   Brave as he was, he seems to have lacked the inspiration which alone could reinvigorate the drooping spirit of the troops.   In a word, though he probably was, in army language, a ' good duty soldier,' he certainly was nothing more.   And something more was needed then.

Action on Shelton's part became necessary the day after he came into cantonments.   The Afghans occupied all the forts on the plain between the Seah Sung heights and the cantonments, and from the nearest of them, the Rika-bashee fort, poured in a heavy fire at close range, which the return artillery fire could not quell. On Macnaghten's urgent requisition the General ordered out a strong force, under Shelton, to storm the obnoxious fort. Captain Bellew missed the gate, and blew open merely a narrow wicket, but the storming party obeyed the signal to advance. Through a heavy fire the leaders reached the wicket, and forced their way in, followed by a few soldiers. The garrison of the fort hastily evacuated it, and all seemed well, when a sudden stampede ensued—the handful which, led by Colonel Mackrell of the 44th and Lieutenant Bird of the Shah's force, had already entered the fort, remaining inside it. The runaway troops were rallied with difficulty by Shelton and the subordinate officers, but a call for volunteers from the European regiment was responded to but by one solitary Scottish private. After a second advance, and a second retreat—a retreat made notwithstanding strong artillery and musketry support—Shelton's efforts brought his people forward yet again, and this time the fort was occupied in force. Of those who had previously entered it but two survivors were found. The Afghans, re-entering the fort, had hacked Mackrell to pieces and slaughtered the men who tried to escape by the wicket. Lieutenant Bird and a sepoy, from a stable the door of which they had barricaded with logs of wood, had fended off their assailants by a steady and deadly fire, and when they were rescued by the entrance of the troops they had to clamber out over a pile of thirty dead Afghans whom the bullets of the two men had struck down.

It had come to our people in those gloomy days, to

regard as a 'triumph' a combat in which they were not
actually worsted; and even of such dubious successes
the last occurred on November 13, when the Afghans,
after having pressed our infantry down the slopes of the
Behmaroo ridge, were driven back by artillery fire, and
forced by a cavalry charge to retreat further, leaving behind them a couple of guns from which they had been
sending missiles into the cantonments. One of those guns
was brought in without difficulty, but the other the Afghans
covered with their jezail fire. The Envoy had sent a message of entreaty that 'the triumph of the day' should be
completed by its capture. Major Scott of the 44th made
appeal on appeal, ineffectually, to the soldierly feelings
of his men, and while they would not move the sepoys
could not be induced to advance. At length Eyre spiked
the piece as a precautionary measure, and finally some
men of the Shah's infantry succeeded in bringing in the
prize. The return march of the troops into cantonments
in the dark, was rendered disorderly by the close pressure
of the Afghans, who, firing incessantly, pursued the broken
soldiery up to the entrance gate.

On the depressed garrison of the Cabul cantonments
tidings of disaster further afield had been pouring in apace.
Soon after the outbreak of the rising, it was known that
Lieutenant Maule, commanding the Kohistanee regiment
at Kurdurrah, had been cut to pieces, with his adjutant
and sergeant-major, by the men of his own corps; and on
November 6th intelligence had come in that the Goorkha
regiment stationed at Charikar in the Kohistan, where
Major Pottinger was Resident, was in dangerous case, and
that Codrington, its commandant, and some of his officers

had already fallen. And now, on the 15th, there rode wearily into cantonments two wounded men, who believed themselves the only British survivors of the Charikar force. Pottinger was wounded in the leg, Haughton, the adjutant of the Goorkha corps, had lost his right hand, and his head hung forward on his breast, half severed from his body by a great tulwar slash. Of the miserable story which it fell to Pottinger to tell only the briefest summary can be given. His residence was at Lughmanee, a few miles from the Charikar cantonments, when early in the month a number of chiefs of the Kohistan and the Nijrao country assembled to discuss with him the terms on which they would reopen the communications with Cabul. Those chiefs proved treacherous, slew Rattray, Pottinger's assistant, and besieged Pottinger in Lughmanee. Finding his position untenable, he withdrew to Charikar under cover of night. On the morning of the 5th the Afghans assailed the cantonments. Pottinger was wounded, Codrington was killed, and the Goorkhas were driven into the barracks. Haughton, who succeeded to the command of the regiment, made sortie on sortie, but was finally driven in, and the enemy renewed their assaults in augmented strength. Thenceforward the position was all but hopeless. On the 10th the last scant remains of water was distributed. Efforts to procure water by sorties on the nights of the 11th and 12th were not successful, and the corps fell into disorganisation because of losses, hardships, exhaustion, hunger and thirst. Pottinger and Haughton agreed that there was no prospect of saving even a remnant of the regiment unless by a retreat to Cabul, which, however, was clearly possible only in the case of the stronger men, unencumbered with women and children, of whom, unfortunately, there was a great number in the garrison.   On the afternoon of the 13th Haughton was cut down by a treacherous native officer of the artillery, who then rushed out of the gate, followed by all the gunners and most of the Mahommedans of the garrison.   In the midst of the chaos of disorganisation, Dr Grant amputated Haughton's hand, dressed his other wounds, and then spiked all the guns. When it was dark, the garrison moved out, Pottinger leading the advance, Dr Grant the main body, and Ensign Rose the rear-guard.   From the beginning of the march, discipline was all but entirely in abeyance ; on reaching the first stream, the last remains of control were lost, and the force was rapidly disintegrating.   Pottinger and Haughton, the latter only just able to keep the saddle, pushed on toward Cabul, rested in a ravine during the day, evaded the partisan detachment sent out from Cabul to intercept them, rode through sleeping Cabul in the small hours of the morning, and after being pursued and fired upon in the outskirts of the city, finally attained the cantonments.   It was afterwards learned that a portion of the regiment had struggled on to within twenty miles from Cabul, gallantly headed by young Rose and Dr Grant.   Then the remnant was destroyed.   Rose was killed, after despatching four Afghans with his own hand. Dr Grant, escaping the massacre, held on until within three miles of the cantonments, when he too was killed.

Macnaghten was naturally much depressed by the news communicated by Pottinger, and realised that the Afghan masses already encompassing the position on the Cabul plain would certainly be increased by bands from the

Kohistan and Nijrao, flushed already with their Charikar
success. He sided strongly with the large party among
the officers who were advocating the measure of abandoning the cantonments altogether, and moving the force now
quartered there to the safer and more commanding position in the Balla Hissar. The military chiefs opposed the
project, and propounded a variety of objections to it, none
of which were without weight, yet all of which might have
been overcome by energy and proper dispositions. Shelton,
however, was opposed to the scheme, since if carried out it
would avert or postpone the accomplishment of his policy
of retreat on Jellalabad; Elphinstone was against it in the
inertia of debility, and the project gradually came to be
regarded as abandoned. Another project, that of driving
the Afghans from Mahmood Khan's fort, commanding
the direct road between the cantonments and the Balla
Hissar, and of occupying it with a British force, was so
far advanced that the time for the attempt was fixed, and
the storming party actually warned, when some petty
objection intervened and the enterprise was abandoned,
never to be revived.

The rising was not three days old when already
Elphinstone had lost heart. On the 5th he had written
to Macnaghten suggesting that the latter should 'consider
what chance there is of making terms,' and since then he
had been repeatedly pressing on the Envoy the 'hopeless-
ness of further resistance.' Macnaghten, vacillating as he
was, yet had more pith in his nature than was left in the
debilitated old general. He wrote to Elphinstone on the
18th recommending, not very strenuously, the policy of
holding out where they were as long as possible, and

indeed throughout the winter, if subsistence could be obtained. He pointed out that in the cantonments, which he believed to be impregnable, there were at least the essentials of wood and water. Arguing that a retreat on Jellalabad must be most disastrous, and was to be avoided except in the last extremity, he nevertheless ended somewhat inconsistently by leaving to the military authorities, if in eight or ten days there should appear no prospect of an improvement of the situation, the decision whether it would be wiser to attempt a retreat or to withdraw from the cantonments into the Balla Hissar.

Far from improving, the situation was speedily to become all but hopeless. The village of Behmaroo, built on the north-eastern slope of the ridge of the same name bounding the plain on the north-west, lay about half a mile due north of the cantonments, part of which some of the houses on the upper slope commanded. From this village, after the loss of the Commissariat fort, our people had been drawing supplies. On the morning of the 22d the Afghans were seen moving in force from Cabul toward Behmaroo, obviously with intent to occupy the village, and so deprive the occupants of the cantonments of the resource it had been affording them. A detachment under Major Swayne, sent out to forestall this occupation, found Behmaroo already in the possession of a body of Kohistanees, who had so blocked the approaches that Swayne did not consider himself justified in attempting the fulfilment of his orders to storm the place; and he contented himself with maintaining all day an ineffectual musketry fire on it. A diversion in his favour by a gun supported by cavalry had no result save that of casualties to the gunners and troopers; reinforcements brought out by Shelton effected nothing, and in the evening the troops were recalled. On this ill-fated day Akbar Khan, Dost Mahomed's fierce and implacable son, arrived in Cabul, and the evil influence on the British fortunes which he exerted immediately made itself felt, for the events of the following day were to bring about a crisis in the fate of our ill-starred people.

Recognising the mischief wrought by the hostile occupation of our only source of supplies, the Envoy strongly urged the immediate despatch of a strong force to occupy the Behmaroo ridge, and dislodge from the village its Kohistanee garrison. Shelton opposed the measure, urging the dispirited state of the troops, their fatigue from constant defensive duty, and their weakened physique because of poor and scanty rations. He was overruled, and before daybreak of the 23d a force under his command, consisting of five companies of the 44th, twelve companies of native infantry, some cavalry, and one horse-artillery gun, was in position on the north-eastern extremity of the ridge overhanging the village. The gun opened fire on the village with grape, and after a short resistance the greater part of its garrison quitted it. The storming party intrusted to Major Swayne did not, however, act, and was withdrawn. Leaving a detachment on the knoll above the village, Shelton moved his force along the upland to a position near the gorge intersecting the ridge, forming his infantry into two squares, with the cavalry in rear. The further hill beyond the gorge was crowded with hostile Afghans from Cabul, and the long-range fire of their jezails across the dividing depression, carried execution into the squares which Shelton had inexplicably formed as if to furnish his foes with a target which they could not miss.   The muskets of his men could not retaliate, and the skirmishers he threw forward to the brow of his hill could not endure the Afghan fire.   Shelton's single gun maintained a hot and telling fire on the Afghan masses on the opposite hill, and baulked an attempt against his right flank made by the Afghan cavalry swarming in the outer plain; but when its vent became too hot for the gunners to serve it, the dullest comprehension became alive to the folly of sending a single gun into the field.

Shelton's men, falling fast though they were, and faint with fatigue and thirst, yet had endured for hours a fusillade to which they could not reply, when a body of Afghan fanatics suddenly sprang up out of the gorge, swept back with their fire the few skirmishers who had been still holding the brow of the hill, and planted their flag within thirty yards of the front of the nearer of the squares. Shelton offered a large reward to the man who should bring it in, but there was no response.   In a passion of soldierly wrath, the veteran commanded a bayonet charge; not a man sprang forward at the summons which British soldiers are wont to welcome with cheers.   The cowed infantry remained supine, when their officers darted forward and threw stones into the faces of the enemy; the troopers heard but obeyed not that trumpet-call to 'Charge!' which so rarely fails to thrill the cavalryman with the rapture of the fray.   The gunners only, men of that noble force the Company's Horse-Artillery, quitted themselves valiantly.   They stood to their piece to the bitter end. Two of them were killed beside it, another was severely wounded, a fourth, refusing to run, took refuge under the gun, and miraculously escaped death. But the gallant example of the artillerymen in their front did not hearten the infantrymen of the leading square. The panic spread among them, and they broke and fled. Fortunately they were not pursued. The rear square stood fast, and the officers by great exertion succeeded in rallying the fugitives under the cover it afforded. The news that a principal chief, Abdoolah Khan, had been severely wounded in the plain gave pause to the offensive vigour of the Afghans, and the assailants fell back, abandoning the gun, but carrying off the limber and gun-team. Our people reoccupied the position, the gun recommenced its fire, and if the cavalry and infantry could have been persuaded to take the offensive the battle might have been retrieved. But they remained passive. The reinforced Afghans renewed their long-range fire with terrible effect ; most of the gunners had fallen, and the Brigadier, recognising the growing unsteadiness of his command and the imminent danger of capture to which the solitary gun was again exposed, ordered a retirement on the detachment left near Behmaroo and the limbering up of the gun, to which a second limber had been sent out from the cantonments. The movement was scarcely begun when a rush of fanatic Afghans completely broke the square, and all order and discipline then disappeared. A regular rout set in down the hill toward cantonments, the fugitives disregarding the efforts of the officers to rally them, and the enemy in full pursuit, the Afghan cavalry making ghastly slaughter among the panic-stricken runaways. The detachment near Behmaroo attempted to fall back in orderly fashion,

but the reinforced garrison of the village swept out upon
it, surrounded it, broke it up, and threw it into utter rout
with the loss of a large proportion of its strength, one
whole company being all but annihilated. It seemed as if
pursued and pursuers would enter the cantonments together
so closely were they commingled; but the fire from the ramparts and an opportune charge of horse arrested the pursuit. Yet Eyre reckons as the chief reason why all the
British force that had gone out to battle was not destroyed,
the fact that a leading Afghan chief forced his men to
spare the fugitives, and ultimately halted and withdrew
his people when the opportunity for wholesale slaughter
lay open to them. Most of the wounded were left on
the field, where they were miserably cut to pieces; and the
gun, which had been overturned in the attempt of the
drivers to gallop down the face of the hill, finally passed
into the possession of the Afghans. Shelton's dispositions
as a commander could not well have been worse; his
bearing as a soldier, although undaunted, imparted to his
hapless troops nothing of inspiration. The obstinacy
with which he held the hill after the impossibility of
even partial success must have been patent to him, was
universally condemned. It need scarcely be added that
his loss was very severe.

No more fighting was possible. What, then, was to
be done? Elphinstone and Shelton were at one in opposing removal into the Balla Hissar. Macnaghten, to whom
Shah Soojah had communicated his urgent recommenda-
tion of that measure as the only expedient which could
secure the safety of the British troops, fell in with the
views of the military authorities. There came to him a

letter from Osman Khan, the chief who had called off his
adherents on the previous day from pursuing the fugitives
fleeing into cantonments. Osman wrote that, if his troops
had followed up their successes, the loss of the cantonments and the destruction of the British force were inevitable; but, he continued, that it was not the wish of
the chiefs to proceed to such extremities, their sole desire
being that our people should quietly evacuate the country,
leaving the Afghan sirdars to govern it according to their
own customs, and with a king of their own choosing. In
communicating this letter to General Elphinstone, Sir
William asked for the latter's opinion on the military
possibility, or the reverse, of the retention of the British
position in Afghanistan. Elphinstone, in reply, enumerated
sundry reasons which led him to the conclusion which
he stated, that 'it is not feasible any longer to maintain
our position in this country, and that you ought to avail
yourself of the offer to negotiate which has been made
to you.'

D

CHAPTER VI

THE ROAD TO RUIN

As the result of the military disaster of November 23d, and of the representations of the General, recorded in the last chapter, Macnaghten, with whatever reluctance, permitted himself to entertain proposals for an arrangement made by the Afghan leaders. From the beginning of the outbreak, while urging on the military authorities to exert themselves in putting down the revolt, he had been engaged in tortuous and dangerous intrigues, with the object of sowing discord among the Afghan chiefs, and thus weakening the league of hostility against Shah Soojah and his British supporters. In the conduct of these intrigues he used the services of Mohun Lal, who had been one of Burnes' assistants, and who, having escaped the fate of his chief, had found refuge in the city residence of a Kuzzilbash chief. Mohun Lal was a fitting agent for the sort of work prescribed to him, and he burrowed and suborned with assiduity, and not altogether without success. But it is unhappily true that he was commissioned to carry out a darker enterprise, the removal by assassination of certain of the more virulently hostile among the Afghan leaders. The incident is the blackest of the many discreditable transactions which chequer the inner political history of this melancholy chapter of our annals. It is unfortunately certain that Lieutenant John Conolly, Macnaghten's kinsman and his confidential representative with Shah Soojah, authorised Mohun Lal, in writing, to compass the taking off of prominent Afghan leaders. In a letter to Mohun Lal, of 5th November, Conolly wrote: 'I promise 10,000 rupees for the head of each rebel chief.' Again, on the 11th, he wrote: 'There is a man called Hadji Ali, who might be induced by a bribe to try and bring in the heads of one or two of the Mufsids. Endeavour to let him know that 10,000 rupees will be given for each head, or even 15,000 rupees.' Two chiefs certainly did die under suspicious circumstances, and in each case the blood-money was claimed. It was refused by Mohun Lal on the plea that the stipulation that the heads of the dead Afghans should be brought in was not fulfilled.

Whether Macnaghten inspired those nefarious machinations, whether indeed he was actively aware of them, are questions which, in the absence of conclusive evidence, may judiciously be left unanswered. There is extant a letter from him to Mohun Lal, written December 1st, which has the following passage: 'I am sorry to find from your letter of last night that you should have supposed it was ever my object to encourage assassination. The rebels are very wicked men, but we must not take unlawful means to destroy them.' And later he is reported to have informed an Afghan deputation that, 'as a British functionary, nothing would induce him to pay a price for

blood.' Durand holds that it was the belief on the part
of the Afghan chiefs that the British Envoy had set a
price on their heads which destroyed all confidence in
Macnaghten's good faith, and which was Akbar Khan's
chief incentive to his murder.

The terms proffered on November 25th by an Afghan
deputation were so humiliating that Macnaghten peremptorily rejected them ; and the threat of immediate
hostilities unless our people promptly surrendered their
arms and withdrew was not carried out. A period
of inaction strangely ensued, which on the Afghan side
was a treacherous lull, but which Macnaghten, hoping
against hope that some turn in our favour might yet
occur, regarded with complacency. The chiefs, aware
that winter was approaching with added hardship to
the forlorn garrison, temporarily desisted from urging
negotiations. But the British military authorities, with
troops living from hand to mouth on precarious half
rations, and with transport cattle dying fast of starvation, kept urging the Envoy to activity in making
terms, if absolute starvation was to be averted. Futile
projects were discussed between Envoy and General,
only to be put aside. As the dreary days of inaction
and depletion passed, the deterioration of military spirit
among our people manifested itself more and more
plainly. British soldiers stolidly watched the Afghans
destroying our bridge across the Cabul river, within a
quarter of a mile from cantonments. Scared by the
threat of an assault, which, in the scornful words of
brave Lady Sale, a child with a stick might have repulsed, the garrison of the Mahomed Shereef fort aban-

doned it in a panic, the white soldiers of the 44th showing the example of pusillanimity to the sepoys whom their cowardice demoralised. Next day the detachment of the 44th which had guarded an exposed position had to be withdrawn, ceding the post of honour to the stauncher sepoys. The camp followers were living on carrion ; the commissaries reported but four days' provisions in store, and their inability to procure any more supplies. At length on December 8th the four senior military officers informed the Envoy that it was imperatively necessary he should negotiate a retreat, on the best terms he could obtain.

Macnaghten had to bring himself to recognise that the alternatives were negotiation or starvation, and on the 11th December, with a draft treaty in his hand, he met the principal Afghan chiefs on the river side between the cantonments and the city. After the introductory palavers, Macnaghten read the proposed treaty, whose purport was as follows : that the British should evacuate Afghanistan forthwith unmolested, furnished with supplies and accompanied by hostages, on their march to India; that the Dost, his family, and other Afghan political exiles, should be allowed to return to their country ; that Shah Soojah should have the option of remaining at Cabul or going down to India ; that amnesty should be accorded to all adherents of Shah Soojah and his British allies ; that all prisoners should be released ; and that perpetual friendship and mutual good offices should thenceforth endure between the British and the Afghans.

Akbar Khan made demur to some of the provisions,

but was overruled, and the main stipulations of the treaty were agreed to by the chiefs. The conference broke up with the understanding that the British troops should evacuate cantonments within three days, and that meanwhile provisions should be sent in for their use. The treaty was simply a virtual capitulation all along the line ; but the inherent falseness of our position, the incapacity of the military chiefs, and the debased spirit of the troops, consequent partly on low rations but mainly because of the utter absence of competent and vigorous leadership such as a Broadfoot or a Havelock would have supplied, enforced on the reluctant Envoy conditions humiliating beyond previous parallel in the history of our nation.

From the outset the Afghan chiefs defaulted from their promise of sending in supplies, but some grain was brought into cantonments by the troops, whose evacuation of the Balla Hissar on the 13th was effected under humiliating circumstances. The Afghans demanded the surrender of the forts in British occupation in the vicinity of the cantonments. The requisition was complied with, and the Magazine fort furnished the enemy with both arms and ammunition.

The three stipulated days passed away, and still the British force remained motionless in the cantonments. Macnaghten was bent on procrastination, and circumstances seemed to favour a policy which to all but himself was inexplicable. By the treaty, Shah Soojah was in effect committed to withdraw to India, but soon after its acceptance the chiefs had invited him to remain in Cabul as king, on the stipulation that he should give his daughters in marriage to leaders of the malcontents. After considerable deliberation, the Shah had consented to remain on the condition named, but a few days later he withdrew his acceptance. His vacillation increased the suspicions of the chiefs, and they demanded the immediate evacuation of the cantonments, refusing to furnish provisions until that was done. Meanwhile they sent in no transport animals, although large sums had been handed over for their purchase. Our people were still immobile, and already, on the 18th, there had occurred a fall of snow several inches deep.

The Envoy was engaged in strange and dubious intrigues, and since the Afghans were not fulfilling their share of the treaty obligations, he appears to have regarded himself as no longer bound by its conditions, and free to try to obtain better terms from other sources, in pursuit of which purpose he was expending money in a variety of directions. The dark and unscrupulous Mohun Lal was his confidant and instrument. Akbar Khan and the chiefs of his party had become aware of Macnaghten's machinations, and they laid a snare for him into which he fell with open eyes. Emissaries were sent to him with the sinister proposals that the British should remain in Afghanistan until the spring, when they were to withdraw as of their own accord; that the head of Ameenoolla Khan, one of the most powerful and obnoxious of the rebel leaders, should be presented to the Envoy in return for a stipulated sum of money; and that for all those services the British Government should requite Akbar Khan with a present of thirty lakhs of rupees, and an annual pension of four lakhs. Macnaghten refused

peremptorily the proffer of Ameenoolla's head, but did
not reject co-operation in that chief's capture by a
dubious device in which British troops were to participate; he did not hesitate to accept the general terms of
the proposals; and he consented to hold a conference
with Akbar Khan on the following day to carry into
effect the projected measures.

On the morning of the 23d the deceived and doomed
man, accompanied by his staff-officers, Lawrence, Trevor
and Mackenzie, rode out from cantonments to keep the
fateful tryst on the bank of the Cabul river. His manner
was 'distracted and hurried.' When he told Lawrence of
the nature of the affair on which he was going, that shrewd
officer immediately warned him that it was a plot against
him. 'A plot!' he replied hastily, 'let me alone for that;
trust me for that!' and Lawrence desisted from useless ex-
postulation. Poor old Elphinstone had scented treachery;
but the Envoy had closed his mouth with the impatient
words: 'I understand these things better than you!' As
he rode out, he admitted the danger of the enterprise, but
argued that if it succeeded it was worth all risks. 'At all
events,' he ended, 'let the loss be what it may, I would
rather die a hundred deaths than live the last six weeks
over again.' The escort halted, and the four British gentlemen advanced to the place of rendezvous, whither came
presently Akbar Khan and his party. Akbar began the
conference by asking the Envoy if he was ready to carry
out the proposals presented to him overnight. 'Why not?'
was Sir William's short reply. A number of Afghans,
armed to the teeth, had gradually formed a circle around
the informal durbar. Lawrence and Mackenzie pointed

out this environment to some of the chiefs, who affected to drive off the intruders with their whips; but Akbar observed that it did not matter, as they 'were all in the secret.' 'Suddenly,' wrote Mackenzie, 'I heard Akbar call out, " Begeer! begeer!" ("Seize! seize!") and turning round I saw him grasp the Envoy's left hand with an expression on his face of the most diabolical ferocity. I think it was Sultan Jan who laid hold of the Envoy's right hand. They dragged him in a stooping posture down the hillock, the only words I heard poor Sir William utter being, " Az barae Khooda " (" For God's sake "). I saw his face, however, and it was full of horror and astonishment.' Neither Mackenzie nor Lawrence, the surviving companions of the Envoy, witnessed the actual end. 'Whether,' writes Kaye, 'he died on the spot, or whether he was slain by the infuriated ghazees, is not very clearly known ; but the fanatics threw themselves on the prostrate body and hacked it with their knives.' There is no doubt that the head of the unfortunate Macnaghten was paraded in triumph through the streets of Cabul, and that the mangled trunk, after being dragged about the city, was hung up in the great bazaar. Of the three officers who accompanied the Envoy to the conference, Trevor was massacred, Lawrence and Mackenzie were saved with difficulty by friendly chiefs, and brought into the city, where they and Captain Skinner joined the hostages, Captains Connolly and Airey, under the safe roof of the venerable Mahomed Zemaun Khan.

That Akbar and the confederate chiefs spread a snare for the Envoy is plain, and that they regarded his acceptance of their deceitful proposals as a proof of his faithless-

ness to the treaty obligations to which he had bound
himself. It was no element in their reasoning that since
they had not regarded the treaty the British functionary
might without breach of faith hold that it did not bind
him. But it is improbable that the murder of Macnaghten was actually included in their scheme of action.
Their intention seems to have been to seize him as a
hostage, with intent thus to secure the evacuation of
Afghanistan and the restoration of Dost Mahomed. The
ill-fated Envoy's expressions on his way to the rendezvous indicate his unhinged state of mind. He went forth
to sure treachery; Akbar's gust of sudden fury converted the planned abduction into savage murder, and his
abrupt pistol bullet baulked the more wily and less ruthless project which had probably been devised in cold
blood.

The escort brought back into cantonments tidings that
the Envoy had been seized. The garrison got under arms,
and remained passive throughout the day. The defences
were manned at night, in the apprehension that the noise
and disturbance in the city portended an assault; but that
clamour was caused by the mustering of the Afghans in
expectation that the British would attack the city, bent on
vengeance on the murderers of the Envoy. Action of that
nature was, however, wholly absent from the prostrate
minds of the military chiefs. On the following afternoon
Captain Lawrence transmitted certain overtures from the
chiefs, as the result of a conference held by them, when,
notwithstanding severe comments on the conduct of the
Envoy, professions were made of sincere regret for his
death. With certain alterations and additions, the treaty

drawn up by Macnaghten was taken by the chiefs as the basis for the negotiations which they desired to renew. Major Pottinger, as now the senior 'political' with the force, was called on by General Elphinstone to undertake the task of conducting negotiations with the Afghan leaders. The high-souled Pottinger rose at the summons from the sickbed to which he had been confined ever since his wonderful escape from Charikar, and accepted the thankless and distasteful duty. It is not necessary to recount the details of negotiations, every article and every stage of which display the arrogance of the men who knew themselves masters of the situation, and reveal not less the degrading humiliation to which was submitting itself a strong brigade of British troops, whose arms were still in the soldiers' hands, and over whose ranks hung banners blazoned with victories that shall be memorable down the ages. On the sombre and cheerless Christmas Day Pottinger rose in the council of men who wore swords, and remonstrated with soldierly vigour and powerful argument against the degrading terms which the chiefs had contumeliously thrown to them. He produced letters from Jellalabad and Peshawur giving information of reinforcements on the way from India, and urging the maintenance of resistance. He argued that to conclude a treaty with the Afghans would be a fatal error, and suggested two alternative courses which offered a prospect of saving their honour and part of the army— the occupation of the Balla Hissar, which was the preferable measure, or the abandonment of camp, baggage, and encumbrances, and forcing a retreat down the passes. The council—Pottinger must have written sarcastically

when he termed it a 'council of war'—unanimously decided that to remain in Cabul and to force a retreat
were alike impracticable, and that nothing remained but
the endeavour to release the army by agreeing to the
conditions offered by the enemy. 'Under these circumstances,' in the words of Pottinger, 'as the Major-General
coincided with the officers of the council, and refused to
attempt occupying the Balla Hissar, and as his second
in command declared that impracticable, I considered it
my duty, notwithstanding my repugnance to and dis-
approval of the measure, to yield, and attempt to carry
on a negotiation.'

This Pottinger accordingly did. The first demand
with which he had to comply was to give bills for the
great sums promised by the Envoy to the chiefs for
their services in furthering and supporting his treaty.
This imposition had to be submitted to, since the Afghans
stopped the supplies until the extortion was complied
with. The next concession required was the surrender
of the artillery of the force, with the exception of six
field and three mule guns; and the military chiefs endured this humiliation, against which even the demoralised soldiery chafed. Then the demand for hostages
had to be complied with, and four officers were sent on to
join the two hostages already in Afghan hands. The chiefs
had demanded four married hostages, with their wives
and children, and a circular was sent round offering to
volunteers the inducement of a large stipend; but the
sentiment of repulsion was too strong to be overcome by
the bribe. The sick and wounded who could not bear
the march were sent into the city in accordance with an

article of the treaty, two surgeons accompanying their patients.

The treaty, ratified by the leading chiefs and sent into cantonments on New Year's Day 1842, provided that the British troops, within twenty-four hours after receiving transport, and under the protection of certain chiefs and an adequate escort, should begin their march of evacuation, the Jellalabad garrison moving down to Peshawur in advance ; that the six hostages left in Cabul should be well treated, and liberated on the arrival at Peshawur of Dost Mahomed ; the sick and wounded left behind to be at liberty to return to India on their recovery ; all small arms and ordnance stores in the cantonment magazine to be made over to the Afghans ' as a token of friendship,' on which account also, they were to have all the British cannon except as above mentioned ; the Afghans to escort the Ghuznee garrison in safety to Peshawur ; and a further stipulation was that the British troops in Candahar and Western Afghanistan were to resign the territories occupied by them and start quickly for India, provisioned and protected from molestation by the way.

Severe and humiliating as were those terms, they were not obtained without difficulty. The terms put forward in the earlier drafts of the treaty were yet more exacting, and the tone of the demands was abrupt, contemptuous, and insulting. Pottinger had to plead, to entreat, to be abject ; to beg the masterful Afghans ' not to overpower the weak with sufferings '; ' to be good enough to excuse the women from the suffering ' of remaining as hostages ; and to entreat them ' not to forget kindness ' shown by us in former days. One blushes not for but with the gallant Pottinger, loyally carrying out the miserable duty put upon him. The shame was not his; it lay on the council of superior officers, who overruled his remonstrances, and ground his face into the dust.

Our people were made to pass under the yoke every hour of their wretched lives during those last winter days in the Cabul cantonments. The fanatics and the common folk of the city and its environs swarmed around our petty ramparts, with their foul sneers and their blackguard taunts, hurled with impunity from where they stood at the muzzles of the loaded guns which the gunners were forbidden to fire. Officers and rank and file were in a condition of smouldering fury, but no act of reprisal or retribution was permitted. If the present was one continuous misery, the future lowered yet more gloomily. It was of common knowledge as well in the cantonments as in the city, that the engagements made by the chiefs were not worth the paper on which they had been written, and that treachery was being concerted against the force on its impending travail through the passes. It was told by a chief to one of the officers who was his friend, that Akbar Khan had sworn to have in his possession the British ladies as security for the safe restoration of his own family and relatives, and, strange forecast to be fulfilled almost to the very letter, had vowed to annihilate every soldier of the British army with the exception of one man, who should reach Jellalabad to tell the story of the massacre of all his comrades. Pottinger was well aware how desperate was the situation of the hapless people on whose behalf he had bent so low his proud soul. Mohun

Lal warned him of the treachery the chiefs were plotting,
and assured him that unless their sons should accompany
the army as hostages, it would be attacked on the march.
Day after day the departure was delayed, on the pretext
that the chiefs had not completed their preparations for
the safe conduct of the force and its encumbrances. Day
after day the snow was falling with a quiet, ruthless
persistency. The bitter night frosts were destroying the
sepoys and the camp followers, their vitality weakened
by semi-starvation and by the lack of firewood which
had long distressed them. At length on January 5th,
Sturt the engineer officer got his instructions to throw
down into the ditch a section of the eastern rampart,
and so furnish a freer exit than the gates could afford.
The supply of transport was inadequate, provisions were
scant, and the escort promised by the chiefs was not
forthcoming. Pottinger advised waiting yet a little
longer, until supplies and escort should arrive; but
for once the military chiefs were set against the
policy of delay, and firm orders were issued that the
cantonments should be evacuated on the following
day.

Shah Soojah remained in Cabul. The resolution
became him better than anything else we know of the
unfortunate man. It may be he reasoned that he had a
chance for life by remaining in the Balla Hissar, and
that from what he knew, there was no chance of life
for anyone participating in the fateful march. He behaved fairly by the British authorities, sending more
than one solemn warning pressing on them the occupation of the Balla Hissar. And there was some dignity in

his appeal to Brigadier Anquetil, who commanded his own contingent, ' if it were well to forsake him in the hour of need, and to deprive him of the aid of that force which he had hitherto been taught to regard as his own ? '

CHAPTER VII

THE CATASTROPHE

THE ill-omened evacuation by our doomed people of the cantonments wherein for two months they had undergone every extremity of humiliation and contumely, was begun on the dreary winter morning of January 6th, 1842. Snow lay deep on plain and hill-side ; the cruel cold, penetrating through the warmest clothing, bit fiercely into the debilitated and thinly clad frames of the sepoys and the great horde of camp followers. The military force which marched out of cantonments consisted of about 4500 armed men, of whom about 690 were Europeans, 2840 native soldiers on foot, and 970 native cavalrymen. The gallant troop of Company's Horse-Artillery marched out with its full complement of six guns, to which, with three pieces of the mountain train, the artillery arm of the departing force was restricted by the degrading terms imposed by the Afghan chiefs. In good heart and resolutely commanded, a body of disciplined troops thus constituted, and of a fighting strength so respectable, might have been trusted not only to hold its own against Afghan onslaught, but if necessary to take the offensive with success. But alas, the heart of the hapless force had gone to water, its discipline was a wreck, its chiefs were feeble and apathetic ; its steps were dogged by the incubus of some 12,000 camp followers, with a great company of women and children. The awful fate brooded over its forlorn banners of expiating by its utter annihilation, the wretched folly and sinister prosecution of the enterprise whose deserved failure was to be branded yet deeper on the gloomiest page of our national history, by the impending catastrophe of which the dark shadow already lay upon the blighted column.

The advance began to move out from cantonments at nine A.M. The march was delayed at the river by the non-completion of the temporary bridge, and the whole of the advance was not across until after noon. The main body under Shelton, which was accompanied by the ladies, invalids, and sick, slowly followed. It as well as the advance was disorganised from the first by the throngs of camp followers with the baggage, who could not be prevented from mixing themselves up with the troops. The Afghans occupied the cantonments as portion after portion was evacuated by our people, rending the air with their exulting cries, and committing every kind of atrocity. It was late in the afternoon before the long train of camels following the main body had cleared the cantonments ; and meanwhile the rear-guard was massed outside, in the space between the rampart and the canal, among the chaos of already abandoned baggage. It was exposed there to a vicious jezail fire poured into it by the Afghans, who abandoned the pleasures of plunder and arson for the yet greater joy of slaughtering the Feringhees. When the rear-guard moved away in the twilight, an officer and fifty men were left dead in the snow, the victims of the Afghan fire from the rampart of the cantonment; and owing to casualties in the gun teams it had been found necessary to spike and abandon two of the horse-artillery guns.

The rear-guard, cut into from behind by the pestilent ghazees, found its route encumbered with heaps of abandoned baggage around which swarmed Afghan plunderers. Other Afghans, greedier for blood than for booty, were hacking and slaying among the numberless sepoys and camp followers who had dropped out of the column, and were lying or sitting on the wayside in apathetic despair, waiting for death and careless whether it came to them by knife or by cold. Babes lay on the snow abandoned by their mothers, themselves prostrate and dying a few hundred yards further on. It was not until two o'clock of the following morning that the rear-guard reached the straggling and chaotic bivouac in which its comrades lay in the snow at the end of the first short march of six miles. Its weary progress had been illuminated by the conflagration raging in the cantonments, which had been fired by the Afghan fanatics, rabid to erase every relic of the detested unbelievers.

It was a night of bitter cold. Out in the open among the snow, soldiers and camp followers, foodless, fireless, and shelterless, froze to death in numbers, and numbers more were frost-bitten. The cheery morning noise of ordinary camp life was unheard in the mournful bivouac. Captain Lawrence outlines a melancholy picture. ' The silence of the men betrayed their despair and torpor. In

the morning I found lying close to me, stiff, cold, and
quite dead, in full regimentals, with his sword drawn in his
hand, an old grey-haired conductor named Macgregor,
who, utterly exhausted, had lain down there silently to
die.' Already defection had set in. One of the Shah's
infantry regiments and his detachment of sappers and
miners had deserted bodily, partly during the march of
the previous day, partly in the course of the night.

No orders were given out, no bugle sounded the
march, on the morning of the 7th. The column heaved
itself forward sluggishly, a mere mob of soldiers, camp
followers and cattle, destitute of any semblance of
order or discipline. Quite half the sepoys were already
unfit for duty ; in hundreds they drifted in among the
non-combatants and increased the confusion. The advance of the previous day was now the rear-guard. After
plundering the abandoned baggage, the Afghans set to
harassing the rear-guard, whose progress was delayed by
the disorderly multitude blocking the road in front. The
three mountain guns, temporarily separated from the
infantry, were captured by a sudden Afghan rush. In vain
Anquetil strove to rouse the 44th to make an effort for
their recapture. Green was more successful with his handful of artillerymen, who followed him and the Brigadier
and spiked the pieces, but being unsupported were compelled a second time to abandon them. On this march it
became necessary also, from the exhaustion of their teams,
to spike and abandon two more of the horse-artillery guns ;
so that there now remained with the force only a couple
of six-pounders. While the rear-guard was in action, a body
of Afghan horse charged on the flank, right into the heart

of the baggage column, swept away much plunder, and spread confusion and dismay far and wide. The rear of the column would probably have been entirely cut off, but that reinforcements from the advance under Shelton pushed back the enemy, and by crowning the lateral heights kept open the thoroughfare. At Bootkhak was found Akbar Khan, who professed to have been commissioned to escort the force to Jellalabad, and who blamed our people for having marched out prematurely from the cantonments. He insisted on the halt of the column at Bootkhak until the following morning, when he would provide supplies, but he demanded an immediate subsidy of 15,000 rupees, and that Pottinger, Lawrence and Mackenzie should be given up to him as hostages that the force would not march beyond Tezeen until tidings should arrive that Sale had evacuated Jellalabad. Those officers by the General's instructions joined the Afghan chief on the following morning, and Akbar's financial requisition was obsequiously fulfilled. After two days' marching our people, who had brought out with them provisions for but five and a half days, expecting within that time to reach Jellalabad, were only ten miles forward on their march.

Another night passed, with its train of horrors—starvation, cold, exhaustion, death. Lady Sale relates that scarcely any of the baggage now remained ; that there was no food for man or beast ; that snow lay a foot deep on the ground ; that even water from the adjacent stream was difficult to obtain, as the carriers were fired on in fetching it ; and that she thought herself fortunate in being sheltered in a small tent in which ' we slept nine,

all touching each other.' Daylight brought merely a
more bitter realisation of utter misery. Eyre expresses
his wonderment at the effect of two nights' exposure to
the frost in disorganising the force. ' It had so nipped
even the strongest men as to completely prostrate their
powers and incapacitate them for service ; even the
cavalry, who suffered less than the rest, were obliged
to be lifted on their horses.' In fact, only a few hundred
serviceable men remained. At the sound of hostile fire
the living struggled to their feet from their lairs in the
snow, stiffened with cold, all but unable to move or hold
a weapon, leaving many of their more fortunate comrades stark in death. A turmoil of confusion reigned.
The Afghans were firing into the rear of the mass, and
there was a wild rush of camp followers to the front, who
stripped the baggage cattle of their loads and carried the
animals off, leaving the ground strewn with ammunition,
treasure, plate, and other property. The ladies were
no longer carried in litters and palanquins, for their
bearers were mostly dead ; they sat in the bullet fire
packed into panniers slung on camels, invalids as some
of them were—one poor lady with her baby only five days
old. Mess stores were being recklessly distributed, and
Lady Sale honestly acknowledges that, as she sat on her
horse in the cold, she felt very grateful for a tumbler of
sherry, which at any other time would have made her
' very unladylike,' but which now merely warmed her.
Cups full of sherry were drunk by young children without in the least affecting their heads, so strong on them
was the hold of the cold.

It was not until noon that the living mass of men and

animals was once more in motion. The troops were in
utter disorganisation; the baggage was mixed up with the
advance guard; the camp followers were pushing ahead
in precipitate panic. The task before the wretched con-
geries of people was to thread the stupendous gorge of
the Khoord Cabul pass—a defile about five miles long,
hemmed in on either hand by steeply scarped hills.
Down the bottom of the ravine dashed a mountain
torrent, whose edges were lined with thick layers of ice,
on which had formed glacier-like masses of snow. The
'Jaws of Death' were barely entered when the slaughter
began. With the advance rode several Afghan chiefs,
whose followers, by their command, shouted to the Ghilzais
lining the heights to hold their fire, but the tribesmen
gave no heed to the mandate. Lady Sale rode with the
chiefs. The Ghilzai fire at fifty yards was close and
deadly. The men of the advance fell fast. Lady Sale
had a bullet in her arm, and three more through her
dress. But the weight of the hostile fire fell on the main
column, the baggage escort, and the rear-guard. Some of
the ladies, who mostly were on camels which were led
with the column, had strange adventures. On one camel
was quite a group. In one of its panniers were Mrs Boyd
and her little son, in the other Mrs Mainwaring, with her
own infant and Mrs Anderson's eldest child. The camel
fell, shot. A Hindustanee trooper took up Mrs Boyd *en
croupe*, and carried her through in safety; another horseman behind whom her son rode, was killed, and the boy
fell into Afghan hands. The Anderson girl shared the
same fate. Mrs Mainwaring, with her baby in her arms,
attempted to mount a baggage pony, but the load upset,

and she pursued her way on foot. An Afghan horseman rode at her, threatened her with his sword, and tried to drag away the shawl in which she carried her child. She was rescued by a sepoy grenadier, who shot the Afghan dead, and then conducted the poor lady along the pass through the dead and dying, through, also, the close fire which struck down people near to her, almost to the exit of the pass, when a bullet killed the chivalrous sepoy, and Mrs Mainwaring had to continue her tramp to the bivouac alone.

A very fierce attack was made on the rear-guard, consisting of the 44th. In the narrow throat of the pass the regiment was compelled to halt by a block in front, and in this stationary position suffered severely. A flanking fire told heavily on the handful of European infantry. The belated stragglers masked their fire, and at length the soldiers fell back, firing volleys indiscriminately into the stragglers and the Afghans. Near the exit of the pass a commanding position was maintained by some detachments which still held together, strengthened by the only gun now remaining, the last but one having been abandoned in the gorge. Under cover of this stand the rear of the mass gradually drifted forward while the Afghan pursuit was checked, and at length all the surviving force reached the camping ground. There had been left dead in the pass about 500 soldiers and over 2500 camp followers.

Akbar and the chiefs, taking the hostages with them, rode forward on the track of the retreating force. Akbar professed that his object was to stop the firing, but Mackenzie writes that Pottinger said to him : ' Mackenzie, remember if I am killed that I heard Akbar Khan shout "Slay them!" in Pushtoo, although in Persian he called out to stop the firing.' The hostages had to be hidden away from the ferocious ghazees among rocks in the ravine until near evening, when in passing through the region of the heaviest slaughter they 'came upon one sight of horror after another. All the bodies were stripped. There were children cut in two. Hindustanee women as well as men—some frozen to death, some literally chopped to pieces, many with their throats cut from ear to ear.'

Snow fell all night on the unfortunates gathered tent-less on the Khoord Cabul camping ground. On the morning of the 9th the confused and disorderly march was resumed, but after a mile had been traversed a halt for the day was ordered at the instance of Akbar Khan, who sent into camp by Captain Skinner a pro-posal that the ladies and children, with whose deplor-able condition he professed with apparent sincerity to sympathise, should be made over to his protection, and that the married officers should accompany their wives; he pledging himself to preserve the party from further hardships and dangers, and afford its mem-bers safe escort through the passes in rear of the force. The General had little faith in the Sirdar, but he was fain to give his consent to an arrangement which promised alleviation to the wretchedness of the ladies, scarce any of whom had tasted a meal since leaving Cabul. Some, still weak from childbirth, were nursing infants only a few days old; other poor creatures were momentarily apprehend-ing the pangs of motherhood. There were invalids whose

only attire, as they rode in the camel panniers or shivered
on the snow, was the nightdresses they wore when leaving
the cantonments in their palanquins, and none possessed
anything save the clothes on their backs. It is not surprising, then, that dark and doubtful as was the future to
which they were consigning themselves, the ladies preferred its risks and chances to the awful certainties which
lay before the doomed column. The Afghan chief had
cunningly made it a condition of his proffer that the
husbands should accompany their wives, and if there
was a struggle in the breasts of the former between
public and private duties, the General humanely decided
the issue by ordering them to share the fortunes of their
families.

Akbar Khan sent in no supplies, and the march was
resumed on the morning of the 10th by a force attenuated
by starvation, cold, and despair, diminished further by
extensive desertion. After much exertion the advance,
consisting of all that remained of the 44th, the solitary
gun, and a detachment of cavalry, forced a passage
to the front through the rabble of camp followers,
and marched unmolested for about two miles until the
Tunghee Tariki was reached, a deep gorge not more
than ten feet wide. Men fell fast in the horrid defile,
struck down by the Afghan fire from the heights; but
the pass, if narrow, was short, and the advance having
struggled through it moved on to the halting-place at
Kubbar-i-Jubbar, and waited there for the arrival of the
main body. But that body was never to emerge from out
the shambles in the narrow throat of the Tunghee Tariki.
The advance was to learn from the few stragglers who

reached it the ghastly truth that it now was all that remained of the strong brigade which four days before had marched out from the Cabul cantonments. The slaughter from the Afghan fire had blocked the gorge with dead and dying. The Ghilzai tribesmen, at the turn into the pen at the other end of which was the blocked gorge, had closed up fiercely. Then the steep slopes suddenly swarmed with Afghans rushing sword in hand down to the work of butchery, and the massacre stinted not while living victims remained. The rear-guard regiment of sepoys was exterminated, save for two or three desperately wounded officers who contrived to reach the advance.

The remnant of the army consisted now of about seventy files of the 44th, about 100 troopers, and a detachment of horse-artillery with a single gun. The General sent to Akbar Khan to remonstrate with him on the attack he had allowed to be made after having guaranteed that the force should meet with no further molestation. Akbar protested his regret, and pleaded his inability to control the wild Ghilzai hillmen, over whom, in their lust for blood and plunder, their own chiefs had lost all control ; but he was willing to guarantee the safe conduct to Jellalabad of the European officers and men if they would lay down their arms and commit themselves wholly into his hands. This sinister proposal the General refused, and the march was continued, led in disorder by the remnant of the camp followers. In the steep descent from the Huft Kotul into the Tezeen ravine, the soldiers following the rabble at some distance, came suddenly on a fresh butchery. The Afghans had suddenly fallen on the confused throng, and the descent was covered with dead and dying.

During the march from Kubbar-i-Jubbar to the Tezeen valley Shelton's dogged valour had mainly saved the force from destruction. With a few staunch soldiers of his own regiment, the one-armed veteran, restored now to his proper *métier* of stubborn fighting man, had covered the rear and repelled the Ghilzai assaults with persevering energy and dauntless fortitude. And he it was who now suggested, since Akbar Khan still held to his stipulation that the force should lay down its arms, that a resolute effort should be made to press on to Jugdulluk by a rapid night march of four-and-twenty miles, in the hope of clearing the passes in that vicinity before the enemy should have time to occupy them.

That the attempt would prove successful was doubtful, since the force was already exhausted ; but it was the last chance, and Shelton's suggestion was adopted. In the early moonlight the march silently began, an ill omen marking the start in the shape of the forced abandonment of the last gun. Fatal delay occurred between Seh Baba and Kutti Sung because of a panic among the camp followers, who, scared by a few shots, drifted backwards and forwards in a mass, retarding the progress of the column and for the time entirely arresting the advance of Shelton's and his rear-guard. The force could not close up until the morning, ten miles short of Jugdulluk, and already the Afghans were swarming on every adjacent height. All the way down the broken slope to Jugdulluk the little column trudged through the gauntlet of jezail fire which lined the road with dead

and wounded. Shelton and his rear-guard handful per-
formed wonders, again and again fending off with close
fire and levelled bayonets the fierce rushes of Ghilzais
charging sword in hand. The harassed advance reached
Jugdulluk in the afternoon of the 11th, and took post
behind some ruins on a height by the roadside, the surviving officers forming line in support of the gallant
rear-guard struggling forward through its environment of
assailants. As Shelton and his brave fellows burst
through the cordon they were greeted by cheers from
the knoll. But there was no rest for the exhausted
people, for the Afghans promptly occupied commanding
positions whence they maintained a fire from which the
ruins afforded but scant protection. To men parched
with thirst the stream at the foot of their knoll was but
a tantalising aggravation, for to attempt to reach it was
certain death. The snow they devoured only increased
their sufferings, and but little stay was afforded by the
raw flesh of a few gun bullocks. Throughout the day
volley after volley was poured down upon the weary band
by the inexorable enemy. Frequent sallies were made,
and the heights were cleared, but the positions were soon
reoccupied and the ruthless fire was renewed.

Captain Skinner, summoned by Akbar, brought back
a message that General Elphinstone should visit him to
take part in a conference, and that Brigadier Shelton and
Captain Johnson should be given over as hostages for the
evacuation of Jellalabad. Compliance was held to be imperative, and the temporary command was entrusted to
Brigadier Anquetil. Akbar was extremely hospitable to
his compulsory guests ; but he insisted on including the

General among his hostages, and was not moved by Elphinstone's representations that he would prefer death to the disgrace of being separated from his command in its time of peril. The Ghilzai chiefs came into conference burning with hatred against the British, and revelling in the anticipated delights of slaughtering them. Akbar seemed sincere in his effort to conciliate them, but was long unsuccessful. Their hatred seemed indeed stronger than their greed ; but at length toward nightfall Akbar announced that pacific arrangements had been accepted by the tribes, and that what remained of the force should be allowed to march unmolested to Jellalabad.

How futile was the compact, if indeed there was any compact, was soon revealed. The day among the ruins on the knoll had passed in dark and cruel suspense— in hunger, thirst, and exhaustion, in the presence of frequent death ; and as the evening fell, in anguish and all but utter despair. As darkness set in the conviction enforced itself that to remain longer in the accursed place was madness ; and the little band, leaving behind perforce the sick and wounded, marched out, resolute to push through or die fighting. In the valley the only molestation at first was a desultory fire from the camping Ghilzais, who were rather taken by surprise, but soon became wide awake to their opportunities. Some hurried forward to occupy the pass rising from the valley to the Jugdulluk crest; others, hanging on the rear and flanks of the column encumbered with its fatal incubus of camp followers, mixed among the unarmed throng with their deadly knives, and killed and plundered with the dexterity of long practice. Throughout the tedious march

up the steeply rising defile a spattering fire came from
the rocks and ridges flanking the track, all but blocked
by the surging concourse of miserable followers. The
advance had to employ cruel measures to force its
way through the chaos toward the crest. As it is approached from the Jugdulluk direction the flanking elevations recede and merge in the transverse ridge, which is
crowned by a low-cut abrupt rocky upheaval, worn down
somewhat where the road passes over the crest by the
friction of traffic. Just here the tribesmen had constructed
a formidable abattis of prickly brushwood, which stretched
athwart the road, and dammed back the fugitives in the
shallow oval basin between the termination of the ravine
and the summit of the ridge. In this trap were caught
our hapless people and the swarm of their native followers,
and now the end was very near. From behind the barrier,
and around the lip of the great trap, the hillmen fired their
hardest into the seething mass of soldiers and followers
writhing in the awful Gehenna on which the calm moon
shone down. On the edges of this whirlpool of death the
fell Ghilzais were stabbing and hacking with the ferocious
industry inspired by thirst for blood and lust for plunder.
It is among the characteristics of our diverse-natured race
to die game, and even to thrill with a strange fierce joy
when hope of escape from death has all but passed away
and there remains only to sell life at the highest possible
premium of exchange. Among our people, face to face
with death on the rocky Jugdulluk, officers and soldiers
alike fought with cool deadly rancour. The brigadier and
the private engaged in the same fierce *mêlée*, fought side
by side, and fell side by side. Stalwart Captain Dodgin

of the 44th slew five Afghans before he fell. Captain
Nicholl of the horse-artillery, gunless now, rallied to him
the few staunch gunners who were all that remained to
him of his noble and historic troop, and led them on to
share with him a heroic death.

All did not perish on the rugged summit of the
Jugdulluk. The barrier was finally broken through, and
a scant remnant of the force wrought out its escape from
the slaughter-pit. Small detachments, harassed by sudden
onslaughts, and delayed by reluctance to desert wounded
comrades, were trudging in the darkness down the long
slope to the Soorkhab. The morning of the 13th dawned
near Gundamuk on the straggling group of some twenty
officers and forty-five European soldiers. Its march
arrested by sharp attacks, the little band moved aside to
occupy a defensive position on an adjacent hillock. A
local sirdar invited the senior officer to consult with
him as to a pacific arrangement, and while Major
Griffiths was absent on this errand there was a temporary suspension of hostilities. The Afghans meanwhile
swarmed around the detachment with a pretence of friendship, but presently attempts were made to snatch from the
soldiers their arms. This conduct was sternly resented,
and the Afghans were forced back. They ascended an
adjacent elevation and set themselves to the work of
deliberately picking off officer after officer, man after man.
The few rounds remaining in the pouches of the soldiers
were soon exhausted, but the detachment stood fast, and
calmly awaited the inevitable end. Rush after rush
was driven back from its steadfast front, but at last,
nearly all being killed or wounded, a final onset of the

enemy, sword in hand, terminated the struggle, and completed the dismal tragedy. Captain Souter of the 44th, with three or four privates all of whom as well as himself were wounded, was spared and carried into captivity ; he saved the colours of his regiment, which he had tied round his waist before leaving Jugdulluk. A group of mounted officers had pushed forward as soon as they had cleared the barrier on the crest. Six only reached Futtehabad in safety. There they were treacherously offered food, and while they halted a few moments to eat two were cut down. Of the four who rode away three were overtaken and killed within four miles of Jellalabad ; one officer alone survived to reach that haven of refuge.

The ladies, the married officers, and the original hostages, followed Akbar Khan down the passes toward Jugdulluk, pursuing the line of retreat strewn with its ghastly tokens of slaughter, and recognising almost at every step the bodies of friends and comrades. At Jugdulluk they found General Elphinstone, Brigadier Shelton, and Captain Johnson, and learned the fate which had overtaken the marching force. On the following day Akbar quitted Jugdulluk with his hostages and the ladies, all of whom were virtually prisoners, and rode away through the mountains in a northerly direction. On the fourth day the fort of Budiabad in the Lughman valley was reached, where Akbar left the prisoners while he went to attempt the reduction of Jellalabad.

E

CHAPTER VIII

THE SIEGE AND DEFENCE OF JELLALABAD

SALE'S brigade, retreating from Gundamuk, reached Jellalabad on the 12th November 1841. An investigation into the state of the fortifications of that place showed them, in their existing condition, to be incapable of resisting a vigorous assault. But it was resolved to occupy the place, and to Captain George Broadfoot, as garrison engineer, was committed the duty of making it defensible. This assuredly was no light task. The enciente was far too extensive for the slender garrison, and its tracing was radically bad. The ramparts were so dilapidated that in places they were scarcely discernible, and the ruins strewn over what should have been the glacis afforded near cover to assailants, whose attitude was already so threatening as to hinder the beginning of repairing operations. Their fire swept the defences, and their braves capered derisively to the strains of a bagpipe on the adjacent rocky elevation, which thenceforth went by the name of 'Piper's Hill.' A sortie on the 15th cleared the environs of the troublesome Afghans, supplies began to come in, and Broadfoot was free to set his sappers to the task of repairing

the fortifications, in which work the entrenching tools he
had wrenched from the Cabul stores proved invaluable.
How greatly Sale had erred in shutting up his force in
Jellalabad was promptly demonstrated. The connecting
posts of Gundamuk and Peshbolak had to be evacuated;
and thus, from Jumrood at the foot of the Khyber up to
Cabul, there remained no intermediate post in British
possession with the solitary exception of Jellalabad, and
communications were entirely interrupted except through
the medium of furtive messengers.

   The Jellalabad garrison was left unmolested for nearly
a fortnight, and the repairs were well advanced when on
the 29th the Afghans came down, invested the place, and
pushed their skirmishers close up to the walls.   On
December 1st Colonel Dennie headed a sortie, which
worsted the besiegers with considerable slaughter and
drove them from the vicinity. Bad news came at intervals from Cabul, and at the new year arrived a melancholy letter from Pottinger, confirming the rumours
already rife of the murder of the Envoy, and of the
virtual capitulation to which the Cabul force had submitted.   A week later an official communication was
received from Cabul, signed by General Elphinstone and
Major Pottinger, formally announcing the convention
which the Cabul force had entered into with the chiefs,
and ordering the garrison of Jellalabad forthwith to
evacuate that post and retire to Peshawur, leaving behind
with 'the new Governor,' an Afghan chief who was the
bearer of the humiliating missive, the fortress guns and
such stores and baggage as there lacked transport to
remove. The council of war summoned by Sale was

unanimous in favour of non-compliance with this mandate. Broadfoot urged with vigour that an order by a
superior who was no longer a free agent and who issued
it under duress, could impose no obligation of obedience.
Sale pronounced himself untrammelled by a convention
forced from people ' with knives at their throats,' and was
resolute in the expression of his determination to hold
Jellalabad unless ordered by the Government to withdraw.

More and more ominous tidings poured in from Cabul.
A letter received on January 10th reported the Cabul
force to be still in the cantonments, living utterly at the
mercy of the Afghans ; another arriving on the 12th told
of the abandonment of the cantonments and the beginning of the march, but that the forlorn wayfarers were
lingering in detention at Bootkhak, halted in their misery
by the orders of Akbar Khan. Those communications in
a measure prepared the people in Jellalabad for disaster,
but not for the awful catastrophe of which Dr Brydon
had to tell, when in the afternoon of the 13th the lone
man, whose approach to the fortress Lady Butler's paint-
ing so pathetically depicts, rode through the Cabul gate
of Jellalabad. Dr Brydon was covered with cuts and
contusions, and was utterly exhausted. His first few
hasty sentences extinguished all hope in the hearts of the
listeners regarding their Cabul comrades and friends.

There was naturally great excitement in Jellalabad,
but no panic. The working parties were called in, the
assembly was sounded, the gates were closed, the walls
were lined, and the batteries were manned ; for it was
believed for the moment that the enemy were in full

pursuit of fugitives following in Brydon's track. The
situation impressed Broadfoot with the conviction that
a crisis had come in the fortunes of the Jellalabad
garrison. He thought it his duty to lay before the
General the conditions of the critical moment which he
believed to have arrived, pointing out to him that the
imperative alternatives were that he should either firmly
resolve on the defence of Jellalabad to the last extremity,
or that he should make up his mind to a retreat that
very night, while as yet retreat was practicable. Sale
decided on holding on to the place, and immediately
announced to the Commander-in-Chief his resolve to
persevere in a determined defence, relying on the promise of the earliest possible relief.

Because of the defection of his Sikh auxiliaries and
the faint-heartedness of his sepoys, Wild's efforts to cross
the threshold of the Khyber had failed, and with the tidings of his failure there came to Sale the information that
the effort for his relief must be indefinitely postponed. It
may be assumed that this intimation weakened in some
degree the General's expressed resolution to hold Jellalabad with determination, and it is not to be denied that
this resolution was in a measure conditional on the not
unwarranted expectation of early relief. Neither he nor
his adviser Macgregor appears to have realised how
incumbent on the garrison of Jellalabad it was to hold
out to the last extremity, irrespective of consequences to
itself, unless it should receive a peremptory recall from
higher authority ; or to have recognised the glorious
opportunity presented of inspiriting by its staunch constancy and high-souled self-abnegation a weak govern-

ment staggering under a burden of calamity. Than Sale
no braver soldier ever wore sword, but a man may delight
to head a forlorn hope and yet lack nerve to carry with
high heart a load of responsibility ; nor was Macgregor so
constituted as to animate his chief to noble emprise.
Fast on the heels of the gloomy tidings from the Khyber
mouth there came to them from Shah Soojah, who was
still the nominal sovereign at Cabul, a curt peremptory
letter obviously written under compulsion, of which the
following were the terms : ' Your people have concluded
a treaty with us ; you are still in Jellalabad ; what are
your intentions ? Tell us quickly.'

Sale summoned a council of war, which assembled at
his quarters on January 27th. Its proceedings were recorded, and the documents laid before it were preserved
by Captain Henry Havelock in his capacity as Sale's staff-
officer. Record and papers were reclaimed from Havelock's custody by General Sale before the evacuation of
Afghanistan, and had been long lost to sight. They have
recently been deposited among the records of the India
Office, but not before their latest non-official possessor had
published some extracts from them. It is to be hoped
that the more important documents may be given to the
public in full, since passages from documents, whether
intentionally or not, may be so extracted as to be mis-
leading. Broadfoot, who had been a member of the
council of war, and who was apparently aware of the
suppression of the official records, wrote in 1843 a detailed narrative of its proceedings while his recollection of
them was still fresh, and this narrative he sent to Havelock, desiring him to note ' any points erroneously stated,

distinguishing between what you may merely not remember and what you know I am mistaken in.' Havelock, who was a loyal and ardent admirer of General Sale, having sparsely annotated Broadfoot's narrative, returned it with the statement that he had compared it with memoranda still in his possession, and that he considered that it 'contributes a fair and correct statement of that which occurred.' The officers comprising the council to whom Sale and Macgregor addressed themselves were Colonel Dennie of the 13th, Colonel Monteath of the 35th N. I., Captains Backhouse and Abbott of the artillery, Captain Oldfield commanding the cavalry, and Captain Broadfoot the garrison engineer. The following is a summary of the proceedings, as recorded by Broadfoot and authenticated by Havelock.

After a few formal words from General Sale, he called on Macgregor to submit a matter on which that political officer and himself were agreed. Macgregor then described the situation from the point of view of Sale and himself, and expressed their united conviction that nothing was to be hoped for from the Government. Reserving his own liberty of action, he sought the opinion of the officers on offers received from Akbar Khan to treat for the evacuation of Afghanistan, and he laid before them a draft answer to Shah Soojah's curt letter, professing the readiness of the garrison to evacuate Jellalabad on his requisition, since it was held only for him, but naming certain conditions: the exchange of hostages, the restoration of British prisoners and hostages in exchange for the Afghan hostages on arrival of the force at Peshawur, escort thither 'in safety and honour,' with arms, colours,

and guns, and adequate assistance of supplies and transport. Both Sale and Macgregor frankly owned that they
were resolved to yield, and negotiate for safe retreat.

Great excitement from the first had pervaded the assemblage, and when Macgregor had finished his statement
Broadfoot arose in his wrath. He declined to believe that
the Government had abandoned the Jellalabad garrison to
its fate, and there was a general outburst of indignation
when Sale produced a letter carrying that significance.
Broadfoot waxed so warm in his remonstrances against
the proposed action that an adjournment was agreed to.
Next day Sale and Macgregor urged that it was impossible to hold out much longer, that later retreat would be
impracticable, and that the scheme they proposed was
safe and honourable. Broadfoot denounced it as disgraceful, contended that they could hold Jellalabad indefinitely—'could colonise if they liked'—and retreat at
discretion. He denied that the place was held for Shah
Soojah, and challenged their right to surrender the post
unless by Government order. Hostages he proclaimed
worthless while the Afghans held heavier pledges of ours
in the shape of prisoners and hostages. He denounced as
disgraceful the giving of hostages on our part. Monteath's
remark that nobody would go as a hostage roused Oldfield
to express himself tersely but pointedly on the subject.
'I for one,' he exclaimed in great agitation, 'will fight
here to the last drop of my blood, but I plainly declare
that I will never be a hostage, and I am surprised that
anyone should propose such a thing, or regard an Afghan's
word as worth anything.' The resolution to treat for the
abandonment of Jellalabad was carried, Oldfield only

voting with Broadfoot against it, but the stipulations regarding hostages were omitted. Broadfoot continued to press modifications of the conditions set out in the proposed reply, pleading, but in vain, that the restoration of the prisoners in Afghan hands before departure of the garrison should be insisted on ; and that since evacuation was resolved on, it should at least be conducted as a military operation, and not degradingly under escort. Then, and little wonder, he objected to expressions in the draft letter as too abject, and he was successful in procuring the alteration of them. The letter was written out, signed by Macgregor, and despatched to Cabul. It was agreed that those members of the council who chose to do should record in writing the reasons for their votes, and this was done by Dennie, Monteath, Abbott, and Broadfoot.

Broadfoot, pending an answer from Cabul, set the garrison to work in digging a ditch round the fortifications. The reply from the Shah, to the effect 'If you are sincere in offers, let all the chief gentlemen affix their seals,' was laid before the reassembled council on February 12th. The implied imputation on the good faith of British officers might well have stung to indignation the meekest ; but the council's opinion was taken as to the expediency of complying with the derogatory request made by the Shah, as well as of a stipulation—a modification of what Broadfoot had originally urged in vain—for the surrender of all prisoners, hostages, sick, and wounded under detention in Afghanistan, on the arrival at Peshawur of the Jellalabad brigade. The members of council, who in the long interval since the previous meeting had been gradually regaining their self-respect and mental equipoise, unanimously declined to accept the proposals tendered them by their commanding officer and his political ally; and a letter written by Monteath was accepted, which 'was not a continuation of the negotiation.'

Thus ended the deliberations of the memorable council of war, whose eleventh hour resolve to 'hold the fort' mainly averted the ruin of British prestige in India and throughout the regions bordering on our Eastern Empire; and the credit of its final decision to repudiate the humiliating proposals of Sale and Macgregor belongs to George Broad-foot, who was firmly though silently backed by Havelock. The day after that decision was formulated a letter came from Peshawur informing the garrison that every effort would be made for its relief; and thenceforth there was no more talk of surrender, nor was the courage of the little brigade impaired even when the earthquake of February 19th shook the newly repaired fortifications into wreck. Broadfoot's vehement energy infected the troops, and by the end of the month the parapets were entirely restored, the bastions repaired, and every battery re-established.

After the council of war had rejected the proposals laid before it, a decision which in effect involved the maintenance of the defence to the last extremity, nearly two months passed without the occurrence of any important event, except the speedily retrieved misfortune of the earthquake of February 19th. The close invest-ment of the place by Akbar Khan thwarted the efforts of the foraging parties to obtain much needed supplies. Those efforts were not vigorous, for Sale, aware of his garrison's poverty of ammunition, was bent on a passive defence, and steadily refused his consent to vigorous sorties. The policy may have had its abstract merits, but it was certainly unsatisfactory in this respect, that perseverance in it involved the unpleasantness of apparently inevitable starvation. General Pollock had arrived in Peshawur, and was making energetic efforts to get his force in order for the accomplishment of the relief of Jellalabad. But he foresaw serious delays, and so late as the middle of March was still unable to specify with any definiteness the probable date of his arrival at that place. The European troops in Jellalabad would be out of meat rations early in April, and Havelock's calculation was that the grain, on which mainly subsisted the native soldiers, who had been on half rations since the new year, would be exhausted before the middle of that month. Sale modified his policy of inactivity when he learned that the blockading Afghans were attempting to drive a mine under a salient of the defences, and Dennie on March 11th led out a sally, destroyed the works, and thrust back Akbar's encroachments. The general lack of vigour, however, on the garrison's part emboldened the Afghans so much that they actually grazed their flocks of sheep within 600 yards of the walls. This was too impudent, and the General consented to a raid, which resulted in the acquisition of some 500 sheep, an invaluable addition to the commissariat resources. It is worth recording that the native regiment gave up its share of the sheep to the soldiers of the 13th, on the ground that Europeans needed animal food more than did natives of India.

On April 6th the Afghan leader fired a salute in triumph for a supposititious repulse of Pollock in the

Khyber.   In regard to what then happened there is a
strange conflict of testimony.   General Sale, in a private
letter written six weeks later, states : 'I made my
arrangements with Macgregor to sally the next day,
provided we did not hear that Pollock had forced the
pass.'   Akbar's salutes, and the information of spies that
Pollock had fallen back, 'made us look very grave—our
case desperate, our provisions nearly out, and no relief
at hand.   I therefore decided to play a bold stroke to
relieve ourselves, and give courage to Pollock's force in
case of success.   If we failed in thrashing Akbar, we
would have left our bones on the field.'   Abbott's diary
of April 5th and 6th records that spies reported that
Pollock had been repulsed at Ali Musjid, and that the
heads of three of his officers had been sent in to Akbar,
whereupon 'all the commanding officers waited on the
General, beseeching him to attack Akbar instantly.
The 13th and the battery got all ready for work, but
the old General was obstinate, and refused to act.'   Backhouse's diary (April 6th) mentions that Pollock having
been reported repulsed, and Akbar having fired a salute,
the officers commanding corps and detachments went
in a body and proposed to the General to attack Akbar
instantly, but without success.   'Immediately the matter
was broached, the General set his face against anything
of the kind, and disagreed about every point—insisted
that the enemy had 5000 or 6000 men in camp, and were
too strong for us ; and then, the next minute, that it was
no use going out as we couldn't punish them, as they
wouldn't stand ; and concluding with usual excuse for inactivity, " It isn't our game."   Words ran precious high. . .'

Whether spontaneously or under pressure, General
Sale must have ordered a sortie in force; for at dawn
of the 7th three infantry columns marched out by the
Cabul gate, the right commanded by Havelock, the
centre by Dennie, the left by Monteath, General Sale
being in command of the whole force. Akbar, reputed
about 5000 strong, was in formation in front of his camp
about three miles west of Jellalabad, his left flank resting on the river, with an advanced post of 300 men in
the 'patched up' fort about midway between his camp
and Jellalabad. The prescribed tactics were to march
straight on the enemy, with which Monteath and Havelock complied; but Dennie, whether with or without
orders is a matter in dispute, diverged to assail the
'patched up' fort. The outer defences were carried,
gallant old Dennie riding at the head of his men to
receive his death wound. In vain did the guns for which
Sale had sent batter at the inner keep, and the General
abandoning the attempt to reduce it, led on in person
the centre column. Meanwhile Havelock and Monteath
had been moving steadily forward, until halted by orders
when considerably advanced. Havelock had to form
square once and again against the Afghan horsemen,
who, however, did not dare to charge home. The artillery
came to the front at the gallop, and poured shot and
shell into Akbar's mass. The three columns, now
abreast of each other, deployed into line, and moving
forward at the double in the teeth of the Afghan
musketry fire, swept the enemy clean out of his position, capturing his artillery, firing his camp, and putting
him to utter rout. Akbar, by seven o'clock in the

April morning, had been signally beaten in the open field by the troops he had boasted of blockading in the fortress.

The garrison of Jellalabad had thus wrought out its own relief. Thenceforth it experienced neither annoyance nor scarcity. Pollock arrived a fortnight after the dashing sally which had given the garrison deliverance, and the head of his column was played into its camp on the Jellalabad plain by the band of the 13th, to the significant tune 'Oh, but ye've been lang o' coming.' The magniloquent Ellenborough dubbed Sale's brigade 'the Illustrious Garrison,' and if the expression is over-strained, its conduct was without question eminently creditable.

CHAPTER IX

RETRIBUTION AND RESCUE

It was little wonder that the unexpected tidings of the Cabul outbreak, and the later shock of the catastrophe in the passes, should have temporarily unnerved the Governor - General. But Lord Auckland rallied his energies with creditable promptitude. His successor was on the voyage out, and in the remnant of his term that remained he could not do more than make dispositions which his successor might find of service. Every soldier of the 'Army of Retribution' was despatched to the frontier during Lord Auckland's rule. Lord Auckland appointed to the command of the troops which he was sending forward a quiet, steadfast, experienced officer of the artillery arm, who had fought under Lake at Deig and Bhurtpore, and during his forty years of honest service had soldiered steadily from the precipices of Nepaul to the rice-swamps of the Irrawaddy. Pollock was essentially the fitting man for the service that lay before him, characterised as he was by strong sense, shrewd sagacity, calm firmness, and self-command. When his superior devolved on him an undue onus of responsibility he was to prove himself thoroughly equal to the occasion, and the sedate, balanced man murmured not, but probably was rather amused when he saw a maker of phrases essaying to deck himself in his laurels. There were many things in Lord Auckland's Indian career of which it behoved him to repent, but it must go to his credit that he gave Pollock high command, and that he could honestly proclaim, as he made his preparations to quit the great possession whose future his policy had endangered, that he had contributed toward the retrieval of the crisis by promptly furthering 'such operations as might be required for the maintenance of the honour and interests of the British Government.'

Brigadier Wild reached Peshawur with a brigade of four sepoy regiments just before the new year. He was destitute of artillery, his sepoys were in poor heart, and the Sikh contingent was utterly untrustworthy. To force the Khyber seemed hopeless. Wild, however, made the attempt energetically enough. But the Sikhs mutinied, expelled their officers, and marched back to Peshawur; Wild's sepoys, behaving badly, were driven back with loss from the mouth of the pass, and Wild himself was wounded. When Pollock reached Peshawur on February 6th, 1842, he found half of Wild's brigade sick in hospital, and the whole of it in a state of utter demoralisation. A second brigade commanded by Brigadier-General M'Caskill, had accompanied Pollock, the sepoys of which promptly fell under the evil influence of Wild's dispirited and disaffected regiments. Pollock had to resist the pressing appeals for speedy relief made to him from Jellalabad, and patiently to devote weeks and months to the restoration of the morale and discipline of the disheartened

Sir F. Grant, P.R.A. pinxt.   Dawsons, Ph. Sc.   J.J. Chant. Sc.

Sir George Pollock.

sepoys of his command, and to the reinvigoration of their physique. By kindness combined with firmness he was able gradually to inspire them with perfect trust and faith in him, and when in the end of March there reached him a third brigade, comprising British cavalry and horse-artillery, ordered forward by Lord Auckland on receipt of tidings of the destruction of the Cabul force, he felt himself at length justified in advancing with confidence.

Before daylight on the morning of April 5th Pollock's army about 8000 strong, consisting of eight infantry regiments, three cavalry corps, a troop and two batteries of artillery, and a mountain train, marched from the Jumrood camping ground into the portals of the Khyber. Pollock's scheme of operations was perfect in conception and complete in detail. His main column, with strong advance and rear-guards, was to pursue the usual road through the pass. It was flanked on each side by a chain of infantry detachments, whose assigned duty was to crown the heights and sweep them clear of assailants in advance of the head of the central column. The Afreedi hillmen had blocked the throat of the pass by a formidable barrier, behind which they were gathered in force, waiting for the opportunity which was never to come to them. For the main body of Pollock's force serenely halted, while the flanking columns, breaking into skirmishing order, hurried in the grey dawn along the slopes and heights, dislodging the Afreedi pickets as they advanced, driving them before them with resolute impetuosity, and pushing forward so far as to take in reverse with their concentrated fire the great barrier and its defenders. The clansmen, recognising the frustration of their devices, deserted the position in its rear, and rushed tumultuously away to crags and sungahs where knife and jezail might still be plied. The centre column then advanced unmolested to the deserted barricade, through which the sappers soon cleared a thoroughfare. The guns swept with shrapnel the hill-sides in front, the flanking detachments pushed steadily further and yet further forward, chasing and slaying the fugitive hillmen; and the Duke of Wellington's observation was that morning fully made good, that 'he had never heard that our troops were not equal, as well in their personal activity as in their arms, to contend with and overcome any natives of hills whatever.' The whole British force, in its order of three columns, the centre in the bed of the hollow, the wings on the flanking ridges, steadily if slowly moved on in the assured consciousness of victory. It was sunset before the rear-guard was in camp under the reoccupied Ali Musjid. The Sikh troops who were to keep open Pollock's communications with Peshawur moved simultaneously on Ali Musjid by a more circuitous route.

While Pollock was halted opposite the throat of the Khyber waiting for the demolition of the Afreedi barricade, the ill-starred Shah Soojah was being murdered, on his way from the Balla Hissar of Cabul to review on the Siah Sung slopes the reinforcements which Akbar Khan was clamouring that he should lead down to aid that Sirdar in reducing Jellalabad before relief should arrive. Ever since the outbreak of November Shah Soojah had led a dog's life. He had reigned in Cabul, but he had not ruled. The Sirdars dunned him for money, and jeered at his protestations of poverty. It is not so much a matter of surprise that he should have been murdered as that, feeble, rich, and loathed, he should have been let live so long. It does not seem worth while to discuss the vexed question whether or not he was faithful to his British allies. He was certainly entitled to argue that he owed us nothing, since what we did in regard to him was nakedly for our own purposes. Shah Soojah's second son Futteh Jung had himself proclaimed his father's successor. The vicissitudes of his short reign need not be narrated. While Pollock was gathering his brigades at Gundamuk in the beginning of the following September, a forlorn Afghan, in dirty and tattered rags, rode into his camp. This scarecrow was Futteh Jung, who, unable to endure longer his sham kingship and the ominous tyranny of Akbar Khan, had fled from Cabul in disguise to beg a refuge in the British camp.

Pollock's march from Ali Musjid to Jellalabad was slow, but almost unmolested. He found, in his own words, 'the fortress strong, the garrison healthy ; and except for wine and beer, better off than we are.' One principal object of his commission had been accomplished ; he had relieved the garrison of Jellalabad, and was in a position to ensure its safe withdrawal. But his commission gave him a considerable discretion, and a great company of his country-men and countrywomen were still in Afghan durance. The calm pulsed, resolute commander had views of his own as to his duty, and he determined in his patient, steadfast way to tarry a while on the Jellalabad plain, in the hope that the course of events might play into his hands.

Maclaren's brigade, which in the beginning of November 1841 General Elphinstone had instructed General Nott to despatch with all speed to Cabul, returned to Candahar early in December. Nott in despatching it had deferred reluctantly to superior authority, and probably Maclaren not sorry to have in the snowfall a pretext for retracing his steps. Atta Mahomed Khan, sent from Cabul to foment mischief in the Candahar regions, had gathered to his banner a considerable force. General Nott quietly waited until the Sirdar, at the head of some 10,000 men, came within five miles of Candahar, and then he crushed him after twenty minutes' fighting. The fugitives found refuge in the camp of the disaffected Dooranee chiefs, whose leader Meerza Ahmed was sedulously trying to tamper with Nott's native troops, severe weather hindering the General from attacking him. Near the end of February there reached Nott a letter two months old from Elphinstone and Pottinger, ordering him to evacuate Candahar and retire to India, in pursuance of the convention into which they had entered. The Dooranee chiefs astutely urged that Shah Soojah, no longer supported by British bayonets, was now ruling in Cabul, as an argument in favour of Nott's withdrawal. Nott's answer was brief : ' I will not treat with any person whatever for the retirement of the British troops from Afghanistan, until I have received instructions from the Supreme Government '—a blunt sentence in curious contrast to the missive which Sale and Macgregor laid before the Jellalabad council of war. When presently there came a communication from Government intimating that the continued occupation of Candahar was regarded as

conducive to the interest of the state, Nott and Rawlinson were in a position to congratulate themselves on
having anticipated the wishes of their superiors. The
situation, however, became so menacing that early in
March its Afghan inhabitants were expelled from the
city of Candahar to the last soul ; and then Nott, leaving
a garrison in the place, took the field in force. The old
soldier, wary as he was, became the victim of Meerza's
wily strategy. As he advanced, the Afghans retired,
skirmishing assiduously. Leaving Nott in the Turnuk
valley, they doubled back on Candahar, and in the early
darkness of the night of the 10th March they furiously
assailed the city gates. They fired one of the gates, and
the swarming ghazees tore down with fury its blazing
planks and the red-hot ironwork. The garrison behaved
valiantly. Inside the burning gate they piled up a rampart of grain bags, on which they trained a couple of guns
loaded with case. For three hours after the gate fell did
the fanatics hurl assault after assault on the interior
barricade. They were terribly critical hours, but the
garrison prevailed, and at midnight, with a loss of many
hundreds, the obstinate assailants sullenly drew off. Nott,
although urgently summoned, was unable to reach Candahar until the 12th.

Candahar was fortunately preserved, but at the end
of March the unpleasant tidings came that Ghuznee,
which British valour had carried by storm three years
before, had now reverted into Afghan possession. The
siege had lasted for nearly three and a half months. In
mid-December the besiegers occupied the city in force,
introduced by the citizens through a subterranean way ;

and the garrison, consisting chiefly of a regiment of
sepoys, withdrew into the citadel. The bitter winter and
the scant rations took the heart out of the natives of the
warm and fertile Indian plains; but nevertheless it was not
until March 6th that the garrison, under pledge of being
escorted to Peshawur with colours, arms, and baggage,
marched out. The unfortunates would have done better
to have died a soldierly death, with arms in their hands
and the glow of fighting in their hearts. As the event
was, faith with them was broken, and save for a few
officers who were made prisoners, most were slaughtered,
or perished in a vain attempt to escape.

During his long isolation Nott's resources had been
seriously depleted, and he had ordered up from Scinde a
brigade, escorting much needed treasure, ammunition, and
medicines. Brigadier England was entrusted with the
command of this force, whose assemblage at Quetta
was expected about the end of March. Pending its
gathering England had moved out toward the entrance
of the Kojuk Pass, where he met with a sharp and
far from creditable repulse, and fell back on Quetta
miserably disheartened, suggesting in his abjectness that
Nott should abandon Candahar and retire on him. The
stout old soldier at Candahar waxed wroth at the limp-
ness of his subordinate, and addressed to England a
biting letter, ordering peremptorily the latter's prompt
advance to Candahar, engaging to dry-nurse him through
the Kojuk by a brigade sent down from Candahar for the
purpose, and remarking sarcastically, ‘ I am well aware
that war cannot be made without loss ; but yet perhaps
British troops can oppose Asiatic armies without defeat.’

Thus exhorted England moved, to find his march through the Kojuk protected by Wymer's sepoys from Candahar, who had crowned the lateral heights before he ventured into the pass; and he reached Candahar without maltreatment on the 10th May, bringing to Nott the much needed supplies which rendered that resolute man equal to any enterprise.

It remained, however, to be seen whether any enterprise was to be permitted to him and to his brother commander lying in camp on the Jellalabad plain. Lord Ellenborough, the successor of Lord Auckland, had struck a firm if somewhat inexplicit note in his earliest manifesto, dated March 13th. A single sentence will indicate its tenor: 'Whatever course we may hereafter take must rest solely on military considerations, and hence in the first instance regard to the safety of our detached garrisons in Afghanistan; to the security of our troops now in the field from unnecessary risks; and finally, to the re-establishment of our military reputation by the infliction upon the Afghans of some signal and decisive blow.' Those were brave words, if only they had been adhered to. But six weeks later his lordship was ordering Nott to evacuate Candahar and fall back on Quetta, until the season should permit further retirement to the Indus; and instructing Pollock, through the Commander-in-Chief, to withdraw without delay every British soldier from Jellalabad to Peshawur, except under certain specified eventualities, none of which were in course of occurrence. Pollock temporised, holding on to his advanced position by the plea of inability to retire for want of transport, claiming mildly to find discretionary powers

in the Government instructions, and cautiously arguing
in favour of an advance by a few marches to a region
where better climate was to be found, and whence he
might bring to bear stronger pressure for the liberation
of the prisoners. Nott was a narrower man than Pollock.
When he got his orders he regarded them as strictly
binding, no matter how unpalatable the injunctions. ' I
shall not lose a moment,' he wrote, ' in making arrangements to carry out my orders, without turning to the
right or the left, and without inquiring into the reasons
for the measures enjoined, whatever our own opinions or
wishes may be.' He reluctantly began preparations for
withdrawal. Carriage was ordered up from Quetta, and
a brigade was despatched to withdraw the garrison of
Khelat-i-Ghilzai, and to destroy the fort which Craigie
had so long and valiantly defended.

It would be tedious to detail the vacillations, the
obscurities, and the tortuosities of Lord Ellenborough's
successive communications to his two Generals in Afghanistan. Pollock had been permitted to remain about Jellalabad until the autumn should bring cooler marching
weather. Nott had been detained at Candahar by the
necessity for crushing menacing bodies of tribal levies,
but as July waned his preparations for withdrawal were
all but complete. On the 4th of that month Lord
Ellenborough wrote to him, reiterating injunctions for
his withdrawal from Afghanistan, but permitting him the
alternatives of retiring by the direct route along his line
of communications over Quetta and Sukkur, or of boxing
the compass by the curiously circuitous 'retirement' *via*
Ghuznee, Cabul, and Jellalabad. Pollock, for his part,

was permitted, if he thought proper, to advance on Cabul in order to facilitate Nott's withdrawal, if the latter should elect to 'retreat' by the circuitous route which has just been described.

One does not care to characterise the 'heads I win, tails you lose' policy of a Governor-General who thus shuffled off his responsibility upon two soldiers who previously had been sedulously restricted within narrow if varying limits. Their relief from those trammels set them free, and it was their joy to accept the devolved responsibility, and to act with soldierly initiative and vigour. The chief credit of the qualified yet substantial triumph over official hesitation certainly belongs to Pollock, who gently yet firmly forced the hand of the Governor-General, while Nott's merit was limited to a ready acceptance of the responsibility of a proffered option. A letter from Nott intimating his determination to retire by way of Cabul and Jellalabad reached Pollock in the middle of August, who immediately advanced from Jellalabad; and his troops having concentrated at Gunda-muk, he marched from that position on 7th September, his second division, commanded by M'Caskill, following next day. Pollock was woefully short of transport, and there-fore was compelled to leave some troops behind at Gundamuk, and even then could carry only half the com-plement of tentage. But his soldiers, who carried in their haversacks seven days' provisions, would gladly have marched without any baggage at all, and the chief him-self was eager to hurry forward, for Nott had written that he expected to reach Cabul on 15th September, and Pollock was burning to be there first. In the Jugdulluk

Pass, on the 8th, he found the Ghilzais in considerable force on the heights. Regardless of a heavy artillery fire they stood their ground, and so galled Pollock's troops with sharp discharges from their jezails that it became necessary to send infantry against them. They were dislodged from the mountain they had occupied by a portion of the Jellalabad brigade, led by gallant old General Sale, who had his usual luck in the shape of a wound.

This Jugdulluk fighting was, however, little more than a skirmish, and Pollock's people were to experience more severe opposition before they should emerge from the passes on to the Cabul plain. On the morning of the 13th the concentrated force had quitted its camp in the Tezeen valley, and had committed itself without due precaution to the passage of the ravine beyond, when the Afghan levies with which Akbar Khan had manned the flanking heights, opened their fire. The Sirdar had been dissuaded by Captain Troup, one of his prisoners, from attempting futile negotiations, and advised not to squander lives in useless opposition. Akbar had replied that he was too deeply committed to recede, and that his people were bent on fighting. They were not baulked in the aspiration, which assuredly their opponents shared with at least equal zeal. Pollock's advance-guard was about the middle of the defile, when the enemy were suddenly discovered blocking the pass in front, and holding the heights which Pollock's light troops should have crowned in advance of the column. Akbar's force was calculated to be about 15,000 strong, and the Afghans fought resolutely against the British regiments which forced their way up the heights on the right and left.

The ghazees dashed down to meet the red soldiers half-way, and up among the precipices there were many hand-to-hand encounters, in which the sword and the bayonet fought out the issue. The Afghans made their last stand on the rocky summit of the Huft Kotul; but from this commanding position they were finally driven by Broad-foot's bloodthirsty little Goorkhas, who, hillmen themselves from their birth, chased the Afghans from crag to crag, using their fell kookeries as they pursued. It was Akbar Khan's last effort, and the quelling of it cost Pollock the trivial loss of thirty-two killed and 130 wounded. There was no more opposition, and it was well for the Afghans, for the awful spectacles presented in the Khoord Cabul Pass traversed on the following day, kindled in Pollock's soldiers a white heat of fury. 'The bodies,' wrote Backhouse in his unpublished diary, 'lay in heaps of fifties and hundreds, our gun wheels crushing the bones of our late comrades at every yard for four or five miles; indeed, the whole march from Gundamuk to Cabul may be said to have been over the bodies of the massacred army.' Pollock marched unmolested to Cabul on the 15th, and camped on the old racecourse to the east of the city.

Nott, in evacuating Candahar, divided his force into two portions, the weaker of which General England took back to India by Quetta and Sukkur, while on August 9th Nott himself, with two European battalions, the 'beautiful sepoy regiments' of which he had a right to be proud, and his field guns, marched away from Candahar, his face set towards Cabul. His march was uneventful until about midway between Khelat-i-Ghilzai

and Ghuznee, when on the 28th the cavalry, unsupported
and badly handled in a stupid and unauthorised foray,
lost severely in officers and men, took to flight in panic,
and so gave no little encouragement to the enemy hanging on Nott's flank. Two days later Shumshoodeen, the
Afghan leader, drew up some 10,000 men in order of battle
on high ground left of the British camp. Nott attacked
with vigour, advancing to turn the Afghan left. In
reprisal the enemy threw their strength on his left, supporting their jezail fire with artillery, whereupon Nott
changed front to the left, deployed, and then charged.
The Afghans did not wait for close quarters, and Nott
was no more seriously molested. Reaching the vicinity of
Ghuznee on September 5th, he cleared away the hordes
hanging on the heights which encircle the place. During the night the Afghans evacuated Ghuznee. Soon after
daylight the British flag was waving from the citadel.
Having fulfilled Lord Ellenborough's ridiculous order to
carry away from the tomb of Sultan Mahmoud in the
environs of Ghuznee, the supposititious gates of Somnath,
a once famous Hindoo shrine in the Bombay province of
Kattiawar, Nott marched onward unmolested till within
a couple of marches of Cabul, when near Maidan he had
some stubborn fighting with an Afghan force which tried
ineffectually to block his way. On the 17th he marched
into camp four miles west of Cabul, whence he could discern, not with entire complacency, the British ensign
already flying from the Balla Hissar, for Pollock had won
the race to Cabul by a couple of days.

For months there had been negotiations for the release
of the British prisoners whom Akbar Khan had kept in

durance ever since they came into his hands in the course
of the disastrous retreat from Cabul in January, but they
had been unsuccessful, and now it was known that the
unfortunate company of officers, women, and children,
had been carried off westward into the hill country of
Bamian. Nott's officers, as the Candahar column was
nearing Cabul, had more than once urged him to detach a
brigade in the direction of Bamian in the hope of effecting
a rescue of the prisoners, but he had steadily refused, lean-
ing obstinately on the absence from the instructions sent
him by Government of any permission to engage in the
enterprise of attempting their release. He was not less
brusque in the intimation of his declinature when Pollock
gave him the opportunity to send a force in support of
Sir Richmond Shakespear, whom, with a detachment of
Kuzzilbash horse, Pollock had already despatched on the
mission of attempting the liberation of the prisoners.
The narrow old soldier argued doggedly that Government
' had thrown the prisoners overboard.' Why, then, should
he concern himself with their rescue ? If his superior
officer should give him a firm order, of course he would
obey, but he would obey under protest. Pollock disdained
to impose so enviable a duty on a recalcitrant man, and
committed to Sale the honourable and welcome service—
all the more welcome to that officer because his wife and
daughter were among the captives. At the head of his
Jellalabad brigade, he was to push forward by forced
marches on the track of Shakespear and his horsemen.

The strange and bitter experiences of the captives,
from that miserable January Sabbath day on which they
passed under the 'protection' of Akbar Khan until the

mid-September noon when Shakespear galloped into
their midst, are recorded in full and interesting detail in
Lady Sale's journal, in Vincent Eyre's *Captivity*, and in
Colin Mackenzie's biography published under the title of
Storms and Sunshine of a Soldier's Life. Here it is
possible only briefly to summarise the chief incidents of
the captivity. The unanimous testimony of the released
prisoners was to the effect that Akbar Khan, violent,
bloody, and passionate man though he was, behaved
toward them with kindness and a certain rude chivalry.
They remained for nearly three months at Budiabad,
living in great squalor and discomfort. For the whole
party there were but five rooms, each of which was
occupied by from five to ten officers and ladies, the few
soldiers and non-commissioned officers, who were mostly
wounded, being quartered in sheds and cellars. Mackenzie drily remarks that the hardships of the common
lot, and the close intimacy of prison life, brought into
full relief good and evil qualities; 'conventional polish
was a good deal rubbed off and replaced by a plainness
of speech quite unheard of in good society.' Ladies and
gentlemen were necessitated to occupy the same room
during the night, but the men 'cleared out' early in the
morning, leaving the ladies to themselves. The dirt and
vermin of their habitation were abominably offensive to
people to whom scrupulous cleanliness was a second
nature. But the captives were allowed to take exercise
within a limited range; they had among them a few
books, and an old newspaper occasionally came on to them
from Jellalabad, with which place a fitful correspondence
in cypher was surreptitiously maintained. They had a few

packs of playing cards ; they made for themselves back-
gammon and draught-boards, and when in good spirits they
sometimes played hopscotch and blindman's - buff with
the children of the party. The Sundays were always
kept scrupulously, Lawrence and Mackenzie conducting
the service in turn.

The earthquake which shook down the fortifications of
Jellalabad brought their rickety fort about the ears of the
captives. Several escaped narrowly with their lives when
walls and roofs yawned and crumbled, and all had to
turn out and sleep in the courtyard, where they suffered
from cold and saturating dews. After the defeat of
Akbar by the Jellalabad garrison on April 7th, there
was keen expectation that Sale would march to their
rescue, but he came not, and there were rumours among
the guards of their impending massacre in revenge for
the crushing reverse Akbar had experienced. Presently,
however, Mahomed Shah Khan, Akbar's lieutenant,
arrived full of courtesy and reassurance, but with the
unwelcome intimation that the prisoners must prepare
themselves to leave Budiabad at once, and move to a
greater distance from Jellalabad and their friends. For
some preparation was not a difficult task. 'All my
worldly goods,' wrote Captain Johnson, ' might be stowed
away in a towel.' Others who possessed heavier impedi-
menta, were lightened of the encumbrance by the Ghilzai
Sirdar, who plundered indiscriminately. The European
soldiers were left behind at Budiabad, and the band of
ladies and gentlemen started on the afternoon of April
10th, in utter ignorance of their destination, under the
escort of a strong band of Afghans. At the ford across

F

the Cabul river the cavalcade found Akbar Khan wounded, haggard, and dejected, seated in a palanquin, which, weak as he was, he gave up to Ladies Macnaghten and Sale, who were ill. A couple of days were spent at Tezeen among the melancholy relics of the January slaughter, whence most of the party were carried several miles further into the southern mountains to the village of Zandeh, while General Elphinstone, whose end was fast approaching, remained in the Tezeen valley with Pottinger, Mackenzie, Eyre, and one or two others. On the evening of April 23d the poor General was finally released from suffering of mind and body. Akbar, who when too late had offered to free him, sent the body down to Jellalabad under a guard, and accompanied by Moore the General's soldier servant ; and Elphinstone lies with Colonel Dennie and the dead of the defence of Jellalabad in their nameless graves in a waste place within the walls of that place. Toward the end of May the captives were moved up the passes to the vicinity of Cabul, where Akbar Khan was now gradually attaining the ascendant. Prince Futteh Jung, however, still held out in the Balla Hissar, and intermittent firing was heard as the weary *cortège* of prisoners reached a fort about three miles short of Cabul, which the ladies of the proprietor's zenana had evacuated in their favour. Here they lived if not in contentment at least in considerable comfort and amenity. They had the privacy of a delightful garden, and enjoyed the freedom of bathing in the adjacent river. After the strife between Akbar Khan and Futteh Jung ceased they were even permitted to exchange visits with their countrymen, the hostages quartered on the Balla Hissar.

They were able to obtain money from the Cabul usurers, and thus to supply themselves with suitable clothing and additions to their rations, and their mails from India and Jellalabad were forwarded to them without hindrance. The summer months were passed in captivity, but it was no longer for them a captivity of squalor and wretchedness. Life was a good deal better worth living in the pleasant garden house on the bank of the Logur than it had been in the noisome squalor of Budiabad and the vermin-infested huddlement of Zandeh. But they still lived under the long strain of anxiety and apprehension, for none of them knew what the morrow might bring forth. While residing in the pleasant quarters in the Logur valley the captives of the passes were joined by nine officers, who were the captives of Ghuznee. After the capitulation the latter had been treated with cruel harshness, shut up in one small room, and debarred from fresh air and exercise. Colonel Palmer, indeed, had undergone the barbarity of torture in the endeavour to force him to disclose the whereabouts of treasure which he was suspected of having buried.

Akbar had full and timely intimation of the mutual intention of the British generals at Jellalabad and Candahar to march on Cabul, and did not fail to recognise of what value to him in extremity might be his continued possession of the prisoners. They had been warned of their probable deportation to the remote and rugged Bamian; and the toilsome journey thither was begun on the evening of August 25th. A couple of ailing families alone, with a surgeon in charge of them, were allowed to remain behind; all the others, hale and sick, had to travel, the former on horseback, the latter carried in camel panniers. The escort consisted of an irregular regiment of Afghan infantry commanded by one Saleh Mahomed Khan, who when a subadar serving in one of the Shah's Afghan regiments had deserted to Dost Mahomed. The wayfarers, female as well as male, wore the Afghan costume, in order that they might attract as little notice as possible.

Bamian was reached on September 3d, where the wretchedness of the quarters contrasted vividly with the amenity of those left behind on the Cabul plain. But the wretchedness of Bamian was not to be long endured. An intimacy had been struck up between Captain Johnson and Saleh Mahomed, and the latter cautiously hinted that a reward and a pension might induce him to carry his charges into the British camp. On September 11th there was a private meeting between the Afghan commandant and three British officers, Pottinger, Johnson, and Lawrence. Saleh Mahomed intimated the receipt of instructions from the Sirdar to carry the prisoners over the Hindoo Koosh into Khooloom, and leave them there to seeming hopeless captivity. But on the other hand a messenger had reached Saleh from Mohun Lal with the assurance that General Pollock, if he restored the prisoners, would ensure him a reward of 20,000 rupees, and a life pension of 12,000 rupees a year. Saleh Mahomed demanded and received a guarantee from the British officers; and the captives bound themselves to make good from their own resources their redemption money. The Afghan ex-Subadar proved himself honest ; the captives were captives no longer, and they proceeded to assert themselves in the masterful British manner. They hoisted the national flag; Pottinger became once again the high-handed 'political,' and ordered the local chiefs to come to his durbar and receive dresses of honour. Their fort was put into a state of defence, and a store of provisions was gathered in case of a siege. But in mid-September came the tidings that Akbar had been defeated at Tezeen, and had fled no one knew whither, whereupon the self-emancipated party set out on the march to Cabul. At noon of the 17th they passed into the safe guardianship of Shakespear and his horsemen. Three days later, within a march of Cabul, there was reached the column which Sale had taken out, and on September 21st Pollock greeted the company of men and women whose rescue had been wrought out by his cool, strong steadfastness.

Little more remains to be told. There was an Afghan force still in arms at Istalif, a beautiful village of the inveterately hostile Kohistanees; a division marched to attack it, carried the place by assault, burnt part of it, and severely smote the garrison. Utter destruction was the fate of Charikar, the capital of the Kohistan, where Codrington's Goorkha regiment had been destroyed. Pollock determined to 'set a mark' on Cabul to commemorate the retribution which the British had exacted. He spared the Balla Hissar, and abstained from laying the city in ruins, contenting himself with the destruction of the principal bazaar, through which the heads of Macnaghten and Burnes had been paraded, and in which their mangled bodies had been exposed. Prince Futteh Jung, tired of his vicissitudes in the character of an Afghan monarch, ceded what of a throne he possessed to another puppet of his race, and gladly accompanied the British armies to India. Other waifs of the wreck of a nefarious and disastrous enterprise, among them old Zemaun Khan, who had been our friend throughout, and the family of the ill-fated Shah Soojah, were well content to return to the exile which afforded safety and quietude. There also accompanied the march of the humane Pollock a great number of the mutilated and crippled camp followers of Elphinstone's army who had escaped with their lives from its destruction. On the 12th of October the forces of Pollock and of Nott turned their backs on Cabul, which no British army was again to see for nearly forty years, and set out on their march down the passes. Jellalabad and Ali Musjid were partially destroyed in passing. Pollock's division reached Peshawur without loss, thanks to the precautions of its chief ; but with M'Caskill and Nott the indomitable Afghans had the last word, cutting off their stragglers, capturing their baggage, and in the final skirmish killing and wounding some sixty men of Nott's command.

Of the bombastic and grotesque pæans of triumph emitted by Lord Ellenborough, whose head had been turned by a success to which he had but scantly contributed, nothing need now be said, nor of the garish pageant with which he received the armies as they re-entered British territory at Ferozepore. As they passed down through the Punjaub, Dost Mahomed passed up on his way to reoccupy the position from which he had been driven. And so ended the first Afghan war, a period of history in which no redeeming features are perceptible except the defence of Jellalabad, the dogged firmness of Nott, and Pollock's noble and successful constancy of purpose. Beyond this effulgence there spreads a sombre welter of misrepresentation and unscrupulousness, intrigue, moral deterioration, and dishonour unspeakable.

Second Afghan War

PART II

THE SECOND AFGHAN WAR

CHAPTER I

THE FIRST CAMPAIGN

A BRIEF period of peace intervened between the ratification of the treaty of Gundamuk on May 30th, 1879, and the renewal of hostilities consequent on the massacre at Cabul of Sir Louis Cavagnari and the whole *entourage* of the mission of which he was the head. There was nothing identical or even similar in the motives of the two campaigns, and regarded purely on principle they might be regarded as two distinct wars, rather than as successive campaigns of one and the same war. But the interval between them was so short that the ink of the signatures to the treaty of Gundamuk may be said to have been scarcely dry when the murder of the British Envoy tore that document into bloody shreds; and it seems the simplest and most convenient method to designate the two years of hostilities from November 1878 to September 1880, as the 'second Afghan war,' notwithstanding the three months' interval of peace in the summer of 1879.

Dost Mahomed died in 1863, and after a long struggle his son Shere Ali possessed himself of the throne bequeathed to him by his father. The relations between Shere Ali and the successive Viceroys of India were friendly, although not close. The consistent aim of the British policy was to maintain Afghanistan in the position of a strong, friendly, and independent state, prepared in certain contingencies to co-operate in keeping at a distance foreign intrigue or aggression ; and while this object was promoted by donations of money and arms, to abstain from interference in the internal affairs of the country, while according a friendly recognition to the successive occupants of its throne, without undertaking indefinite liabilities in their interest. The aim, in a word, was to utilise Afghanistan as a 'buffer' state between the north-western frontier of British India and Russian advances from the direction of Central Asia. Shere Ali was never a very comfortable ally ; he was of a saturnine and suspicious nature, and he seems also to have had an overweening sense of the value of the position of Afghanistan, interposed between two great powers profoundly jealous one of the other. He did not succeed with Lord Northbrook in an attempt to work on that Viceroy by playing off the bogey of Russian aggression ; and as the consequence of this failure he allowed himself to display marked evidences of disaffected feeling. Cognisance was taken of this 'attitude of extreme reserve,' and early in 1876 Lord Lytton arrived in India charged with instructions to break away from the policy designated as that of 'masterly inactivity,' and to initiate a new basis of relations with Afghanistan and its Ameer.

Lord Lytton's instructions directed him to despatch without delay a mission to Cabul, whose errand would be to require of the Ameer the acceptance of a permanent Resident and free access to the frontier positions of Afghanistan on the part of British officers, who should have opportunity of conferring with the Ameer on matters of common interest with 'becoming attention to their friendly councils.' Those were demands notoriously obnoxious to the Afghan monarch and the Afghan people. Compliance with them involved sacrifice of independence, and the Afghan loathing of Feringhee officials in their midst had been fiercely evinced in the long bloody struggle and awful catastrophe recorded in earlier pages of this volume. Probably the Ameer, had he desired, would not have dared to concede such demands on any terms, no matter how full of advantage. But the terms which Lord Lytton was instructed to tender as an equivalent were strangely meagre. The Ameer was to receive a money gift, and a precarious stipend regarding which the new Viceroy was to 'deem it inconvenient to commit his government to any permanent pecuniary obligation.' The desiderated recognition of Abdoolah Jan as Shere Ali's successor was promised with the qualifying reservation that the promise 'did not imply or necessitate any intervention in the internal affairs of the state.' The guarantee against foreign aggression was vague and indefinite, and the Government of India reserved to itself entire 'freedom of judgment as to the character of circumstances involving the obligation of material support.'

The Ameer replied to the notice that a mission was about to proceed to Cabul by a courteous declinature to receive an Envoy, assigning several specious reasons. He was quite satisfied with the existing friendly relations, and desired no change in them; he could not guarantee the safety of the Envoy and his people; if he admitted a British mission, he would have no excuse for refusing to receive a Russian one. An intimation was conveyed to the Ameer that if he should persist in his refusal to receive the mission, the Viceroy would have no other alternative than to regard Afghanistan as a state which had 'voluntarily isolated itself from the alliance and support of the British Government.' The Ameer arranged that the Vakeel of the Indian Government should visit Simla, carrying with him full explanations, and charged to lay before the Viceroy sundry grievances which were distressing Shere Ali. That functionary took back to Cabul certain minor concessions, but conveyed the message also that those concessions were contingent on the Ameer's acceptance of British officers about his frontiers, and that it would be of no avail to send an Envoy to the conference at Peshawur for which sanction was given, unless he were commissioned to agree to this condition as the fundamental basis of a treaty. Before the Vakeel quitted Simla he had to listen to a truculent address from Lord Lytton, in the course of which Shere Ali's position was genially likened to that of 'an earthen pipkin between two iron pots.' Before Sir Lewis Pelly and the Ameer's representative met at Peshawur in January 1877, Shere Ali had not unnaturally been perturbed by the permanent occupation of Quetta, on the southern verge of his dominions, as indicating, along with other military dispositions, an intended invasion. The Peshawur con-

ference, which from the first had little promise, dragged
on unsatisfactorily until terminated by the death of the
Ameer's representative, whereupon Sir Lewis Pelly was
recalled by Lord Lytton, notwithstanding the latter's
cognisance that Shere Ali was despatching to Peshawur
a fresh Envoy authorised to assent to all the British demands. The justification advanced by Lord Lytton for
this procedure was the discovery purported to have been
made by Sir Lewis Pelly that the Ameer was intriguing
with General Kaufmann at Tashkend. Since Shere Ali
was an independent monarch, it was no crime on his part
to enter into negotiations with another power than Great
Britain, although if the worried and distracted man did so
the charge of folly may be laid to him, since the Russians
were pretty certain to betray him after having made a
cat's-paw of him, and since in applying to them he involved himself in the risk of hostile action on the part of
the British. The wisdom of Lord Lytton's conduct is not
apparent. The truculent policy of which he was the
instrument was admittedly on the point of triumphing ;
and events curiously falsified his short-sighted anticipation of the unlikelihood, because of the Russo-Turkish
war then impending, of any *rapprochement* between the
Ameer and the Russian authorities in Central Asia. The
Viceroy withdrew his Vakeel from Cabul, and in the
recognition of the Ameer's attitude of ' isolation and
scarcely veiled hostility ' Lord Salisbury authorised Lord
Lytton to protect the British frontier by such measures
as circumstances should render expedient, ' without regard
to the wishes of the Ameer or the interests of his
dynasty.' Lord Lytton took no measures, expedient or

otherwise, in the direction indicated by Lord Salisbury; the Ameer, as if he had been a petted boy consigned to the corner, was abandoned to his sullen 'isolation,' and the Russians adroitly used him to involve us in a war which lasted two years, cost us the lives of many valiant men, caused us to incur an expenditure of many millions, and left our relations with Afghanistan in all essential respects in the same condition as Lord Lytton found them when he reached India with the 'new policy' in his pocket.

If the Russians could execute as thoroughly as they can plan skilfully, there would be hardly any limit to their conquests. When England was mobilising her forces after the treaty of San Stefano, and ordering into the Mediterranean a division of sepoys drawn from the three presidencies of her Indian Empire, Russia for her part was concerting an important diversion in the direction of the north-western frontier of that great possession. But for the opportune conclusion of the treaty of Berlin, the question as to the ability of sepoy troops stiffened by British regiments to cope with the mixed levies of the Tzar might have been tried out on stricken fields between the Oxus and the Indus. When Gortschakoff returned from Berlin to St Petersburg with his version of 'Peace with Honour'—Bessarabia and Batoum thrown in—Kaufmann had to countermand the concentration of troops that had been in progress on the northern frontier of Afghanistan. But the Indian division was still much in evidence in the Mediterranean, its tents now gleaming on the brown slopes of Malta, now crowning the upland of Larnaca and nestling among the foliage of Kyrenea.

Kaufmann astutely retorted on this demonstration by despatching, not indeed an expedition, but an embassy to Cabul ; and when Stolietoff, the gallant defender of the Schipka Pass, rode into the Balla Hissar on August 11th, 1878, Shere Ali received him with every token of cordiality and regard.

No other course was now open to Her Majesty's Government than to insist on the reception at Cabul of a British mission. The gallant veteran officer Sir Neville Chamberlain, known to be held in regard by the Ameer, was named as Envoy, and an emissary was sent to Cabul in advance with information of the date fixed for the setting out of the mission. Shere Ali was greatly per-plexed, and begged for more time. ' It is not proper,' he protested, ' to use pressure in this way ; it will tend to a complete rupture.' But Sir Neville Chamberlain was satisfied that the Ameer was trifling with the Indian Government ; and he had certain information that the Ameer, his Ministers, and the Afghan outpost officers, had stated plainly that, if necessary, the advance of the mission would be arrested by force. This was what in effect happened when on September 21st Major Cavagnari rode forward to the Afghan post in the Khyber Pass. The officer who courteously stopped him assured him that he had orders to oppose by force the progress of Sir Neville and his mission, so Cavagnari shook hands with the Afghan major and rode back to Peshawur.

The Viceroy sought permission to declare war im-mediately, notwithstanding his condition of unprepared-ness ; but the Home Government directed him instead to require in temperate language an apology and the accept-

ance of a permanent mission, presenting at the same time
the ultimatum that if a satisfactory reply should not be
received on or before the 20th November hostilities would
immediately commence.   Meanwhile military preparations were actively pushed forward.   The scheme of
operations was as follows : three columns of invasion
were to move simultaneously, one through the Khyber
Pass to Dakka, another through the Kuram valley, south
of the Khyber, with the Peiwar Pass as its objective, and
a third from Quetta into the Pisheen valley, to march
forward to Candahar after reinforcement by a division
from Mooltan.   To General Sir Sam Browne was assigned the command of the Khyber column, consisting
of about 10,000 men, with thirty guns; to General
Roberts the command of the Kuram valley column,
of about 5,500 men, with twenty - four guns ; and to
General Biddulph the command of the Quetta force,
numbering some 6000 men, with eighteen guns.   When
General Donald Stewart should bring up from Mooltan
the division which was being concentrated there, he
was to command the whole southern force moving on
Candahar.   The reserve division gathering at Hassan
Abdul and commanded by General Maude, would support the Khyber force ; another reserve division massing
at Sukkur under General Primrose, would act in support of the Candahar force ; and a contingent contributed by the Sikh Feudatory States and commanded
by Colonel Watson, was to do duty on the Kurum line of
communication.   The Generals commanding columns
were to act independently of each other, taking instructions direct from Army and Government headquarters.

No answer to the ultimatum was received from the Ameer, and on the morning of November 21st Sir Sam Browne crossed the Afghan frontier and moved up the Khyber on Ali Musjid with his third and fourth brigades and the guns. Overnight he had detached Macpherson's and Tytler's brigades with the commission to turn the Ali Musjid position by a circuitous march, the former charged to descend into the Khyber Pass in rear of the fortress, and block the escape of its garrison; the latter instructed to find, if possible, a position on the Rhotas heights on the proper left of the fortress from which a flank attack might be delivered. About noon Sir Sam reached the Shagai ridge and came under a brisk fire from the guns of Ali Musjid, to which his heavy cannon and Manderson's horse-battery replied with good results. The Afghan position, which was very strong, stretched right athwart the valley from an entrenched line on the right to the Rhotas summit on the extreme left. The artillery duel lasted about two hours, and then Sir Sam determined to advance, on the expectation that the turning brigades had reached their respective objectives. He himself moved forward on the right upland; on the opposite side of the Khyber stream Appleyard led the advance of his brigade against the Afghan right. No co-operation on the part of the turning brigades had made itself manifest up till dusk; the right brigade had been brought to a halt in face of a precipitous cliff crowned by the enemy, and it was wisely judged that to press the frontal attack further in the meantime would involve a useless loss of life. Sir Sam therefore halted, and sent word to Appleyard to stay for the night his further advance, merely holding the ridge which he had already carried. But before this order reached him Appleyard was sharply engaged with the enemy in their entrenched position, and in the fighting which occured before the retirement was effected two officers were killed, a third wounded, and a good many casualties occurred among the rank and file of the native detachments gallantly assailing the Afghan entrenchments.

Early next morning offensive operations were about to be resumed, when a young officer of the 9th Lancers brought intelligence that the Afghan garrison had fled under cover of night, whereupon the fort was promptly occupied. The turning brigades had been delayed by the difficult country encountered, but detachments from both had reached Kata Kustia in time to capture several hundred fugitives of the Ali Musjid garrison. The mass of it, however—its total strength was about 4000 men— effected a retreat by the Peshbolak track from the right of the entrenched position. Sir Sam Browne's advance to Dakka was made without molestation, and on 20th December he encamped on the plain of Jellalabad, where he remained throughout the winter, Maude's reserve division keeping open his communications through the Khyber Pass. The hill tribes, true to their nature, gave great annoyance by their continual raids, and several punitive expeditions were sent against them from time to time, but seldom with decisive results. The tribesmen for the most part carried off into the hills their moveable effects, and the destruction of their petty forts apparently gave them little concern. For the most part they maintained their irreconcilable attitude, hanging on the flanks of our detachments on their return march through the lateral passes to their camps, and inflicting irritating if not very severe losses. Occasionally they thought proper to make nominal submission with tongue in cheek, breaking out again when opportunity or temptation presented itself. Detailed description of those raids and counter-raids would be very tedious reading. It was when starting to co-operate in one of those necessary but tantalising expeditions that a number of troopers of the 10th Hussars were drowned in a treacherous ford of the Cabul river near Jellalabad.

General Roberts, to whom the conduct of operations in the Kuram district had been entrusted, crossed the frontier on November 21st, and marched up the valley with great expedition. The inhabitants evinced friendliness, bringing in live stock and provisions for sale. Reaching Habib Killa on the morning of the 28th, he received a report that the Afghan force which he knew to be opposed to him had abandoned its guns on the hither side of the Peiwar Kotul, and was retreating in confusion over that summit. Roberts promptly pushed forward in two columns. Building on the erroneous information that the enemy were in a hollow trying to withdraw their guns—in reality they were already in their entrenched position on the summit of the Kotul—he ordered Cobbe's (the left) column to turn the right of the supposed Afghan position, and debar the enemy from the Kotul, while the other column (Thelwall's) was ordered to attack in front, the object being to have the enemy between two fires. Cobbe's leading regiment near the village of Turrai found its advance blocked by precipices, and a withdrawal was

ordered, the advantage having been attained of forcing
the enemy to disclose the position which he was holding.
Further reconnaissances proved that the Afghan line of
defence extended along the crest of a lofty and broken
mountainous range from the Spingawai summit on the
left to the Peiwar Kotul on the right centre, the right
itself resting on commanding elevations a mile further
south. The position had a front in all of about four miles.
It was afterwards ascertained to have been held by about
3500 regulars and a large number of tribal irregulars.
General Roberts' force numbered about 3100 men.

His scheme of operations he explained to his commanding officers on the evening of December 1st. With
the bulk of the force he himself was to make a circuitous
night march by his right on the Spingawai Kotul, with
the object of turning that position and taking the main
Afghan position on the Peiwar Kotul in reverse; while
Brigadier Cobbe, with whom were to remain the 8th
(Queen's) and 5th Punjaub Infantry regiments, a cavalry
regiment and six guns, was instructed to assail the
enemy's centre when the result of the flank attack on his
left should have made itself apparent.

The turning column, whose advance the General led
in person, consisted of the 29th N. I. (leading), 5th
Goorkhas, and a mountain battery, all under Colonel
Gordon's command; followed by a wing of the 72d
Highlanders, 2d Punjaub Infantry, and 23d Pioneers,
with four guns on elephants, under Brigadier Thelwall.
The arduous march began at ten P.M. Trending at first
rearward to the Peiwar village, the course followed was
then to the proper right, up the rugged and steep Spin-

gawai ravine. In the darkness part of Thelwall's force lost its way, and disappeared from ken. Further on a couple of shots were fired by disaffected Pathans in the ranks of the 29th N. I. That regiment was promptly deprived of the lead, which was taken by the Goorkha regiment, and the column toiled on by a track described by General Roberts as 'nothing but a mass of stones, heaped into ridges and furrowed into deep hollows by the action of the water.' Day had not broken when the head of the column reached the foot of the steep ascent to the Spingawai Kotul. The Goorkhas and the 72d rushed forward on the first stockade. It was carried without a pause save to bayonet the defenders, and stockade after stockade was swept over in rapid and brilliant succession. In half-an-hour General Roberts was in full possession of the Spingawai defences, and the Afghan left flank was not only turned but driven in. Cobbe was ordered by signal to co-operate by pressing on his frontal attack ; and Roberts himself hurried forward on his enterprise of rolling up the Afghan left and shaking its centre. But this proved no easy task. The Afghans made a good defence, and gave ground reluctantly. They made a resolute stand on the further side of a narrow deep-cut ravine, to dislodge them from which effort after effort was ineffectually made. The General then determined to desist from pressing this line of attack, and to make a second turning movement by which he hoped to reach the rear of the Afghan centre. He led the 72d wing, three native regiments, and ten guns, in a direction which should enable him to threaten the line of the Afghan retreat. Brigadier Cobbe since morning had been steadily although slowly climbing toward the front of the Peiwar Kotul position. After an artillery duel which lasted for three hours the Afghan fire was partially quelled ; Cobbe's infantry pushed on and up from ridge to ridge, and at length they reached a crest within 800 yards of the guns on the Kotul, whence their rifle fire compelled the Afghan gunners to abandon their batteries. Meanwhile Roberts' second turning movement was developing, and the defenders of the Kotul placed between two fires and their line of retreat compromised, began to waver. Brigadier Cobbe had been wounded, but Colonel Drew led forward his gallant youngsters of the 8th, and after toilsome climbing they entered the Afghan position, which its defenders had just abandoned, leaving many dead, eighteen guns, and a vast accumulation of stores and ammunition. Colonel H. Gough pursued with his cavalry, and possessed himself of several more guns which the Afghans had relinquished in their precipitate flight. The decisive success of the Peiwar Kotul combat had not cost heavily ; the British losses were twenty-one killed and seventy-two wounded.

His sick and wounded sent back to Fort Kuram, General Roberts advanced to Ali Khel, and thence made a reconnaissance forward to the Shutargurdan Pass, whose summit is distant from Cabul little more than fifty miles. Its height is great—upwards of 11,200 feet—but it was regarded as not presenting serious obstacles to the advance by this route of a force from the Kuram valley moving on Cabul. A misfortune befell the baggage guard on one of the marches in the trans-

Peiwar region when Captains Goad and Powell lost their lives in a tribal onslaught. The somewhat chequered experiences of General Roberts in the Khost valley need not be told in detail. After some fighting and more marching he withdrew from that turbulent region altogether, abjuring its pestilent tribesmen and all their works. The Kuram force wintered in excellent health spite of the rigorous climate, and toward the end of March 1879 its forward concentration about Ali Kheyl was ordered, which was virtually accomplished before the snow had melted from the passes in the later weeks of April. Adequate transport had been got together and supplies accumulated ; Colonel Watson's contingent was occupying the posts along the valley ; and General Roberts was in full readiness promptly to obey the orders to advance which he had been led to expect, and on which his brother-general Sir Sam Browne had already acted to some extent.

The march on Candahar of the two divisions under the command of General Stewart had the character, for the most part, of a military promenade. The tramp across the deserts of Northern Beloochistan was arducus ; the Bolan, the Gwaga, and the Kojuk passes had to be surmounted, and the distances which both Biddulph and Stewart had to traverse were immensely in excess of those covered by either of the forces operating from the north-western frontier line. But uneventful marches, however long and toilsome, do not call for detailed description. Stewart rcde into Candahar on January 8th, 1879, and the troops as they arrived encamped on the adjacent plain. The Governor and most of his officials, together with the Afghan cavalry, had fled toward Herat ; the Deputy-Governor remained to hand over the city to General Stewart. For commissariat reasons one division under Stewart presently moved by the Cabul road on Khelat-i-Ghilzai, which was found empty, the Afghan garrison having evacuated it. Simultaneously with Stewart's departure from Candahar Biddulph marched out a column westward toward the Helmund, remaining in that region until the third week in February. On its return march to Candahar the rear-guard had a sharp skirmish at Khushk-i-Nakhud with Alizai tribesmen, of whom 163 were left dead on the field. Soon after the return of Stewart and Biddulph to Candahar, orders arrived that the former should retain in Candahar, Quetta, and Pishin a strong division of all arms, sending back to India the remainder of his command under Biddulph—the march to be made by the previously unexplored Thal-Chotiali route to the eastward of the Pisheen valley.

Before Sir Sam Browne moved forward from Jellalabad to Gundamuk he had been able to report to the Viceroy the death of Shere Ali. That unfortunate man had seen with despair the departure on December 10th of the last Russian from Cabul—sure token that he need hope for nothing from Kaufmann or the Tzar. His chiefs unanimous that further resistance by him was hopeless, he released his son Yakoub Khan from his long harsh imprisonment, constituted him Regent, and then followed the Russian mission in the direction of Tashkend. Kaufmann would not so much as allow him to cross the frontier, and after a painful illness Shere

Ali died on February 21st, 1879, near Balkh in northern
Afghanistan. He was a man who deserved a better
fate than that which befell him. His aspiration was
to maintain the independence of the kingdom which he
ruled with justice if also with masterfulness, and he
could not brook the degradation of subjection. But,
unfortunately for him, he was the 'earthen pipkin' which
the 'iron pot' found inconvenient. There had been
plenty of manhood originally in his son and successor
Yakoub Khan, but much of that attribute had withered
in him during the long cruel imprisonment to which he
had been subjected by his father. Shere Ali's death
made him nominal master of Afghanistan, but the
vigour of his youth-time no longer characterised him.
He reigned but did not rule, and how precarious was
his position was evidenced by the defection of many
leading chiefs who came into the English camps and
were ready to make terms.

After the flight of Shere Ali some correspondence
had passed between Yakoub Khan and Major Cavagnari,
but the former had not expressed any willingness for the
re-establishment of friendly relations. In February of
his own accord he made overtures for a reconciliation, and
soon after intimated the death of his father and his own
accession to the Afghan throne. Major Cavagnari, acting
on the Viceroy's authorisation, wrote to the new sovereign
stating the terms on which the Anglo-Indian Government
was prepared to engage in negotiations for peace. Yakoub
temporised for some time, but influenced by the growing
defection of the Sirdars from his cause, as well as by the
forward movements of the forces commanded by Browne

and Roberts, he intimated his intention of visiting Gundamuk in order to discuss matters in personal conference with Major Cavagnari. A fortnight later he was on his way down the passes.

Instructions had been given by the Viceroy that Yakoub Khan should be received in the British camp with all honour and distinction. When his approach was announced on May 8th, Cavagnari and a number of British officers rode out to meet him; when he reached the camp, a royal salute greeted him, a guard of honour presented arms, and Sir Sam Browne and his staff gave him a ceremonious welcome. Cavagnari had full powers to represent his Government in the pending negotiations, as to the terms of which he had received from the Viceroy detailed instructions. The Ameer and his General-in-Chief, Daoud Shah, came to the conference attired in Russian uniforms. The negotiations were tedious, for the Ameer, his Minister, and his General made difficulties with a somewhat elaborate stupidity, but Cavagnari as a diplomatist possessed the gift of being at once patient and firm; and at length on May 26th the treaty of peace was signed, and formally ratified by the Viceroy four days later. By the treaty of Gundamuk Afghanistan was deprived for the time of its traditional character of a 'buffer state,' and its Ameer became virtually a feudatory of the British Crown. He was no longer an independent prince; although his titular rank and a nominal sovereignty remained to him, his position under its articles was to be analagous to that of the mediatised princes of the German Empire. The treaty vested in the British Government the control of

the external relations of Afghanistan. The Ameer consented to the residence of British Agents within his
dominions, guaranteeing their safety and honourable
treatment, while the British Government undertook that
its representatives should not interfere with the internal
administration of the country. The districts of Pisheen,
Kuram, and Sibi were ceded to the British Government
along with the permanent control of the Khyber and
Michnai passes, and of the mountain tribes inhabiting the
vicinity of those passes ; all other Afghan territory in
British occupation was to be restored. The obligations
to which the treaty committed the British Government
were that it should support the Ameer against foreign
aggression with arms, money, or troops at its discretion,
and that it should pay to him and his successor an annual
subsidy of £60,000. Commercial relations between India
and Afghanistan were to be protected and encouraged ;
a telegraph line between Cabul and the Kuram was forthwith to be constructed ; and the Ameer was to proclaim
an amnesty relieving all and sundry of his subjects from
punishment for services rendered to the British during
the war.

That the treaty of Gundamuk involved our Indian
Empire in serious responsibilities is obvious, and those
responsibilities were the more serious that they were
vague and indefinite, yet none the less binding on this
account. It is probable that its provisions, if they had
remained in force, would have been found in the long run
injurious to the interests of British India. For that realm
Afghanistan has the value that its ruggedness presents
exceptional obstacles to the march through it of hostile

armies having the Indian frontier for their objective, and this further and yet more important value that the Afghans by nature are frank and impartial Ishmaelites, their hands against all foreigners alike, no matter of what nationality. If this character be impaired, what virtue the Afghan has in our eyes is lost. In his implacable passion for independence, in his fierce intolerance of the Feringhee intruder, he fulfils in relation to our Indian frontier a kindred office to that served by abattis, *cheveux de frise*, and wire entanglements in front of a military position. The short-lived treaty, for which the sanguine Mr Stanhope claimed that it had gained for England 'a friendly, an independent, and a strong Afghanistan,' may now be chiefly remembered because of the circumstance that it gave effect for the moment to Lord Beaconsfield's 'scientific frontier.'

The withdrawal of the two northern forces to positions within the new frontier began immediately on the ratification of the treaty of Gundamuk, the evacuation of Candahar being postponed for sanitary reasons until autumn. The march of Sir Sam Browne's force from the breezy upland of Gundamuk down the passes to Peshawur, made as it was in the fierce heat of midsummer through a region of bad name for insalubrity, and pervaded also by virulent cholera, was a ghastly journey. That melancholy pilgrimage, every halting-place in whose course was marked by graves, and from which the living emerged 'gaunt and haggard, marching with a listless air, their clothing stiff with dried perspiration, their faces thick with a mud of dust and sweat through which their red bloodshot eyes looked forth, many suffering from heat prostration,' dwells in the memory of British India as the 'death march,' and its horrors have been recounted in vivid and pathetic words by Surgeon-Major Evatt, one of the few medical officers whom, participating in it, it did not kill.

CHAPTER II

THERE were many who mistrusted the stability of the treaty of Gundamuk. Perhaps in his heart Sir Louis Cavagnari may have had his misgivings, for he was gifted with shrewd insight, and no man knew the Afghan nature better; but outwardly, in his quiet, resolute manner, he professed the fullest confidence. Cavagnari was a remarkable man. Italian and Irish blood commingled in his veins. Both strains carry the attributes of vivacity and restlessness, but Cavagnari to the superficial observer appeared as phlegmatic as he was habitually taciturn. This sententious imperturbability was only on the surface; whether it was a natural characteristic or an acquired manner is not easy to decide. Below the surface of measured reticent composure there lay a temperament of ardent enthusiasm, and not less ardent ambition. In subtlety he was a match for the wiliest Oriental, whom face to face he dominated with a placid dauntless masterfulness that was all his own. The wild hill tribes among whom he went about escortless, carrying his life continually in his hand, recognised the complex strength of his personal sway, and feared at once and loved the quiet, firm man, the flash of whose eye was sometimes ominous,

Dawsons, Ph. Sc.

Sir Louis Cavagnari and Sirdars.

but who could cow the fiercest hillman without losing a tittle of his cool composure.

Cavagnari had negotiated the treaty of Gundamuk, the real importance of which consisted in the Afghan acceptance of a British Resident at Cabul. The honour, the duty, and the danger naturally fell to him of being the first occupant of a post created mainly by his own mingled tact and strength. Many of his friends regarded him in the light of the leader of a forlorn hope, and probably Cavagnari recognised with perfect clearness the risks which encompassed his embassy ; but apart from mayhap a little added gravity in his leave-takings when he quitted Simla, he gave no sign. It was not a very imposing mission at whose head he rode into the Balla Hissar of Cabul on July 24th, 1879. His companions were his secretary, Mr William Jenkins, a young Scotsman of the Punjaub Civil Service, Dr Ambrose Kelly, the medical officer of the embassy, and the gallant, stalwart young Lieutenant W. R. P. Hamilton, V.C., commanding the modest escort of seventy-five soldiers of the Guides. It was held that an escort so scanty was sufficient, since the Ameer had pledged himself personally for the safety and protection of the mission. The Envoy was received with high honour, and conducted to the roomy quarters in the Balla Hissar which had been prepared as the Residency, within easy distance of the Ameer's palace. Unquestionably the mission was welcome neither to the Afghan ruler nor to the people, but Cavagnari, writing to the Viceroy, made the best of things. The arrival at the adjacent Sherpur cantonments of the Herat regiments in the beginning of August was extremely

unfortunate for the mission. Those troops had been inspired by their commander Ayoub Khan with intense
hatred to the English, and they marched through the
Cabul streets shouting objurgations against the British
Envoy, and picking quarrels with the soldiers of his
escort. A pensioned sepoy who had learned that the
Afghan troops had been ordered to abuse the Eltchi,
warned Cavagnari of the danger signals. Cavagnari's
calm remark was, ' Dogs that bark don't bite.' The old
soldier earnestly urged, ' But these dogs do bite, and
there is danger.' ' Well,' said Cavagnari, ' they can only
kill the handful of us here, and our death will be
avenged.' The days passed, and it seemed that Cavagnari's diagnosis of the situation was the accurate one.
The last words of his last message to the Viceroy, despatched on September 2d, were ' All well.' The writer
of those words was a dead man, and his mission had
perished with him, almost as soon as the cheerful
message borne along the telegraph wires reached its
destination.

In the morning of September 3d some Afghan regiments paraded without arms in the Balla Hissar to
receive their pay. An instalment was paid, but the
soldiers clamoured for arrears due. The demand was
refused, a riot began, and the shout rose that the British
Eltchi might prove a free-handed paymaster. There was
a rush toward the Residency, and while some of the
Afghan soldiers resorted to stone-throwing, others ran
for arms to their quarters, and looted the Arsenal in the
upper Balla Hissar. The Residency gates had been
closed on the first alarm, and fire was promptly opened

on the rabble. The place was never intended for defence, commanded as it was at close range from the higher level of the Arsenal, whence a heavy continuous fire was from the first poured down. The mob of the city in their thousands hurried to co-operate with the mutinied soldiers and share in the spoils of the sack, so that the Residency was soon besieged. As soon as the outbreak manifested itself Cavagnari had sent a message to the Ameer, and the communication admittedly reached the latter's hands. He had more than 2000 troops in the Balla Hissar, still at least nominally loyal; he had guaranteed the protection of the mission, and it behoved him to do what in him lay to fulfil his pledge. But the Ameer sat supine in his palace, doing no more than send his General-in-Chief Daoud Shah to remonstrate with the insurgents. Daoud Shah went on the errand, but it is questionable whether he showed any energy, or indeed desired that the besiegers should desist. It was claimed by and for him that he was maltreated and indeed wounded by the mob, and it appears that he did ride into the throng and was forcibly dismounted. He might perhaps have exerted himself with greater determination if he had received more specific orders from his master the Ameer. That feeble or treacherous prince never stirred. To the frequent urgent messages sent him by Lieutenant Hamilton, he replied vaguely: 'As God wills; I am making preparations.' Meanwhile the little garrison maintained with gallant staunchness hour after hour the all but hopeless defence. 'While the fighting was going on,' reported the pensioner who had previously warned Cavagnari, 'I myself saw the four European

officers charge out at the head of some twenty-five of the
garrison ; they drove away a party holding some broken
ground.   When chased, the Afghan soldiers ran like
sheep before a wolf.   Later, another sally was made by
a detachment, with but three officers at their head.
Cavagnari was not with them this time.   A third sally
was made with only two officers leading, Hamilton and
Jenkins ; and the last of the sallies was made by a Sikh
Jemadar bravely leading.   No more sallies were made
after this.'   About noon the gates were forced, and the
Residency building was fired ; but the defenders long
maintained their position on the roof and in a detached
building.   At length the fire did its work, the walls and
roof fell in, and soon the fell deed was consummated by
the slaughter of the last survivors of the ill-fated garrison.
Hamilton was said to have died sword in hand in a final
desperate charge.   Tidings of the massacre were carried
with great speed to Massy's outposts in the Kuram
valley.   The news reached Simla by telegraph early on
the morning of the 5th.   The authorities there rallied
from the shock with fine purposeful promptitude, and
within a few hours a telegram was on its way to General
Massy's headquarters at Ali Khel instructing him to
occupy the crest of the Shutargurdan Pass with two
infantry regiments and a mountain battery, which force
was to entrench itself there and await orders.

The policy of which Lord Lytton was the figurehead
had come down with a bloody crash, and the ' masterly
inactivity' of wise John Lawrence stood vindicated in
the eyes of Europe and of Asia.   But if his policy had
gone to water, the Viceroy, although he was soon to

default from the constancy of his purpose, saw for the present clear before him the duty that now in its stead lay upon him of inflicting summary punishment on a people who had ruthlessly violated the sacred immunity from harm that shields alike among civilised and barbarous communities the person and suite of an ambassador accepted under the provisions of a deliberate treaty.   Burnes and Macnaghten had met their fate because they had gone to Cabul the supporters of a detested intruder and the unwelcome representatives of a hated power.   But Cavagnari had been slaughtered notwithstanding that he dwelt in the Balla Hissar Residency in virtue of a solemn treaty between the Empress of India and the Ameer of Afghanistan, notwithstanding that the latter had guaranteed him safety and protection, notwithstanding that Britain and Afghanistan had ratified a pledge of mutual friendship and reciprocal good offices. Lord Lytton recognised, at least for the moment, that no consideration of present expediency or of ulterior policy could intervene to deter him from the urgent imperative duty which now suddenly confronted him. The task, it was true, was beset with difficulties and dangers.   The forces on the north-western frontier had been reduced to a peace footing, and the transport for economical reasons had been severely cut down.   The bitter Afghan winter season was approaching, during which military operations could be conducted only under extremely arduous conditions, and when the line of communications would be liable to serious interruptions. The available troops for a prompt offensive did not amount to more than 6500 men all told, and it was apparent that many circumstances might postpone their reinforcement.

When men are in earnest, difficulties and dangers are recognised only to be coped with and overcome. When the Simla council of war broke up on the afternoon of September 5th the plan of campaign had been settled, and the leader of the enterprise had been chosen. Sir Frederick Roberts was already deservedly esteemed one of the most brilliant soldiers of the British army. He had fought with distinction all through the Great Mutiny, earning the Victoria Cross and rapid promotion; he had served in the Abyssinian campaign of 1868, and been chosen by Napier to carry home his final despatches; and he had worthily shared in the toil, fighting, and honours of the Umbeyla and Looshai expeditions. In his command of the Kuram field force during the winter of 1878-9 he had proved himself a skilful, resolute, and vigorous leader. The officers and men who served under him believed in him enthusiastically, and, what with soldiers is the convincing assurance of whole-souled confidence, they had bestowed on him an affectionate nickname—they knew him among themselves as ' little Bobs.' His administrative capacity he had proved in the post of Quartermaster-General in India. Ripe in experience of war, Roberts at the age of forty-seven was in the full vigour of manhood, alert in mind, and of tough and enduring physique. He was a very junior Major-General, but even among his seniors the conviction was general that Lord Lytton the Viceroy, and Sir F. Haines the Commander-in-Chief, acted wisely in entrusting to him the most active command in the impending campaign.

Our retention of the Kuram valley was to prove very useful in the emergency which had suddenly occurred. Its occupation enabled Massy to seize and hold the Shutargurdan, and the force in the valley was to constitute the nucleus of the little army of invasion and retribution to the command of which Sir Frederick Roberts was appointed. The apex at the Shutargurdan of the salient angle into Afghanistan which our possession of the Kuram valley furnished was within little more than fifty miles of Cabul, whereas the distance of that city from Lundi Kotul, our advanced position at the head of the Khyber Pass, was about 140 miles, and the route exceptionally difficult. Roberts' column of invasion was to consist of a cavalry brigade commanded by Brigadier-General Dunham-Massy, and of two infantry brigades, the first commanded by Brigadier-General Macpherson, the second by Brigadier-General Baker, three batteries of artillery, a company of sappers and miners, and two Gatling guns. The Kuram valley between the Shutargurdan and the base was to be garrisoned adequately by a force about 4000 strong, in protection of Roberts' communications by that line until snow should close it, by which time it was anticipated that communication by the Khyber-Jellalabad-Gundamuk line would be opencd up, for gaining and maintaining which a force of about 6600 men was to be detailed under the command of Major-General Bright, which was to furnish a movable column to establish communications onward to Cabul. A strong reserve force was to be gathered between Peshawur and Rawal Pindi under the command of Major-General Ross, to move forward

as occasion might require.   In the south-west Sir Donald
Stewart was to recall to Candahar his troops, which,
having begun their march toward India, were now mainly
echeloned along the route to Quetta, when that General
would have about 9000 men at his disposition to
dominate the Candahar province, reoccupy Khelat-i-
Ghilzai, and threaten Ghuznee, his communications with
the Indus being kept open by a brigade of Bombay
troops commanded by Brigadier-General Phayre.

Sir Frederick Roberts left Simla on 6th September
along with Colonel Charles Macgregor, C.B., the brilliant
and daring soldier whom he had chosen as chief of staff,
and travelling night and day they reached Ali Khel on
the 12th. The transport and supply difficulty had to be
promptly met, and this was effected only by making a
clean sweep of all the resources of the Peshawur district,
greatly but unavoidably to the hindrance of the advance
of the Khyber column, and by procuring carriage and
supplies from the friendly tribes of the Kuram.   Notwithstanding the most strenuous exertions it was not
until the 1st October that Roberts' little army, having
crossed the Shutargurdan by detachments, was rendez-
voused at and about the village of Kushi in the Logur
plain, within forty-eight miles of Cabul.   Some sharp
skirmishes had been fought as the troops traversed the
rugged ground between Ali Khel and the Shutargurdan,
but the losses were trivial, although the General himself
had a narrow escape.   A couple of regiments and four
guns under the command of Colonel Money were left in
an entrenched camp to hold the Shutargurdan.

The massacre of the British mission had no sooner

been perpetrated than Yakoub Khan found himself in a
very bad way.   The Cabul Sirdars sided with the disaffected soldiery, and urged the Ameer to raise his banner
for a *jehad* or religious war, a measure for which he had
no nerve.   Nor had he the nerve to remain in Cabul until
Roberts should camp under the Balla Hissar and demand
of him an account of the stewardship he had undertaken
on behalf of the ill-fated Cavagnari.   What reasons actuated the anxious and bewildered man cannot precisely be
known ; whether he was simply solicitous for his own
wretched skin, whether he acted from a wish to save
Cabul from destruction, or whether he hoped that his
entreaties for delay might stay the British advance until
the tribesmen should gather to bar the road to the capital.
He resolved to fly from Cabul, and commit himself to the
protection of General Roberts and his army.   The day
before General Roberts arrived at Kushi the Ameer presented himself in Baker's camp, accompanied by his eldest
son and some of his Sirdars, among whom was Daoud
Shah the Commander-in-Chief of his army.   Sir Frederick
on his arrival at Kushi paid a formal visit to the Ameer,
which the latter returned the same afternoon and took
occasion to plead that the General should delay his
advance.   The reply was that not even for a single day
would Sir Frederick defer his march on Cabul.   The
Ameer remained in camp, his personal safety carefully
protected, but under a species of honourable surveillance,
until it should be ascertained judicially whether or not
he was implicated in the massacre of the mission.

Yakoub had intimated his intention of presenting
himself in the British camp some days in advance of

his arrival, and as telegraphic communication with headquarters was open, his acceptance in the character of an
honoured guest was presumably in accordance with instructions from Simla. The man who had made himself
personally responsible for the safety of Cavagnari's
mission was a strange guest with an army whose avowed
errand was to exact retribution for the crime of its destruction. It might seem not unreasonable to expect
that, as an indispensable preliminary to his entertain-
ment, he should have at least afforded some *prima facie*
evidence that he had been zealous to avert the fate which
had befallen the mission, and stern in the punishment
of an atrocity which touched him so nearly. But instead,
he was taken on trust so fully that Afghans resisting the
British advance were not so much regarded as enemies
resisting an invasion and as constructive vindicators of the
massacre, as they were held traitors to their sovereign
harbouring in the British camp.

On the morning of October 2d the whole force
marched from Kushi toward Cabul, temporarily cutting
loose from communication with the Shutargurdan, to avoid
diminishing the strength of the column by leaving detachments to keep the road open. All told, Roberts' army
was the reverse of a mighty host. Its strength was little
greater than that of a Prussian brigade on a war footing.
Its fate was in its own hands, for befall it what might it
could hope for no timely reinforcement. It was a mere
detachment marching against a nation of fighting men
plentifully supplied with artillery, no longer shooting
laboriously with jezails, but carrying arms of precision
equal or little inferior to those in the hands of our own

soldiery. But the men, Europeans and Easterns, hillmen of Scotland and hillmen of Nepaul, plainmen of Hampshire and plainmen of the Punjaub, strode along buoyant with confidence and with health, believing in their leader, in their discipline, in themselves.   Of varied race, no soldier who followed Roberts but came of fighting stock ; ever blithely rejoicing in the combat, one and all burned for the strife now before them with more than wonted ardour, because of the opportunity it promised to exact vengeance for a deed of foul treachery.

The soldiers had not long to wait for the first fight of the campaign.   On the afternoon of the 5th Baker's brigade, with most of the cavalry and artillery, and with the 92d Highlanders belonging to Macpherson's brigade, camped on the plain to the south of the village of Charasiah, Macpherson remaining one march in rear to escort the convoy of ammunition and stores.   North of Charasiah rises a semicircular curtain of hills ascending in three successive tiers, the most distant and loftiest range closing in the horizon and shutting out the view of Cabul, distant only about eleven miles.   The leftward projection of the curtain, as one looks northward, comes down into the plain almost as far as and somewhat to the left of Charasiah, dividing the valley of Charasiah from the outer plain of Chardeh.   To the right front of Charasiah, distant from it about three miles, the range is cleft by the rugged and narrow Sung-i-Nawishta Pass, through which run the Logur river and the direct road to Cabul by Beni Hissar.   Information had been received that the Afghans were determined on a resolute attempt to prevent the British force from reaching Cabul, and the position beyond Charasiah seemed so tempting that it was regarded as surprising that cavalry reconnaissances sent forward on three distinct roads detected no evidences of any large hostile gathering.

But next morning 'showed another sight.' At dawn on the 6th General Roberts, anxious to secure the Sung-i-Nawishta Pass and to render the track through it passable for guns, sent forward his pioneer battalion with a wing of the 92d and two mountain guns. That detachment had gone out no great distance when the spectacle before it gave it pause. From the Sung-i-Nawishta defile, both sides of which were held, the semicircular sweep of the hill-crests was crowned by an Afghan host in great strength and regular formation. According to subsequent information no fewer than thirteen regiments of the Afghan regular army took part in the combat, as well as large contingents of irregular fighting men from Cabul and the adjoining villages, while the British camp was threatened from the heights on either side by formidable bodies of tribesmen, to thwart whose obviously intended attack on it a considerable force had to be retained. The dispositions of the Afghan commander Nek Mahomed Khan were made with some tactical skill. The Sung-i-Nawishta Pass itself, the heights on either side, and a low detached eminence further forward, were strongly held by Afghan infantry; in the mouth of the pass were four Armstrong guns, and on the flanking height twelve mountain guns were in position. The projecting spur toward Charasiah which was the extreme right of the Afghan position, was held in force, whence an effective fire would bear on the left flank of a force advancing to a direct attack on the pass. But Roberts was not the man to play into the hands of the Afghan tactician. He humoured his conception so far as to send forward on his right toward the pass, a small detachment of all arms under Major White of the 92d, with instructions to maintain a threatening attitude in that direction, and to seize the opportunity to co-operate with the flanking movement entrusted to General Baker as soon as its development should have shaken the constancy of the enemy. To Baker with about 2000 infantry and four guns, was assigned the task of attacking the Afghan right on the projecting spur and ridge, forcing back and dispersing that flank ; and then, having reached the right of the Afghan main position on the farthest and loftiest range, he was to wheel to his right and sweep its defenders from the chain of summits.

Baker moved out toward his left front against the eminences held by the Afghan right wing, which Nek Mahomed, having discerned the character of Roberts' tactics, was now reinforcing with great activity. The 72d Highlanders led the attack, supported vigorously by the 5th Goorkhas and the 5th Punjaub Infantry. The resistance of the Afghans was stubborn, especially opposite our extreme left, whence from behind their sungahs on a steep hill they poured a heavy fire on the assailants. A yet heavier fire came from a detached knoll on Baker's right, which the artillery fire gradually beat down. The Afghans continued to hold the advanced ridge constituting their first position until two o'clock, when a direct attack, accompanied by a double flanking fire, compelled their withdrawal. They, however, fell back only to an intermediate

loftier position about 700 yards in rear of the ridge from
which they had been driven. Approached by successive
rushes under cover of artillery fire, they were then attacked
vigorously and fell back in confusion. No rally was permitted them, and by three o'clock the whole Afghan right
was shattered and in full flight along the edge of the
Chardeh valley. Baker unfortunately had no cavalry,
else the fugitives would have suffered severely. But the
rout of the Afghan right had decided the fortune of the
day. Its defenders were already dribbling away from
the main position when Baker, wheeling to his right,
marched along the lofty crest, rolling up and sweeping
away the Afghan defence as he moved toward the Sung-
i-Nawishta gorge. That defile had already been entered
by the cavalry of White's detachment, supported by some
infantry. While Baker had been turning the Afghan
right, White and his little force had been distinguishing
themselves not a little. After an artillery preparation
the detached hill had been won as the result of a hand-to-
hand struggle. Later had fallen into the hands of White's
people all the Afghan guns, and the heights to the immediate right and left of the gorge had been carried, the
defenders driven away, and the pass opened up. But
the progress through it of the cavalry was arrested by
a strongly garrisoned fort completely commanding the
road. On this fort Baker directed his artillery fire, at
the same time sending down two infantry regiments to
clear away the remnants of the Afghan army still lingering in the pass. This accomplished, the fighting ceased.
It had been a satisfactory day. Less than half of Roberts'
force had been engaged, and this mere brigade had routed

the army of Cabul and captured the whole of the artillery it had brought into the field. The Afghan loss was estimated at about 300 killed. The British loss was twenty killed and sixty-seven wounded. On the night of the combat part of Baker's troops bivouacked beyond the Sung-i-Nawishta, and on the following day the whole division passed the defile and camped at Beni Hissar, within sight of the Balla Hissar and the lofty ridge overhanging Cabul.

On the afternoon of the 7th a violent explosion was heard in the Beni Hissar camp from the direction of the Sherpur cantonment north of Cabul, near the site of the British cantonments of 1839-41. Next morning information came in that the Sherpur magazine had been blown up, and that the cantonment had been abandoned by the Afghan regiments which had garrisoned that vast unfinished structure. General Massy led out part of his brigade on a reconnaissance, and took possession of the deserted Sherpur cantonment, and of the seventy-five pieces of ordnance parked within the walls. Massy had observed from the Siah Sung heights that the Asmai heights, overhanging the Cabul suburb of Deh Afghan, were held by a large body of Afghan soldiery, a force, it was afterwards learned, composed of the remnants of the regiments defeated at Charasiah, three fresh regiments from the Kohistan, and the rabble of the city and adjacent villages, having a total strength of nearly 3000 men, with twelve guns, under the leadership of Mahomed Jan, who later was to figure prominently as the ablest of our Afghan enemies. Massy heliographed his information to General Roberts, who sent Baker with a force to drive

the enemy from the heights ; and Massy was instructed
to pass through a gap in the ridge and gain the Chardeh
valley, where he might find opportunity to intercept the
Afghan retreat toward the west.   Massy pierced the
ridge at the village of Aushar, and disposed his troops
on the roads crossing the Chardeh valley.   Meanwhile
Baker found the ascent of the Sher Derwaza heights so
steep that the afternoon was far spent before his guns
came into action, and it was still later before part of his
infantry effected their descent into the Chardeh valley.
Reinforcements necessary to enable him to act did not
reach him until dusk, when it would have been folly to
commit himself to an attack.   A night patrol ascertained
that the Afghans had evacuated the position under cover
of darkness, leaving behind their guns and camp equipage.   On the 9th the divisional camp moved forward to
the Siah Sung heights, a mile eastward from the Balla
Hissar, and there it was joined by Baker, and by Massy,
who on his way to camp led his wearied troopers through
the city of Cabul without mishap or insult.   The Goorkha
regiment was detached to hold the ridge commanding the Balla Hissar, and a cavalry regiment was quartered in the Sherpur cantonment to protect it from the
ravages of the villagers.

A melancholy interest attaches to the visit paid by
Sir Frederick Roberts to the Balla Hissar on the 11th.
Through the dirt and squalor of the lower portion he
ascended the narrow lane leading to the ruin which a
few weeks earlier had been the British Residency.   The
commander of the avenging army looked with sorrowful
eyes on the scene of heroism and slaughter, on the

smoke-blackened walls, the blood splashes on the white-washed walls, the still smouldering *débris*, the half-burned skulls and bones in the blood-dabbled chamber where apparently the final struggle had been fought out. He stood in the great breach in the quarters of the Guides where the gate had been blown in after the last of the sorties made by the gallant Hamilton, and lingered in the tattered wreck of poor Cavagnari's drawing-room, its walls dinted with bullet-pits, its floor and walls brutally defiled. Next day he made a formal entry into the Balla Hissar, his road lined with his staunch troops, a royal salute greeting the banner of Britain as it rose on the tall flagstaff above the gateway. He held a Durbar in the 'Audience Chamber' in the garden of the Ameer's palace; in front and in flank of him the pushing throng of obsequious Sirdars of Cabul arrayed in all the colours of the rainbow; behind them, standing immobile at attention, the guard of British infantry with fixed bayonets which the soldiers longed to use. The General read the mild proclamation announcing the disarmament of the Cabulese and the punishment of fine which was laid upon the city, but which never was exacted. And then he summarily dismissed the Sirdars, three only, the Mustaphi, Yahuja Khan the Ameer's father-in-law, and Zakariah Khan his brother, being desired to remain. Their smug complacency was suddenly changed into dismay when they were abruptly told that they were prisoners.

Another ceremonial progress the General had to perform. On the 13th he marched through the streets of Cabul at the head of his little army, the bazaars and dead walls echoing to the music of the bands and the wild scream of the bagpipes.　In the Afghan quarter no salaams greeted the conquering Feringhees, and scowling faces frowned on the spectacle from windows and side-streets.　Three days later occurred an event which might have been a great catastrophe.　Captain Shafto of the ordnance was conducting an examination into the contents of the arsenal in the upper Balla Hissar, and had already discovered millions of cartridges, and about 150,000 lbs. of gunpowder.　Daoud Shah, however, expressed his belief that at least a million pounds were in store.　Captain Shafto, a very cautious man, was pursuing his researches; the Goorkhas were quartered in the upper Balla Hissar near the magazine shed, and the 67th occupied the Ameer's garden lower down.　On the 16th a dull report was heard in the Siah Sung camp, followed immediately by the rising above the Balla Hissar of a huge column of grey smoke, which as it drifted away disclosed flashes of flame and sudden jets of smoke telling of repeated gunpowder explosions.　The 67th, powdered with dust, escaped all but scathless; but the Goorkha regiment had been heavily smitten.　Twelve poor fellows were killed, and seven wounded; among the former were five principal Goorkha officers.

The Balla Hissar was promptly evacuated.　Occasional explosions occurred for several days, the heaviest of those on the afternoon of the 16th, which threw on the city a great shower of stones, beams, and bullets.　By a jet of stones blown out through the Balla Hissar gate four Afghans were killed, and two sowars and an Afghan badly hurt.　Captain Shafto's body and the remains of the Goorkhas were found later, and buried; and the determination was formed to have no more to do with the Balla Hissar, but to occupy the Sherpur cantonment. Meanwhile General Hugh Gough was despatched with a small force of all arms to escort to Cabul Money's gallant garrison of the Shutargurdan, and to close for the winter the line of communication *via* the Kuram valley. Colonel Money had undergone with fine soldierly spirit and action not a few turbulent experiences since Roberts had left him and his Sikhs on the lofty crest of the Shutargurdan. The truculent Ghilzais gave him no peace; his method of dealing with them was for the most part with the bayonet point. The last attempt on him was made by a horde of Ghilzais some 17,000 strong, who completely invested his camp, and after the civility of requesting him to surrender, a compliment which he answered by bullets, made a close and determined attack on his position. This was on the 18th October; on the following day Gough heliographed his arrival at Kushi, whereupon Money took the offensive with vigour and scattered to the winds his Ghilzai assailants. On 30th October the Shutargurdan position was evacuated, and on the 3d November the Cabul force received the welcome accession of headquarters and two squadrons 9th Lancers, Money's 3d Sikhs, and four mountain guns.

CHAPTER III

SIR FREDERICK ROBERTS had been hurried forward on Cabul charged with the duty of avenging the perpetration of a foul and treacherous crime, 'which had brought indelible disgrace upon the Afghan nation.' The scriptural injunction to turn the other cheek to the smiter has not yet become a canon of international law or practice; and the anti-climax to an expedition engaged in with so stern a purpose, of a nominal disarmament and a petty fine never exacted, is self-evident. Our nation is given to walk in the path of precedent; and in this juncture the authorities had to their hand the most apposite of precedents. Pollock, by destroying the Char bazaar in which had been exposed the mangled remains of Burnes and Macnaghten, set a 'mark' on Cabul the memory of which had lasted for decades. Cavagnari and his people had been slaughtered in the Balla Hissar, and their bones were still mingled with the smouldering ruins of the Residency. Wise men discerned that the destruction of the fortress followed by a homeward march as swift yet as measured as had been the march of invasion, could not but have made a deep and lasting impression on the Afghans; while the complications, humiliations, and expense of the long futile occupation would have been obviated. Other counsels prevailed.

To discover, in a nation virtually accessory as a whole after the fact to the slaughter of the mission, the men on whom lay the suspicion of having been the instigators and the perpetrators of the cruel deed, to accord them a fair trial, and to send to the gallows those on whose hands was found the blood of the massacred mission, was held a more befitting and not less telling course of retributive action than to raze the Balla Hissar and sow its site with salt. Skilfully and patiently evidence was gathered, and submitted to the Military Commission which General Roberts had appointed. This tribunal took cognisance of crimes nominally of two classes. It tried men who were accused of having been concerned in the destruction of the British mission, and those charged with treason in having offered armed resistance to the British troops acting in support of the Ameer, who had put himself under their protection. Of the five prisoners first tried, condemned, and duly hanged, two were signal criminals. One of them, the Kotwal or Mayor of Cabul, was proved to have superintended the contumelious throwing of the bodies of the slaughtered Guides of the mission escort into the ditch of the Balla Hissar. Another was proved to have carried away from the wrecked Residency a head believed to have been Cavagnari's, and to have exhibited it on the ridge above the city. The other three and many of those who were subsequently executed, suffered for the crime of 'treason' against Yakoub Khan. Probably there was no Afghan who did not approve of the slaughter of the Envoy, and who would not in his heart have rejoiced at the annihilation of the British force ; but it seems strange law and stranger justice to hang men for 'treason' against a Sovereign who had gone over to the enemy. On the curious expedient of temporarily governing in the name of an Ameer who had deserted his post to save his skin, comment would be superfluous. Executions continued; few, however, of the mutinous sepoys who actually took part in the wanton attack on the British Residency had been secured, and it was judged expedient that efforts should be made to capture and punish those against whom there was evidence of that crime, in the shape of the muster-rolls of the regiments now in the possession of the military authorities. It was known that many of the disbanded and fugitive soldiers had returned to their homes in the villages around Cabul, and early in November General Baker took out a force and suddenly encircled the village of Indikee, on the edge of the Chardeh valley—a village reported full of Afghan sepoys. A number of men were brought out by the scared headmen and handed over, answering to their names called over from a list carried by Baker; and other villages in the vicinity yielded a considerable harvest of disbanded soldiers. Before the Commission the prisoners made no attempt to conceal their names, or deny the regiments to which they had belonged; and forty-nine of them were found guilty and hanged, nearly all of whom belonged to the regiments that had assailed the Residency.

On 12th November Sir Frederick Roberts proclaimed an amnesty in favour of all who had fought against the British troops, on condition that they should surrender

their arms and return to their homes ; but exempted
from the benefit were all concerned in the attack on the
Residency. The amnesty was well timed, although
most people would have preferred that fewer sepoys
and more Sirdars should have been hanged.

Our relations with the Ameer during the earlier part
of his residence in the British camp were not a little
peculiar. Nominally he was our guest, and a certain freedom was accorded to him and his retinue. There was
no doubt that the Sirdars of the Ameer's suite grossly
abused their privileges. Whether with Yakoub Khan's
cognisance or not, they authorised the use of his name
by the insurgent leaders. Nek Mahomed, the insurgent
commander at Charasiah, was actually in the tents of
the Ameer on the evening before the fight. To all
appearance our operations continued to have for their
ultimate object the restoration of Yakoub Khan to his
throne. Our administrative measures were carried on
in his name. The hostile Afghans we designated as
rebels against his rule ; and his authority was proclaimed as the justification of much of our conduct.
But the situation gradually became intolerable to
Yakoub Khan. He was a guest in the British camp,
but he was also in a species of custody. Should our
arms reinstate him, he could not hope to hold his throne.
His harassed perplexity came to a crisis on the morning
of the 12th October, the day of General Roberts' durbar
in the Balla Hissar, which he had been desired to attend.
What he specifically apprehended is unknown ; what
he did was to tell General Roberts, with great excitement, that he would not go to the durbar, that his life

was too miserable for long endurance, that he would rather be a grass-cutter in the British camp than remain Ameer of Afghanistan. He was firmly resolved to resign the throne, and begged that he might be allowed to do so at once. General Roberts explained that the acceptance of his resignation rested not with him but with the Viceroy, pending whose decision matters, the General desired, should remain as they were, affairs continuing to be conducted in the Ameer's name as before. To this the Ameer consented; his tents were moved to the vicinity of General Roberts' headquarters, and a somewhat closer surveillance over him was maintained.

Secrecy meanwhile was preserved until the Viceroy's reply should arrive. The nature of that reply was intimated by the proclamation which General Roberts issued on the 28th October. It announced that the Ameer had of his own free will abdicated his throne and left Afghanistan without a government. 'The British Government,' the proclamation continued, 'now commands that all Afghan authorities, chiefs, and sirdars, do continue their functions in maintaining order. . . The British Government, after consultation with the principal sirdars, tribal chiefs, and others representing the interests and wishes of the various provinces and cities, will declare its will as to the future permanent arrangements to be made for the good government of the people.'

This *ad interim* assumption of the rulership of Afghanistan may have been adopted as the only policy which afforded even a remote possibility of tranquillity. But it was essentially a policy of speculative makeshift. The retributive and punitive object of the swift march on

Cabul can scarcely be regarded as having been fulfilled by the execution of a number of subordinate participants and accessories in the destruction of the mission and by the voluntary abdication of Yakoub Khan. That the Afghan ' authorities, chiefs, and sirdars,' would obey the command to ' maintain order ' issued by the leader of a few thousand hostile troops, masters of little more than the ground on which they were encamped, experience and common sense seemed alike to render improbable. The Afghans subordinated their internal quarrels to their common hatred of the masterful foreigners, and the desperate fighting of December proved how fiercely they were in earnest.

Yakoub Khan had been regarded as merely a weak and unfortunate man, but the shadows gradually darkened around him until at length he came to be a man under grave suspicion. General Roberts became satisfied from the results of the proceedings of the court of inquiry, that the attack on the Residency, if not actually instigated by him, might at least have been checked by active exertion on his part. Information was obtained which convinced the General that the ex-Ameer was contemplating a flight toward Turkestan, and it was considered necessary to place him in close confinement. He remained a close prisoner until December 1st. On the early morning of that day he was brought out from his tent, and after taking farewell of the General and his staff, started on his journey to Peshawur, surrounded by a strong escort. If the hill tribes along his route had cared enough about him to attempt his rescue, the speed with which he travelled afforded them no time to gather for that purpose.

During those uneventful October and November days, when the little army commanded by General Roberts lay in its breezy camp on the Siah Sung heights, there was no little temptation for the unprofessional reader of the telegraphic information in the newspapers to hold cheap those reputedly formidable Afghans, whose resistance a single sharp skirmish had seemingly scattered to the winds, and who were now apparently accepting without active remonstrance the dominance of the few thousand British bayonets glittering there serenely over against the once turbulent but now tamed hill capital. One may be certain that the shrewd and careful soldier who commanded that scant array did not permit himself to share in the facile optimism whether on the part of a government or of the casual reader of complacent telegrams. It was true that the Government of India had put or was putting some 30,000 soldiers into the field on the apparent errand of prosecuting an Afghan war. But what availed Roberts this host of fighting men when he had to realise that, befall him what might in the immediate or near future, not a man of it was available to strengthen or to succour him? The quietude of those cool October days was very pleasant, but the chief knew well how precarious and deceitful was the calm. For the present the Afghan unanimity of hostility was affected in a measure by the fact that the Ameer, who had still a party, was voluntarily in the British camp. But when Yakoub's abdication should be announced, he knew the Afghan nature too well to doubt that the tribal blood-feuds would be soldered for the time, that Dooranee and Barakzai would strike hands, that Afghan regulars and

Afghan irregulars would rally under the same standards, and that the fierce shouts of 'Deen! deen!' would resound on hill-top and in plain. Cut loose from any base, with slowly dwindling strength, with waning stock of ammunition, it was his part to hold his ground here for the winter, he and his staunch soldiers, a firm rock in the midst of those surging Afghan billows that were certain to rise around him. Not only would he withstand them, but he would meet them, for this bold man knew the value in dealing with Afghans of a resolute and vigorous offensive. But it behoved him above all things to make timely choice of his winter quarters where he should collect his supplies and house his troops and the followers. After careful deliberation the Sherpur cantonment was selected. It was overlarge for easy defence, but hard work, careful engineering, and steadfast courage would redeem that evil. And Sherpur had the great advantage that besides being in a measure a ready-made defensive position, it had shelter for all the European troops and most of the native soldiery, and that it would accommodate also the horses of the cavalry, the transport animals, and all the needful supplies and stores.

An Afghan of the Afghans, Shere Ali nevertheless had curiously failed to discern that the warlike strength of the nation which he ruled lay in its intuitive aptitude for irregular fighting; and he had industriously set himself to the effort of warping the combative genius of his people and of constituting Afghanistan a military power of the regular and disciplined type. He had created a large standing army the soldiery of which wore uniforms, underwent regular drill, obeyed words of command, and carried arms of precision.   He had devoted great pains to the manufacture of a formidable artillery, and what with presents from the British Government and the imitative skill of native artificers he was possessed at the outbreak of hostilities of several hundred cannon.   His artisans were skilful enough to turn out in large numbers very fair rifled small-arms, which they copied from British models ; and in the Balla Hissar magazine were found by our people vast quantities of gunpowder and of admirable cartridges of local manufacture.   There were many reasons why the Cabul division of Shere Ali's army should be quartered apart from his turbulent and refractory capital, and why its cantonment should take the form of a permanent fortified camp, in which his soldiers might be isolated from Cabul intrigues, while its proximity to the capital should constitute a standing menace to the conspirators of the city.   His original design apparently was to enclose the Behmaroo heights within the walls of his cantonment, and thus form a great fortified square upon the heights in the centre of which should rise a strong citadel dominating the plain in every direction. The Sherpur cantonment as found by Roberts consisted of a fortified enciente, enclosing on two sides a great open space in the shape of a parallelogram lying along the southern base of the Behmaroo heights.   When the British troops took possession, only the west and south faces of the enciente were completed ; although not long built those were already in bad repair, and the explosion of the great magazine when the Afghan troops abandoned the cantonment had wrecked a section of the western face. The eastern face had been little more than traced, and the

northern side had no artificial protection, but was closed
in by the Behmaroo heights, whose centre was cleft by a
broad and deep gorge. The design of the enciente was
peculiar. There was a thick and high exterior wall of
mud, with a banquette for infantry protected by a
parapet. Inside this wall was a dry ditch forty feet wide,
on the inner brink of which was the long range of barrack-
rooms. Along the interior front of the barrack-rooms
was a verandah faced with arches supported by pillars, its
continuity broken occasionally by broad staircases conducting to the roof of the barracks, which afforded a
second line of defence. The closing in of the verandah
would of course give additional barrack accommodation,
but there were quarters in the barrack-rooms for at least
all the European troops. In the southern face of the
enciente were three gateways, and in the centre of the
western face there was a fourth, each gate covered adequately by a curtain. Between each gate were semicircular bastions for guns. In the interior there was
space to manœuvre a division of all arms. There was a
copious supply of water, and if the aspect of the great
cantonment was grim because of the absence of trees and
the utter barrenness of the enclosed space, this æsthetic
consideration went for little against its manifest advantages as snug and defensible winter quarters. Shere Ali
had indeed been all unconsciously a friend in need to the
British force wintering in the heart of that unfortunate
potentate's dominions. Human nature is perverse and
exacting, and there were those who objurgated his
memory because he had constructed his cantonment a
few sizes too large to be comfortably defended by Sir

Frederick Roberts' little force. But this was manifestly unreasonable; and in serious truth the Sherpur cantonment was a real godsend to our people. Supplies of all kinds were steadily being accumulated there, and the woodwork of the houses in the Balla Hissar was being carried to Sherpur for use as firewood. On the last day of October the force quitted the Siah Sung position and took possession of Sherpur, which had undergone a rigorous process of fumigation and cleansing. The change was distinctly for the better. The force was compacted, and the routine military duties were appreciably lightened since there were needed merely piquets on the Behmaroo heights and sentries on the gates; the little army was healthy, temperate, and in excellent case in all respects.

The dispositions for field service made at the outset of the campaign by the military authorities have already been detailed. Regarded simply as dispositions they left nothing to be desired, and certainly Sir Frederick Roberts' force had been organised and equipped with a fair amount of expedition. But it was apparent that the equipment of that body of 6500 men—and that equipment by no means of an adequate character, had exhausted for the time the resources of the Government as regarded transport and supplies. Promptitude of advance on the part of the force to which had been assigned the line of invasion by the Khyber-Jellalabad route, was of scarcely less moment than the rapidity of the stroke which Roberts was commissioned to deliver. The former's was a treble duty. One of its tasks was to open up and maintain Roberts' communications with India, so that the closing of the Shutargurdan should not leave him isolated. Another duty resting on the Khyber force was to constitute for Roberts a ready and convenient reserve, on which he might draw when his occasions demanded. No man could tell how soon after the commencement of his invasion that necessity might arise ; it was a prime *raison d'être* of the Khyber force to be in a position to give him the hand when he should intimate a need for support. Yet again, its presence in the passes dominantly thrusting forward, would have the effect of retaining the eastern tribes within their own borders, and hindering them from joining an offensive combination against the little force with which Roberts was to strike at Cabul. But delay on delay marked the mobilisation and advance of the troops operating in the Khyber line. There was no lack of earnestness anywhere ; the eagerness to push on was universal from the commander to the corporal. But the barren hills and rugged passes could furnish no supplies ; the base had to furnish everything, and there was nothing at the base, neither any accumulation of supplies nor means to transport supplies if they had been accumulated. Weeks elapsed before the organisation of the force approached completion, and it was only by a desperate struggle that General Charles Gough's little brigade received by the end of September equipment sufficient to enable that officer to advance by short marches. Roberts was holding his durbar in the Balla Hissar of Cabul on the day that the head of Gough's advance reached Jellalabad. No man can associate the idea of dawdling with Jenkins and his Guides, yet the Guides reaching Jellalabad on October 12th were not at

H

Gundamuk until the 23d, and Gundamuk is but thirty
miles beyond Jellalabad.   The anti-climax for the time
of General Bright's exertions occurred on November 6th.
On that day he with Gough's brigade reached so far
Cabulward as Kutti Sung, two marches beyond Gundamuk.   There he met General Macpherson of Roberts'
force, who had marched down from Cabul with his
brigade on the errand of opening communications with
the head of the Khyber column.   The two brigades had
touch of each other for the period of an interview between
the Generals, and then they fell apart and the momentary
union of communication was disrupted.   General Bright
had to fall back toward Gundamuk for lack of supplies.
The breach continued open only for a few days, and
then it was closed, not from down country but from up
country.   Roberts, surveying the rugged country to the
east of Cabul, had discerned that the hill road toward
Jugdulluk by Luttabund, was at once opener and shorter
than the customary tortuous and overhung route through
the Khoord Cabul Pass and by Tezeen.   The pioneers
were set to work to improve the former.   The Luttabund road became the habitual route along which, from
Cabul downwards, were posted detachments maintaining
the communications of the Cabul force with the Khyber
column   and   India.   Nearly   simultaneous   with   this
accomplishment was the accordance to Sir Frederick
Roberts of the local rank of Lieutenant-General, a
promotion which placed him in command of all the
troops in Eastern Afghanistan down to Jumrood, and
enabled him to order up reinforcements from the
Khyber column at his discretion, a power he refrained

from exercising until the moment of urgent need was impending.

After his interview at Kutti Sung with General Bright, Macpherson, before returning to Cabul, made a short reconnaissance north of the Cabul river toward the Lughman valley and into the Tagao country inhabited by the fanatic tribe of the Safis. From his camp at Naghloo a foraging party, consisting of a company of the 67th escorting a number of camels and mules, moved westward toward a village near the junction of the Panjshir and Cabul rivers, there to obtain supplies of grain and forage. The little detachment on its march was suddenly met by the fire of about 1000 Safi tribesmen. Captain Poole, observing that the tribesmen were moving to cut him off, withdrew his party through a defile in his rear, and taking cover under the river bank maintained a steady fire while the camels were being retired. The Safis were extremely bold and they too shot very straight. Captain Poole was severely wounded and of his handful of fifty-six men eight were either killed or wounded, but their comrades resolutely held their position until reinforcements came out from the camp. The Safis, who retired with dogged reluctance, were not finally routed until attacked by British infantry in front and flank. After they broke the cavalry pursued them for six miles, doing severe execution; the dead of the 67th were recovered, but the poor fellows had been mutilated almost past recognition. General Macpherson returned to Sherpur on the 20th November, having left a strong garrison temporarily at Luttabund to strengthen communications and open out effectually the new route eastward.

General Roberts, with all his exertions, had been unable to accumulate sufficient winter of grain for his native troops and forage for his cavalry and baggage animals. Agents had been purchasing supplies in the fertile district of Maidan, distant from Cabul about twenty-five miles in the Ghuznee direction, but the local people lacked carriage to convey their stocks into camp, and it was necessary that the supplies should be brought in by the transport of the force. The country toward Ghuznee was reported to be in a state of disquiet, and a strong body of troops was detailed under the command of General Baker for the protection of the transport. This force marched out from Sherpur on November 21st, and next day camped on the edge of the pleasant Maidan plain. Baker encountered great difficulties in collecting supplies. The villages readily gave in their tribute of grain and forage, but evinced extreme reluctance to furnish the additional quantities which our necessities forced us to requisition. With the villagers it was not a question of money ; the supplies for which Baker's commissaries demanded money in hand constituted their provision for the winter season. But the stern maxim of war is that soldiers must live although villagers starve, and this much may be said in our favour that we are the only nation in the world which, when compelled to resort to forced requisitions, invariably pays in hard cash and not in promissory notes. Baker's ready-money tariff was far higher than the current rates, but nevertheless he had to resort to strong measures. In one instance he was defied outright. A certain Bahadur Khan inhabiting a remote valley in the Bamian direction, refused to sell any portion of his great store of grain and forage, and declined to comply with a summons to present himself in Baker's camp. It was known that he was under the influence of the aged fanatic Moulla the Mushk-i-Alum, who was engaged in fomenting a tribal rising, and it was reported that he was affording protection to a number of the fugitive sepoys of the ex-Ameer's army. A political officer with two squadrons of cavalry was sent to bring into camp the recalcitrant Bahadur Khan. His fort and village were found prepared for a stubborn defence. Received with a heavy fire from a large body of men while swarms of hostile tribesmen showed themselves on the adjacent hills, the horsemen had to withdraw. It was judged necessary to punish the contumacious chief and to disperse the tribal gathering before it should make more head, and Baker led out a strong detachment in light marching order. There was no fighting, and the only enemies seen were a few tribesmen, who drew off into the hills as the head of Baker's column approached. Fort, villages, and valley were found utterly deserted. There were no means to carry away the forage and grain found in the houses, so the villages belonging to Bahadur Khan were destroyed by fire. Their inhabitants found refuge in the surrounding villages, and there was absolutely no foundation for the statements which appeared in English papers to the effect that old men, women, and children were turned out to die in the snow. In the words of Mr Hensman, a correspondent who accompanied the column: 'There were no old men, women, and children, and there was no snow.' British officers cannot be supposed to have found pleasure, on the verge of the bitter

Afghan winter, in the destruction of the hovels and the winter stores of food belonging to a number of miserable villagers ; but experience has proved that only by such stern measures is there any possibility of cowing the rancour of Afghan tribesmen.   No elation can accompany an operation so pitiless, and the plea of stern necessity must be advanced alike and accepted with a shudder.   Of the necessity of some such form of reprisals an example is afforded in an experience which befell General Baker a few days later in this same Maidan region.   He visited the village of Beni-Badam with a small cavalry escort. The villagers with every demonstration of friendliness entertained the officers and men with milk and fruit, and provided corn and forage for their horses.   There were only old men in the village with the women and children, but no treachery was suspected until suddenly two large bodies of armed men were seen hurrying to cut off the retreat, and it was only by hard fighting that the General with his escort succeeded in escaping from the snare. Next day he destroyed the village.   Baker probably acted on general principles, but had he cared for precedents he would have found them in the conduct of the Germans in the Franco-Prussian war.   He remained in the Maidan district until the transport of the army had brought into Sherpur all the supplies which he had succeeded in obtaining in that region, and then returned to the cantonment.

By the terms of the proclamation which he issued on the 28th October Sir Frederick Roberts was announced as the dominant authority for the time being in Eastern and Northern Afghanistan.   He occupied this position

just as far as and no further than he could make it good.
And he could make it good only over a very circum-
scribed area. Even more than had been true of Shah
Soojah's government forty years previously was it true
of Roberts' government now that it was a government
of sentry-boxes. He was firm master of the Sherpur
cantonment. General Hills, his nominee, held a somewhat precarious sway in Cabul in the capacity of its
Governor, maintaining his position there in virtue of the
bayonets of his military guard, the support of the
adjacent Sherpur, and the waiting attitude of the populace of the capital. East of Cabul the domination of
Britain was represented by a series of fortified posts
studding the road to Gundamuk, whence to Jumrood the
occupation was closer, although not wholly undisturbed.
When a column marched out from Sherpur the British
power was dominant only within the area of its fire zone.
The stretch of road it vacated as it moved on ceased to
be territory over which the British held dominion. This
narrowly restricted nature of his actual sway Sir Frederick
Roberts could not but recognise, but how with a force of
7000 men all told was it possible for him to enlarge its
borders? One expedient suggested itself which could
not indeed extend the area of his real power, but which
might have the effect, to use a now familiar expression, of
widening the sphere of his influence. From among the
Sirdars who had regarded it as their interest to cast in
their lot with the British, he selected four to represent
him in the capacity of governors of provinces which his
bayonets were not long enough to reach. The experiment
made it disagreeably plain that the people of the pro-

vinces to which he had deputed governors were utterly indisposed to have anything to do either with them or with him. The governors went in no state, they had no great sums to disburse, they were protected by no armed escorts, and they were regarded by the natives much as the Southern states of the American Union after the Civil War regarded the 'carpet bag' governors whom the North imposed upon them. The Logur Governor was treated with utter contempt. The Kohistanees despitefully used Shahbaz Khan, and when a brother of Yakoub Khan was sent to use his influence in favour of the worried and threatened governor, he was reviled as a 'Kafir' and a 'Feringhee,' and ordered peremptorily back to Sherpur if he had any regard for his life. Sirdar Wali Mahomed, the governor-nominate to the remote Turkestan, found pretext after pretext for delaying to proceed to take up his functions, and had never quitted the British camp. When Baker returned from Maidan he reported that he had left the district peaceful in charge of the governor whom he had installed, the venerable and amiable Hassan Khan. Baker's rear-guard was scarcely clear of the valley when a mob of tribesmen and sepoys attacked the fort in which the old Sirdar was residing, shot him through the head, and then hacked his body to pieces. It was too clear that governors unsupported by bayonets, and whose only weapons were tact and persuasiveness, were at an extreme discount in the condition which Afghanistan presented in the end of November and the beginning of December.

CHAPTER IV

THE DECEMBER STORM

THE invader of Afghanistan may count as inevitable a national rising against him, but the Afghans are a people so immersed in tribal quarrels and domestic blood feuds that the period of the outbreak is curiously uncertain. The British force which placed Shah Soojah on the throne and supported him there, was in Afghanistan for more than two years before the waves of the national tempest rose around it. The national combination against Roberts' occupation was breaking its strength against the Sherpur defences while as yet the Cabul field force had not been within sight of the capital for more than two months. There seems no relation between opportunity and the period of the inevitable outburst. If in November 1841 the Cabul Sirdars had restrained themselves for a few days longer two more regiments would have been following on Sale's track, and the British force in the cantonments would have been proportionately attenuated. Roberts might have been assailed with better chance of success when his force was dispersed between the Siah Sung camp, the Balla Hissar, and Sherpur, than when concentrated in the strong defensive position against which the Afghans beat in vain. Perhaps the rising ripened faster in 1879 than in 1841

because in the former period no Macnaghten fomented
intrigues and scattered gold.   Perhaps Shere Ali's military
innovations may have instilled into the masses of his time
some rough lessons in the art and practice of speedy
mobilisation.   The crowning disgrace of 1842 was that
a trained army of regular soldiers should have been annihilated by a few thousand hillmen, among whom there was
no symptom either of real valour or of good leadership.
To Roberts and his force attaches the credit of having
defeated the persistent and desperate efforts of levies at
least ten times superior in numbers, well armed, far from
undisciplined, courageous beyond all experience of Afghan
nature, and under the guidance of a leader who had some
conception of strategy, and who certainly was no mean
tactician.

In the Afghan idiosyncrasy there is a considerable
strain of practical philosophy.   The blood of the massacred mission was not dry when it was recognised in
Cabul that stern retribution would inevitably follow.
Well, said the Afghans among themselves, what must
be must be, for they are all fatalists.   The seniors recalled the memory of the retribution Pollock exacted—
how he came, destroyed Istalif, set a 'mark' on Cabul
by sending the great bazaar in fragments into the air, and
then departed.   This time Istalif was not compromised ;
if Roberts Sahib should be determined to blow up the
Char Chowk again, why, that infliction must be endured.
It had been rebuilt after Pollock Sahib's engineers had
worked their will on it ; it could be rebuilt a second time
when Roberts Sahib should have turned his back on
the city, as pray God and the Prophet he might do with

no more delay than Pollock Sahib had made out yonder
on the Logur plain. So after a trial of Roberts' mettle
at Charasiah, and finding the testing sample not quite to
their taste, the Afghans fell into an attitude of expectancy,
and were mightily relieved by his proclamation read at
the Balla Hissar durbar of October 12th. After a reason-
able amount of hanging and the exaction of the fine laid
on the city, it was assumed that he would no doubt de-
part so as to get home to India before the winter snows
should block the passes. But the expected did not hap-
pen. The British General established a British Governor
in Cabul who had a heavy hand, and policed the place
in a fashion that stirred a lurid fury in the bosoms of
haughty Sirdars who had been wont to do what seemed
good in their own eyes. He engaged in the sacrilegious
work of dismantling the Balla Hissar, the historic fortress
of the nation, within whose walls were the royal palace
and the residences of the principal nobles. Those were
bitter things, but they could be borne if they were mere
temporary inflictions, and if the hated Feringhees would
but take themselves away soon. But that hope was
shattered by the proclamation of October 28th, when the
abdication of the Ameer was intimated and the British
raj in Afghanistan was announced. Yes, that pestilent
zabardasti little General, who would not follow the example of good old Pollock Sahib, and who held Yakoub
Khan and sundry of his Sirdars in close imprisonment
in his camp, had now the insolence to proclaim himself
virtually the Ameer of Afghanistan! Far from showing symptom of budging, he was sending out his governors
into the provinces, he was gathering tribute in kind, and

he had taken possession of Shere Ali's monumental cantonment, under the shadow of the Behmaroo heights
on which Afghan warriors of a past generation had
slaughtered the Feringhee soldiers as if they had been
sheep ; and it was the Feringhee General's cantonment
now, which he was cunningly strengthening as if he
meant to make it his permanent fortress.

Yakoub Khan had gained little personal popularity
during his brief and troubled reign, but he was an Afghan
and a Mahomedan ; and his deportation to India, followed shortly afterwards by that of his three Ministers,
intensified the rancour of his countrymen and co-reli-
gionists against the handful of presumptuous foreigners
who arrogantly claimed to sway the destinies of Afghanistan. *Cherchez la femme* is the keynote among Western
peoples of an investigation into the origin of most
troubles and strifes ; the watchword of the student of
the springs of great popular outbursts among Eastern
nations must be *Cherchez les prêtres*.   The Peter the
Hermit of Afghanistan was the old Mushk-i-Alum, the
fanatic Chief Moulla of Ghuznee. This aged enthusiast
went to and fro among the tribes proclaiming the sacred
duty of a *Jehad* or religious war against the unbelieving
invaders, stimulating the pious passions of the followers
of the Prophet by fervent appeals, enjoining the chiefs to
merge their intestine strifes in the common universal
effort to crush the foreign invaders of the Afghan soil.
The female relatives of the abdicated Ameer fomented
the rising by appeals to popular sympathy, and by the
more practical argument of lavish distribution of treasure.
The flame spread, tribesmen and disbanded soldiers sprang

to arms, the banner of the Prophet was unfurled, and the nation heaved with the impulse of fanaticism. Musa Khan, the boy heir of Yakoub, was in the hands of the Mushk-i-Alum, and the combination of fighting tribes found a competent leader in Mahomed Jan, a Warduk general of proved courage and capacity. The plan of campaign was comprehensive and well devised. The contingent from the country to the south of the capital, from Logur, Zurmat, and the Mangal and Jadran districts, was to seize that section of the Cabul ridge extending from Charasiah northward to the cleft through which flows the Cabul river. The northern contingent from the Kohistan and Kohdaman was to occupy the Asmai heights and the hills further to the north-west; while the troops from the Maidan and Warduk territories, led by Mahomed Jan in person, were to come in from the westward across the Chardeh valley, take possession of Cabul, and rally to their banners the disaffected population of the capital and the surrounding villages. The concentration of the three bodies effected, the capital and the ridge against which it leans occupied, the next step would be the investment of the Sherpur cantonment, preparatory to an assault upon it in force.

The British general through his spies had information of those projects. To allow the projected concentration to be effected would involve serious disadvantages, and both experience and temperament enjoined on Roberts the offensive. The Logur contingent was regarded as not of much account, and might be headed back by a threat. Mahomed Jan's force, which was reckoned some 5000 strong, needed to be handled with greater vigour.

Meer Butcha and his Kohistanees were less formidable, and might be dealt with incidentally. Roberts took a measure of wise precaution in telegraphing to Colonel Jenkins on the 7th December to march his Guides (cavalry and infantry) from Jugdulluk to Sherpur.

On the 8th General Macpherson was sent out toward the west with a column consisting of 1300 bayonets, three squadrons, and eight guns. Following the Ghuznee road across the Chardeh valley, he was to march to Urgundeh, in the vicinity of which place it was expected that he would find Mahomed Jan's levies, which he was to attack and drive backward on Maidan, taking care to prevent their retreat to the westward in the direction of Bamian. On the following day General Baker marched out with a force made up of 900 infantrymen, two and a half squadrons, and four guns, with instructions to march southward toward the Logur valley, deal with the tribal gathering there, then bend sharply in a south-westerly direction and take up a position across the Ghuznee road in the Maidan valley on the line of retreat which it was hoped that Macpherson would succeed in enforcing on Mahomed Jan. In that case the Afghan leader would find himself between two fires, and would be punished so severely as to render it unlikely that he would give further trouble. To afford time for Baker to reach the position assigned to him Macpherson remained halted during the 9th at Aushar, a village just beyond the debouche of the Nanuchee Pass, at the north-western extremity of the Asmai heights. On that day a cavalry reconnaissance discovered that the Kohistanee levies in considerable strength had already gathered about Karez

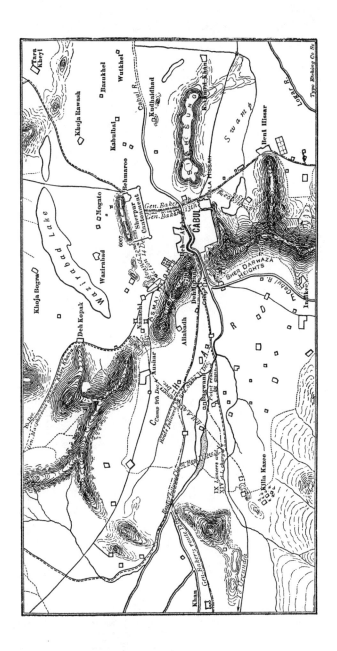

Meer, some ten miles north-west of Cabul, and that
masses of Afghans presumably belonging to the force of
Mahomed Jan were moving northward in the Kohistan
direction, apparently with the object of joining Meer
Butcha's gathering at Karez. It was imperative that the
latter should be dispersed before the junction could be
effected, and Sir Frederick Roberts had no option but to
order Macpherson to alter his line of advance and move
against the Kohistanees. Necessary as was this diverg-
ence from the original plan of operation, it had the effect
of sending to wreck the combined movement from which
so much was hoped, and of bringing about a very critical
situation. If Lockhart's reconnaissance had been made
a day earlier, Macpherson might probably have utilised
to good purpose by dispersing the Kohistanees, the day
which as it was he spent halted at Aushar. He might
have accomplished that object equally well if, instead of
the cavalry reconnaissance made by Lockhart, Macpherson himself had been instructed to devote the 9th to a
reconnaissance in force in the direction of Karez Meer.

The country being held unsuited for the action of
wheeled artillery and cavalry, Macpherson left his details
of those arms at Aushar, and marched on the morning
of the 10th on Karez with his infantry and mountain
guns. As his troops crowned the Surkh Kotul they saw
before them an imposing spectacle. The whole terrain
around Karez swarmed with masses of armed tribesmen,
whose banners were flying on every hillock. Down in the
Pughman valley to the left rear, were discerned bodies of
the hostile contingent from the west, between which and
the Kohistanees no junction had fortunately as yet

been made. Macpherson's dispositions were simple. His mountain guns shelled with effect the Kohistanee tribesmen, and then he moved forward from the Surkh Kotul in three columns. His skirmishers drove back the forward stragglers, and then the main columns advancing at the double swept the disordered masses before them, and forced them rearward into their in-trenched position in front of the Karez village. There the resistance was half-hearted. After a brief artillery preparation the columns carried the position with a rush, and the Kohistanees were routed with heavy loss. Meer Butcha and his Kohistanees well beaten, Macpherson camped for the night near Karez. Baker had reached his assigned position in the Maidan valley, and there seemed a fair prospect that the operation against Mahomed Jan as originally designed might be carried out notwithstanding the interruption to its prosecution which had been found necessary. For there was good reason to believe that the Afghan commander and his force, whose strength was estimated at about 5000 men, were in the vicinity of Urgundeh, about midway between Macpherson at Karez and Baker in the Maidan valley. If Mahomed Jan would be so complaisant as to remain where he was until Macpherson could reach him, then Roberts' strategy would have a triumphant issue, and the Warduk general and his followers might be relegated to the category of negligable quantities.

Orders were sent to Macpherson to march as early as possible on the morning of the 11th, follow up the enemy who had been observed retiring toward the west and south, and endeavour to drive them down toward General

Baker. He was further informed that the cavalry and horse-artillery which he had left at Aushar would leave that village at nine A.M. under the command of Brigadier-General Massy, and would cross the Chardeh valley by the Urgundeh road, on which he was directed to join them on his march. The specific instructions given to General Massy were as follows : ' To advance from Aushar by the road leading directly from the city of Cabul toward Urgundeh and Ghuznee' (the main Ghuznee road), 'to proceed cautiously and quietly feeling for the enemy, to communicate with General Macpherson, and to act in conformity with that officer's movements, but on no account to commit himself to an action until General Macpherson had engaged the enemy.'

Macpherson marched at eight A.M., moving in a south-westerly direction toward Urgundeh by a direct track in rear of the range of hills bounding the western edge of the Chardeh valley. To the point at which it was pro-bable that he and Massy should meet he had considerably further to travel than had the latter from the Aushar camp, and Macpherson's force consisted of infantry while that of Massy was cavalry and horse-artillery. Massy left Aushar at nine A.M. in consideration of the shorter dis-tance he had to traverse, and he headed for Killa Kazee, a village near the foothills of the western ridge about four miles from Aushar as the crow flies. He did not comply with the letter of his instructions to follow the Ghuznee road because of the wide detour marching by it would have involved, but instead made his way straight across country. That he should have done this was un-fortunate, since the time he thus gained threw him forward

into a position involving danger in advance of any possible
co-operation on the part of Macpherson, who was still far
away from the point of intended junction while Massy
was comparatively near it. Massy's force consisted of
two squadrons 9th Lancers and a troop of 14th Bengal
Lancers, escorting four horse-artillery guns. He had
detached a troop of 9th Lancers to endeavour to open
communication with Macpherson, in compliance with his
instructions. As he approached Killa Kazee, Captain
Gough commanding the troop of 9th Lancers forming
the advance guard, sent back word that the hills on
either side of the Ghuznee road some distance beyond
the village were occupied by the enemy in considerable
force. Massy, in his unsupported condition and destitute
of any information as to Macpherson's whereabouts, would
have shown discretion by halting on receipt of this intelligence pending further developments. But he probably
believed that the Afghans flanking the road were casual
tribesmen from the adjacent villages who were unlikely
to make any stand, and he determined to move on.

What he presently saw gave him pause. A great
mass of Afghans some 2000 strong were forming across
the Ghuznee road. From the hills to right and left
broad streams of armed men were pouring down the hill-
slopes and forming on the plain. The surprise was
complete, the situation full of perplexity. That gathering host in Massy's front could be none other than
Mahomed Jan's entire force. So far from being in retreat southward and westward, so far from waiting
supinely about Urgundeh until Macpherson as per programme should drive it on to the muzzles of Baker's

Martinis, here it was inside our guard, in possession of the interior line, its front facing toward turbulent Cabul and depleted Sherpur, with no obstruction in its path save this handful of lancers and these four guns ! Massy's orders, it was true, were to act in conformity with Macpherson's movements, and on no account to commit himself to an action until that officer had engaged the enemy. Yes, but could the framer of those orders have anticipated the possibility of such a position as that in which Massy now found himself? There was no Macpherson within ken of the perplexed cavalryman, nor the vaguest indication of his movements. The enemy had doubled on that stout and shrewd soldier ; it was clear that for the moment he was not within striking distance of his foe, whether on flank or on rear. No course of action presented itself to Massy that was not fraught with grave contingencies. If he should keep to the letter of his orders, the Afghan host might be in Cabul in a couple of hours. Should he retire slowly, striving to retard the Afghan advance by his cannon fire and by the threatening demonstrations of his cavalry, the enemy might follow him up so vigorously as to be beyond Macpherson's reach when that officer should make good his point in the direction of Urgundeh. If on the other hand he should show a bold front, and departing from his orders in the urgent crisis face to face with which he found himself should strain every nerve to 'hold' the Afghan masses in their present position, there was the possibility that, at whatever sacrifice to himself and his little force, he might save the situation and gain time for Macpherson to come up and strike Mahomed Jan on flank and in rear.

For better or for worse Massy committed himself to the rasher enterprise, and opened fire on the swiftly growing Afghan masses. The first range was held not sufficiently effective, and in the hope by closer fire of deterring the enemy from effecting the formation they were attempting, the guns were advanced to the shorter ranges of 2500 and 2000 yards. The shells did execution, but contrary to precedent did not daunt the Afghans. They made good their formation under the shell fire. Mahomed Jan's force had been estimated of about 5000 strong; according to Massy's estimate it proved to be double that number. The array was well led; it never wavered, but came steadily on with waving banners and loud shouts. The guns had to be retired; they came into action again, but owing to the rapidity of the Afghan advance at shorter range than before. The carbine fire of thirty dismounted lancers 'had no appreciable effect.' The outlook was already ominous when at this moment Sir Frederick Roberts came on the scene. As was his wont, he acted with decision. The action, it was clear to him, could not be maintained against odds so overwhelming and in ground so unfavourable. He immediately ordered Massy to retire slowly, to search for a road by which the guns could be withdrawn, and to watch for an opportunity to execute a charge under cover of which the guns might be extricated. He despatched an aide-de-camp in quest of Macpherson, with an order directing that officer to wheel to his left into the Chardeh valley and hurry to Massy's assistance; and he ordered General Hills to gallop to Sherpur and warn General Hugh Gough, who had charge in the cantonment, to be

on the alert, and also to send out at speed a wing of the
72d to the village of Deh Mazung, in the throat of
the gorge of the Cabul river, which the Highlanders were
to hold to extremity.

The enemy were coming on, the guns were in imminent danger, and the moment had come for the action of
the cavalry. The gallant Cleland gave the word to his
lancers and led them straight for the centre of the Afghan
line, the troop of Bengal Lancers following in support.
Gough, away on the Afghan left, saw his chief charging
and he eagerly 'conformed,' crushing in on the enemy's
flank at the head of his troop. ' Self-sacrifice ' the
Germans hold the duty of cavalry ; and there have been
few forlorner hopes than the errand on which on this ill-
starred day our 200 troopers rode into the heart of
10,000 Afghans flushed with unwonted good fortune.
Through the dust-cloud of the charge were visible the
flashes of the Afghan volleys and the sheen of the British
lance heads as they came down to the 'engage.' There
was a short interval of suspense, the stour and bicker of
the *mêlée* faintly heard, but invisible behind the bank of
smoke and dust. Then from out the cloud of battle
riderless horses came galloping back, followed by
broken groups of troopers. Gallantly led home, the
charge had failed—what other result could have been
expected ? Its career had been blocked by sheer weight
of opposing numbers. Sixteen troopers had been killed,
seven were wounded, two officers had been slain in the
hand-to-hand strife. Cleland came out with a sword cut
and a bullet wound. Captain Stewart Mackenzie had
been crushed under his fallen horse, but distinguished

himself greatly, and brought the regiment out of action. As the dust settled it was apparent that the charge had merely encouraged the enemy, who as they steadily pressed on in good order, were waving their banners in triumph and brandishing their tulwars and knives. The fire from the Sniders and Enfields of their marksmen was well directed and deliberate. While Cleland's broken troopers were being rallied two guns were brought into action, protected in a measure by Gough's troop and the detachment of Bengal Lancers, which had not suffered much in the charge. But the Afghans came on so ardently that there was no alternative but prompt retreat. One gun had to be spiked and abandoned, Lieutenant Hardy of the Horse-Artillery remaining by it until surrounded and killed. Some 500 yards further back, near the village of Baghwana, the three remaining guns stuck fast in a deep watercourse. At General Roberts' instance a second charge was attempted, to give time for their extrication; but it made no head, so that the guns had to be abandoned, and the gunners and drivers with their teams accompanied the retirement of the cavalry. Some fugitives both of cavalry and artillery hurried to the shelter of the cantonment somewhat precipitately; but the great majority of Massy's people behaved well, rallying without hesitation and constituting the steady and soldierly little body with which Roberts, retiring on Deh Mazung as slowly as possible to give time for the Highlanders from Sherpur to reach that all-important point, strove to delay the Afghan advance. This in a measure was accomplished by the dismounted fire of the troopers, and the retirement was distinguished by the steady coolness displayed by Gough's men and Neville's Bengal Lancers. Deh Mazung was reached, but no Highlanders had as yet reached that place. The carbines of the cavalrymen were promptly utilised from the cover the village afforded ; but they could not have availed to stay the Afghan rush. There was a short interval of extreme anxiety until the 200 men of the 72d, Brownlow leading them, became visible advancing at the double through the gorge. 'It was literally touch and go who should reach the village first, the Highlanders or the Afghans,' who were streaming toward it 'like ants on a hill,' but the men of the 72d swept in, and swarming to the house tops soon checked with their breechloaders the advancing tide. After half-an-hour of futile effort the Afghans saw fit to abandon the attempt to force the gorge, and inclining to their right they occupied the Takht-i-Shah summit, the slopes of the Sher Derwaza heights, and the villages in the south-eastern section of the Chardeh valley.

Macpherson, marching from the Surkh Kotul toward Urgundeh, had observed parties of Afghans crossing his front in the direction of the Chardeh valley, and when the sound reached him of Massy's artillery fire he wheeled to his left through a break in the hills opening into the Chardeh valley, and approached the scene of the discomfiture of Massy's force. This he did at 12.30 P.M., four and a half hours after leaving the Surkh Kotul. As the length of his march was about ten miles, it may be assumed that he encountered difficulties in the rugged track by which he moved, for Macpherson was not the man to linger by the way when there was the prospect of a fight. Had it been possible for him to have marched two hours earlier than he did—and his orders were to march as early as possible—his doing so would have made all the difference in the world to Massy, and could scarcely have failed to change the face of the day. He did not discover the lost guns, but he struck the Afghan rear, which was speedily broken and dispersed by the 67th and 3d Sikhs. Macpherson's intention to spend the night at Killa Kazee was changed by the receipt of an order from General Roberts calling him in to Deh Mazung, where he arrived about nightfall. Sir Frederick Roberts then returned to Sherpur, for the defence of which General Hugh Gough had made the best disposi- tions in his power, and the slender garrison of which was to receive in the course of the night an invaluable acces- sion in the shape of the Guides, 900 strong, whom Jenkins had brought up by forced marches from Jug- dulluk.

The misfortunes of the day were in a measure retrieved by a well-timed, ready-witted, and gallant action on the part of that brilliant and lamented soldier Colonel Mac- gregor. A wing of the 72d had been called out to hold the gorge of the Cabul river, but the Nanuchee Pass, through which led the direct road from the scene of the combat to Sherpur, remained open ; and there was a time when the Afghan army was heading in its direction. Macgregor had hurried to the open pass in time to rally about him a number of Massy's people, who had lost their officers and were making their way confusedly toward the refuge of Sherpur. Remaining in possession of this important point until all danger was over, he noticed that the ground about Bagwana, where the guns had been abandoned, was not held by the enemy, and there seemed to him that the opportunity to recover them presented itself. Taking with him a detachment of lancers and artillerymen, he rode out and met with no molestation beyond a few shots from villagers. From Macpherson's baggage guard, met as it crossed the valley toward Sherpur, he requisitioned sixty infantrymen who entered and held Bagwana, and covered him and the gunners during the long and arduous struggle to extricate the guns from their lair in the deep and rugged watercourse. This was at length accomplished, scratch teams were improvised, and the guns, which were uninjured although the ammunition boxes had been emptied, were brought into the cantonment to the general joy.

The result of the day's operations left General Baker momentarily belated. But on the morning of the 11th that officer, finding that no Afghans were being driven down upon him in accordance with the programme, quitted the Maidan country and marched northward toward Urgundeh. An attack on his baggage and rear-guard was foiled; but as he reached his camping ground for the night at Urgundeh the Afghans were found in possession of the gorge opening into the Chardeh valley, through which ran his road to Cabul. They were dislodged by a dashing attack of part of the 92d Highlanders led by Lieutenant Scott Napier. It was not until the morning of the 12th that Baker was informed by heliograph from Sherpur of the occurrences of the previous day, and received directions to return to the cantonment without delay. In the course of a few hours he was inside

Sherpur, notwithstanding that his march had been constantly molested by attacks on his rear-guard.

The casualties of the 11th had been after all not very serious. All told they amounted to thirty men killed and forty-four wounded; fifty-one horses killed and sixteen wounded. But the Afghans were naturally elated by the success they had unquestionably achieved; the national rising had been inaugurated by a distinct triumph, the news of which would bring into the field incalculable swarms of fierce and fanatical partisans. It was clear that Mahomed Jan had a quick eye for opportunities, and some skill in handling men. That he could recognise the keypoint of a position and act boldly and promptly on that recognition, his tactics of the 11th made abundantly obvious, and his commanding position on the morning of the 12th still further demonstrated his tactical ability. *L'audace, encore l'audace, et toujours l'audace* is the game to be played by the commander of disciplined troops against Asiatic levies, and no man was more sensible of this than the gallant soldier who now from the bastion of Sherpur could see the Afghan standards waving on the summit of the Takht-i-Shah. Indeed he was impressed so thoroughly by the force of the maxim as to allow himself to hope that some 560 soldiers, of whom about one-third were Europeans, backed by a couple of mountain guns, would be able to carry by assault the lofty peak, strongly held by resolute Afghans in protected positions, supported by several thousands of their fellows lying out of sight until an attack should develop itself, to meet which they were at hand to reinforce the garrison of the Takht-i-Shah. From the gorge of the Cabul river there runs due south to near Charasiah a lofty and rugged range, the highest point of which, the Takht-i-Shah, is about midway from either extremity. From this main ridge there project eastward at right angles two lateral spurs. The shorter and more northerly of those runs down to the Balla Hissar, the longer and more southerly obtruding itself into the plain as far as the village of Beni Hissar. This latter spur quits the main ridge no great distance south of the Takht-i-Shah peak, and on the 12th the Afghan reserves were massed in rear of the peak, both on the main ridge and on this spur. The steep faces of the mountain were strewn with great smooth boulders and jagged masses of rock ; the ascent, everywhere laborious, was complicated in places by sheer scarps, and those formidable impediments were made still more difficult by frequent sungahs, strong stone curtains behind which the defenders lay safe or fired with a minimum of exposure. On the summit was a great natural cavity which had been made bomb proof by art, and further cover was afforded by caves and lines of rock. The most northerly portion of the ridge described is known as the Sher Derwaza heights, which Macpherson had occupied on the morning of the 12th, and his brigade it was which furnished the little force already mentioned as charged to attempt the task of storming the Takht-i-Shah.

For several hours Morgan's two mountain guns industriously shelled that peak, and then the infantry made their effort. The Afghans fought stubbornly in defence of a lower hill they held in advance of the Takht-i-Shah, but after a hard struggle they had to abandon it to Macpherson's resolute men. But the exertions of the latter to ascend the peak were baulked by its rugged steepness and the fire of the Afghans holding the sungahs on its face. Sir Frederick Roberts had to recognise that the direct attack by so weak a force unaided by a diversion, could not succeed, and he ordered further efforts to be deferred. The casualties of the abortive attempt included three officers, one of whom, Major Cook, V.C. of the Goorkhas, than whom the British army contained no better soldier, died of his wound. Macpherson was directed to hold the ground he had won, including the lower advanced hill, and was informed that on the following morning he was to expect the co-operation of General Baker from the direction of Beni Hissar.

The lesson of the result of attempting impossibilities had been taken to heart, and the force which Baker led out on the morning of the 13th was exceptionally strong, consisting as it did of the 92d Highlanders and Guides infantry, a wing of the 3d Sikhs, a cavalry regiment, and eight guns. Marching in the direction of the lateral spur extending from the main ridge eastward to Beni Hissar, Baker observed that large masses of the enemy were quitting the plain villages about Beni Hissar in which they had taken shelter for the night, and were hurrying to gain the summit of the spur which constituted the defensive position of the Afghan reserve. Baker's *coup d'œil* was quick and true. By gaining the centre of the spur he would cut in two the Afghan line along its summit, and so isolate and neutralise the section of it from the centre to the Beni Hissar extremity, toward which section the reinforcements from the plain villages were climbing. But to accomplish this shrewd stroke it was necessary that he should act with promptitude and energy. His guns opened fire on the summit. The Sikhs, extended athwart the plain, protected his right flank. His cavalry on the left cut into the bodies of Afghans hurrying to ascend the eastern extremity of the spur. With noble emulation the Highlanders and the Guides sprang up the rugged slope, their faces set towards the centre of the summit line. Major White, who already had earned many laurels in the campaign, led on his Highlanders; the Guides, burning to make the most of their first opportunity to distinguish themselves, followed eagerly the gallant chief who had so often led them to victory on other fields. Lieutenant Forbes, a young officer of the 92d heading the advance of his regiment, reached the summit accompanied only by his colour-sergeant. A band of ghazees rushed on the pair and the sergeant fell. As Forbes stood covering his body he was overpowered and slain. The sudden catastrophe staggered for a moment the soldiers following their officer, but Lieutenant Dick Cunyngham rallied them immediately and led them forward at speed. For his conduct on this occasion Cunyngham received the Victoria Cross.

With rolling volleys Highlanders and Guides reached and won the summit. The Afghans momentarily clung to the position, but the British fire swept them away and the bayonets disposed of the ghazees, who fought and died in defence of their standards. The severance of the Afghan line was complete. A detachment was left to maintain the isolation of some 2000 of the enemy who had been cut off; and then swinging to their right Baker's regiments swept along the summit of the spur toward the main ridge and the Takht-i-Shah, the High-landers leading. As they advanced they rolled up the Afghan line and a panic set in among the enemy, who sought safety in flight. Assailed from both sides, for Macpherson's men from the conical hill were passing up the north side of the peak, and shaken by the steady fire of the mountain guns, the garrison of the Takht-i-Shah evacuated the position. Baker's soldiers toiled vigorously upward toward the peak, keen for the honour of winning it; but the credit of that achievement justly fell to their comrades of Macpherson's command, who had striven so valiantly to earn it the day before, and who had gained possession of the peak and the Afghan standards flying on its summit, a few minutes before the arrival of White's Highlanders and Jenkins' Guides. As the midday gun was fired in the cantonment the flash of the heliograph from the peak told that the Takht-i-Shah was won.

While Baker was sweeping the spur and climbing the lofty peak of the main ridge, his reserve, which remained in the plain, was in sharp action against masses of assailants from the city and other bodies from the villages about Beni Hissar. Those were beaten off by the 3d Sikhs and Baker's flanks were thus cleared, but the resolute Afghans, bent on interfering with his return march, surged away in the direction of the Siah Sung ridge and gathered thereon in considerable strength. The guns of Sherpur shelled them smartly, but they held their ground; and Massy went out to disperse them with the cavalry. The Afghans showed unwonted resolution, confronting the cavalry with extraordinary steadiness in regular formation and withholding their fire until the troopers were close upon them. But the horsemen were not to be denied. Captains Butson and Chisholme led their squadrons against the Afghan flanks, and the troopers of the 9th avenged the mishap which had befallen that gallant regiment two days before, riding through and through the hostile masses and scattering them over the plain. But in the charge Butson was killed, Chisholme and Trower were wounded ; the sergeant-major and three men were killed and seven were wounded. Brilliant charges were delivered by the other cavalry detachments, and the Siah Sung heights were ultimately cleared. The Guides' cavalry attacked, defeated, and pursued for a long distance a body of Kohistanees marching from the north-east apparently with intent to join Mahomed Jan. The casualties of the day were sixteen killed and forty-five wounded ; not a heavy loss considering the amount of hard fighting. The Afghans were estimated to have lost in killed alone from 200 to 300 men.

The operations of the day were unquestionably successful so far as they went, but the actual results attained scarcely warranted the anticipation that the Afghans would acknowledge themselves defeated by breaking up their combination and dispersing to their homes. It was true that they had been defeated, but they had fought with unprecedented stubbornness and gave little evidence of being cowed. Throughout the day the villages around Cabul had evinced a rancorous hostility which had a marked significance. Not less significant was the participation in the fighting of the day on the part of the population of Cabul. As Baker was returning to Sherpur

J

in the evening he had been fired upon from the Balla Hissar, and his flanking parties had found ambushes of armed Afghans among the willows between the city and the cantonment. But for the skill and courage of the non-commissioned officer in charge a convoy of wounded on its way to Sherpur would certainly have been destroyed. But there was a stronger argument than any of those indications, significant as they were of the un-broken spirit of the Afghans, telling against the pro-bability that the operations of the day would have the effect of putting down the national rising. The hordes which had gathered to the banners of the Mushk-i-Alum and Mahomed Jan combined with the fanaticism of the *jehad* a fine secular greed for plunder. Was it likely that they would scatter resignedly, leaving untouched the rich booty of the city that had been almost within arm's-length as they looked down on it from the peak of the Takht-i-Shah, and whose minarets they were within sight of on the spur and in the villages of Beni-Hissar? Was that ever likely? And was it not made more and yet more unlikely when on the afternoon of the 13th Macpherson, acting on orders, moved his camp to the Balla Hissar heights, evacuating Deh Mazung and leaving open to the enemy the road into the city through the Cabul gorge? The following morning was to show how promptly and how freely the Afghans had taken advant-age of the access to the capital thus afforded them. It must never be forgotten that at this time our people in Afghanistan held no more territory than the actual ground they stood upon and the terrain swept by their fire. No trustworthy intelligence from outside that region was procurable ; and of this there can be no clearer evidence than that the General was under the belief that the enemy had been ' foiled in their western and southern operations.'

The morning of the 14th effectually dispelled the optimistic anticipations indulged in overnight. At day-break a large body of Afghans, with many standards, were discerned on a hill about a mile northward of the Asmai ridge, from which and from the Kohistan road they were moving on to the crest of that ridge. They were joined there by several thousands coming up the slopes from out the village of Deh Afghan, the northern suburb of Cabul. It was estimated that there were about 8000 men in position along the summit of the ridge, and occupying also a low conical hill beyond its north-western termination. The array of Afghans displayed itself within a mile of the west face of the Sherpur canton-ment, and formed a menace which could not be brooked. To General Baker was entrusted the task of dislodging the enemy from the threatening position, and there was assigned to him for this purpose a force consisting of about 1200 bayonets, eight guns, and a regiment of native cavalry. His first object was to gain possession of the conical hill already mentioned, and thus debar the Afghan force on the Asmai heights from receiving accessions either from the masses on the hill further north or by the Kohistan road. Under cover of the artillery fire the Highlanders and Guides occupied this conical hill after a short conflict. A detachment was left to hold it and then Colonel Jenkins, who commanded the attack, set about the arduous task of storming from the northward the

formidable position of the Asmai heights. The assault
was led by Brownlow's staunch Highlanders, supported
on the right by the Guides operating on the enemy's
flank ; and the Afghan position was heavily shelled by
four of Baker's guns, and by four more in action near
the south-western corner of the Sherpur cantonment.
Macpherson from his position on the Balla Hissar
hill aided the attack by the fire of his guns, and
also by despatching two companies of the 67th to
cross the Cabul gorge and operate against the enemy's
left rear.

In the face of a heavy fire the Highlanders and Guides
climbed with great speed and steadiness the rugged hill-
side leading upward to the Afghan breastwork on the
northern edge of the summit. Their approach and the
crushing shrapnel fire from the guns near Sherpur had
caused numerous Afghans to move downward from the
position toward Deh Afghan, heavily smitten as they
went ; but the ghazees in the breastworks made a strenuous resistance and died under their banners as the
Highlanders carried the defences with a rush. The crest,
about a quarter of a mile long, was traversed under heavy
fire and the southern breastwork on the peak was approached. It was strong and strongly held, but a cross
fire was brought to bear on its garrison, and then the
frontal attack led by a lance-corporal of the 72d was
delivered. After a hand-to-hand grapple in which
Highlanders and Guides were freely cut and slashed by
the knives of the ghazees, the position, which was found
full of dead, was carried, but with considerable loss. The
whole summit of the Asmai heights was now in British

possession, and everything seemed auspicious. The Afghans streaming down from the heights toward the city were being lacerated by shell fire and musketry fire as they descended. When they took refuge in Deh Afghan that suburb was heavily shelled, and it was gradually evacuated.

Scarcely had Jenkins won the summit of the Asmai ridge when the fortune of the day was suddenly overcast; indeed while he was still engaged in the attainment of that object premonitory indications of serious mischief were unexpectedly presenting themselves. A vast host of Afghans described as numbering from 15,000 to 20,000, debouched into the Chardeh valley from the direction of Indikee, and were moving northwards, apparently with the object of forming a junction with the masses occupying the hills to the north-west of the Asmai heights. About the same time cavalry scouting in the Chardeh valley brought in the information that large parties of hostile infantry and cavalry were hurrying across the valley in the direction of the conical hill the defence of which had been entrusted to Lieutenant-Colonel Clark with 120 Highlanders and Guides. Recognising Clark's weakness, General Baker had judiciously reinforced that officer with four mountain guns and 100 bayonets. The guns opened fire on the Afghan bodies marching from the Killa Kazee direction, and drove them out of range. But they coalesced with the host advancing from Indikee, and the vast mass of Afghans, facing to the right, struck the whole range of the British position from near the Cabul gorge on the south to and beyond the conical hill on the north. The most vulnerable point was

the section at and about that eminence, and the necessity
for supplying Clark with further reinforcements became
urgently manifest. Baker sent up a second detachment, and
200 Sikhs came out from Sherpur at the double. But the
Afghans, creeping stealthily in great numbers up the slope
from out the Chardeh valley, had the shorter distance to
travel, and were beforehand with the reinforcements.
Their tactics were on a par with their resolution. The
left of their attack grasped and held a knoll north of the
conical hill, and from this position of vantage brought a
cross fire to bear on Clark's detachment. As their direct
attack developed itself it encountered from the conical
hill a heavy rifle fire, and shells at short range tore
through the loose rush of ghazees, but the fanatics sped
on and up without wavering. As they gathered behind a
mound for the final onslaught, Captain Spens of the 72d
with a handful of his Highlanders went out on the forlorn
hope of dislodging them. A rush was made on him ; he
was overpowered and slaughtered after a desperate resistance, and the Afghan charge swept up the hill-side. In
momentary panic the defenders gave ground, carrying
downhill with them the reinforcement of Punjaubees
which Captain Hall was bringing up. Two of the
mountain guns were lost, but there was a rally at the foot
of the hill under cover of which the other two were extricated. The Afghans refrained from descending into
the plain, and directed their efforts toward cutting off the
occupants of the position on the Asmai summit. They
ascended by two distinct directions. One body from
the conical hill followed the route taken by Jenkins in the
morning ; another scaled a spur trending downward to

the Chardeh valley from the southern extremity of the Asmai ridge.

It was estimated that the Afghan strength disclosed this day did not fall short of 40,000 men ; and General Roberts was reluctantly compelled to abandon for the time any further offensive efforts. His reasons, stated with perfect frankness, may best be given in his own words. ' Up to this time,' he wrote, ' I had no reason to apprehend that the Afghans were in sufficient force to cope successfully with disciplined troops, but the resolute and determined manner in which the conical hill had been recaptured, and the information sent to me by Brigadier-General Macpherson that large masses of the enemy were still advancing from the north, south, and west, made it evident that the numbers combined against us were too overwhelming to admit of my comparatively small force meeting them. I therefore determined to withdraw from all isolated positions, and to concentrate the whole force at Sherpur, thus securing the safety of our large cantonment, and avoiding what had now become a useless sacrifice of life.' The orders issued to Generals Baker and Macpherson to retire into the cantonment were executed with skill and steadiness. Jenkins' evacuation of the Asmai position was conspicuously adroit. When the order to quit reached that able officer, Major Stockwell of the 72d was out with a small detachment, maintaining a hot fire on the Afghan bodies ascending by the southern spur from the Chardeh valley. He fell back with great deliberation, and when he rejoined the retirement down the hill face looking toward Sherpur was leisurely proceeded with, the hostile advance from the northern side being held in check by the fire of covering parties from Jenkins' left flank. General Macpherson's retirement was masterly. Flanking his march through the Cabul gorge with two companies of the 67th who stalled off a rush of ghazees from the Asmai crest, he continued his march through the suburb of Deh Afghan, his baggage in front under a strong guard. Some few shots were exchanged before the suburb was cleared, but the casualties were few and presently the brigade entered the cantonment. General Baker continued to hold a covering position with part of his force, until the troops from the heights and Macpherson's command had made good their retirement, and he was the last to withdraw. By dusk the whole force was safely concentrated within the cantonment, and the period of the defensive had begun. The casualties of the day were serious; thirty-five killed, and 107 wounded. During the week of fighting the little force had lost somewhat heavily ; the killed numbered eighty-three, the wounded 192. Eight officers were killed, twelve were wounded.

CHAPTER V

ON THE DEFENSIVE IN SHERPUR

ALTHOUGH overlarge for its garrison, the Sherpur cantonment had many of the features of a strong defensive position. On the southern and western faces the massive and continuous enciente made it impregnable against any force unprovided with siege artillery. But on the eastern face the wall had been built to the elevation only of seven feet, and at either end of the Behmaroo heights, which constituted the northern line of defence, there were open gaps which had to be made good. The space between the north western bastion and the heights was closed by an entrenchment supported by a 'laager' of Afghan guncarriages and limbers, the ground in front strengthened by abattis and wire entanglements, beyond which a village flanking the northern and western faces was occupied as a detached post. The open space on the north-eastern angle was similarly fortified; the village of Behmaroo was loopholed, and outlying buildings to the front were placed in a state of defence. The unfinished eastern wall was heightened by logs built up in tiers, and its front was covered with abattis, a tower and garden outside being occupied by a detachment. A series of block houses had been built along the crest of the Behmaroo heights supporting a continuous entrenchment, gun emplacements made in the line of defence, and the gorge dividing the heights strongly fortified against an attack from the northern plain. The enciente was divided into sections to each of which was assigned a commanding officer with a specified detail of troops ; and a strong reserve of European infantry was under the command of Brigadier-General Baker, ready at short notice to reinforce any threatened point. It was presumably owing to the absorption of the troops in fighting, collecting supplies, and providing winter shelter, that when the concentration within Sherpur became suddenly necessary the defences of the position were still seriously defective ; and throughout the period of investment the force was unremittingly engaged in the task of strengthening them. Nor had the military precaution been taken of razing the villages and enclosures within the fire zone of the enciente, and they remained to afford cover to the enemy during the period of investment.

Before the enemy cut the telegraph wire in the early morning of the 15th Sir Frederick Roberts had informed the authorities in India of his situation and of his need for reinforcements ; and he had also ordered up General Charles Gough's brigade without loss of time. Gough was already at Jugdulluk when he received the order calling him to Cabul, but he had to wait for reinforcements and supplies, and the tribesmen were threatening his position and the line of communication in rear of it. He did not move forward until the 21st. On the following day he reached Luttabund, whence he took on with him the garrison of that post, but although his march was unmolested it was not until the 24th that he reached

Sherpur, a day too late to participate in repelling the assault on the cantonment.

While General Roberts' force was busily engaged in making good the defences of Sherpur, the Afghans refrained from attempting to back their success on the Asmai heights by an assault on the defensive position which seemed to invite an attack. During the first two days of their possession of the city they were enjoying the fruits of their occupation in their own turbulent manner. Roberts' spies reported them busily engaged in sacking the Hindoo and Kuzzilbash quarters, in looting and wrecking the houses of chiefs and townsfolk who had shown friendliness to the British, and in quarrelling among themselves over the spoils. Requisitioning was in full force. The old Moulla Mushk-i-Alum was the temporary successor of General Hills in the office of Governor of Cabul; and spite of his ninety years he threw extraordinary energy into the work of arousing fanaticism and rallying to Cabul the fighting men of the surrounding country. The *jehad* of which he had been the chief instigator had certainly attained unexampled dimensions, and although it was not in the nature of things that every Afghan who carried arms should be inspired with religious fanaticism to such a pitch as to be utterly reckless of his life, swarms of fierce ghazees made formidable the levies which Mahomed Jan commanded.

On the 17th and 18th the Afghans made ostentatious demonstrations against Sherpur, but those were never formidable, although they made themselves troublesome with some perseverance during the daytime, consistently refraining from night attacks, which was remarkable since ordinarily they are much addicted to the *chapao*. There never was any investment of Sherpur, or indeed any approximation to investment. Cavalry reconnaissances constantly went out, and piquets and videttes were habitually on external duty; infantry detachments sallied forth whenever occasion demanded to dislodge the assailants from points occupied by them in inconvenient proximity to the defences. The Afghan offensive was not dangerous, but annoying and wearying. It was indeed pushed with some resolution on the 18th, when several thousand men poured out of the city, and skirmished forward under cover of the gardens and enclosures on the plain between Cabul and Sherpur, in the direction of the southern front and the south-western bastions. The Afghans are admirable skirmishers, and from their close cover kept up for hours a brisk fire on the soldiers lining the Sherpur defences, but with singularly little effect. The return rifle fire was for the most part restricted to volleys directed on those of the enemy who offered a sure mark by exposing themselves; and shell fire was chiefly used to drive the Afghan skirmishers from their cover in the gardens and enclosures. Some of those, notwithstanding, were able to get within 400 yards of the enciente, but could make no further headway. On the morning of the 19th it was found that in the night the enemy had occupied the Meer Akhor fort, a few hundred yards beyond the eastern face, and close to the Residency compound of the old cantonments of 1839-42. The fire from this fort was annoying, and General Baker went out on the errand of destroying it, with 800 bayonets, two mountain guns, and a party of sappers. As the fort was

being approached through the dense mist a sudden volley
from it struck down several men, and Lieutenant Monte-
naro of the mountain battery was mortally wounded.
The fort was heavily shelled from the south-eastern
bastion ; its garrison evacuated it, and it was blown up.

Mahomed Jan and his coadjutors could hardly flatter
themselves that as yet they had made any impression on
the steadfast defence which the British force was maintaining in the Sherpur cantonment. The Afghan leader
had tried force in vain ; he knew the history of that
strange period in the winter of 1841 during which Afghan
truculence and audacity had withered the spirit of a
British force not much less numerically strong than the
little army now calmly withstanding him. Things had
not gone very well with that little army of late, possibly
its constancy might have been impaired, and its chief
might be willing, as had been Elphinstone and the Eltchi,
to listen to terms. Anyhow there could be no harm in
making a proffer based on the old lines. So the Afghan
leader proposed to General Roberts, apparently in all
seriousness, that the British army should forthwith
evacuate Afghanistan, encountering no molestation in
its march ; that the British General before departing
should engage that Yakoub Khan should return to
Afghanistan as its Ameer ; and that there should be left
behind two officers of distinction as hostages for the
faithful fulfilment of the contract. 'We have a lakh of
men ; they are like wolves eager to rush on their prey !
We cannot much longer control them !'—such were said
to have been the terms of a message intended to disturb
the equanimity of the British commander. Meer Butcha

and his Kohistanees, again, were not to all appearance anxious for the restoration of Yakoub. They professed themselves content to accept our staunch friend Wali Mahomed as Ameer, if only the British army would be good enough to march home promptly and leave to Afghans the administration of Afghan affairs. It was not likely that a man of Roberts' nature would demean himself to take any notice of such overtures. For the moment circumstances had enforced on him the wisdom of accepting the defensive attitude, but he knew himself, nevertheless, the virtual master of the situation. He had but one serious anxiety—the apprehension lest the Afghans should not harden their hearts to deliver an assault on his position.

That apprehension was not long to give him concern. On the 20th, as a menace against the southern face of Sherpur, the enemy took strong possession of the Mahomed Shereef fort, stormed so gallantly by Colonel Griffiths on 6th November 1841 ; and they maintained themselves there during the two following days in face of the fire of siege guns mounted on the bastions of the enciente. On the 21st and 22d large numbers of Afghans quitted the city, and passing eastward behind the Siah Sung heights, took possession in great force of the forts and villages outside the eastern face of Sherpur. On the 22d a spy brought in the intelligence that Mahomed Jan and his brother-chiefs had resolved to assault the cantonment early on the following morning, and the spy was able to communicate the plan of attack. The 2000 men holding the King's Garden and the Mahomed Shereef fort had been equipped with scaling ladders, and were to make a false attack which might become a real one, against the western section of the southern front. The principal assault, however, was to be made against the eastern face of the Behmaroo village —unquestionably the weakest part of the defensive position. The 23d was the last day of the Mohurrum—the great Mahomedan religious festival, when fanaticism would be at its height; and further to stimulate that incentive to valour, the Mushk-i-Alum would himself kindle the beacon fire on the Asmai height which was to be the signal to the faithful to rush to the assault.

The information proved perfectly accurate. All night long the shouts and chants of the Afghans filled the air. Purposeful silence reigned throughout the cantonment. In the darkness the soldiers mustered and quietly fell into their places ; the officers commanding sections of the defence made their dispositions ; the reserves were silently standing to their arms. Every eye was toward the Asmai heights, shrouded still in the gloom of the night. A long tongue of flame shot up into the air, blazed brilliantly for a few moments, and then waned. At the signal a fierce fire opened from the broken ground before one of the gateways of the southern face, the flashes indicating that the marksmen were plying their rifles within 200 yards of the enciente. The bullets sped harmlessly over the defenders sheltered behind the parapet, and in the dusk of the dawn reprisals were not attempted. But this outburst of powder-burning against the southern face was a mere incident ; what men listened and watched for was the development of the true assault on the

eastern end of the great parallelogram. The section commanders there were General Hugh Gough in charge of
the eastern end of the Behmaroo heights, and Colonel
Jenkins from the village down to the Native Hospital
and beyond to the bastion at the south-eastern corner.
The troops engaged were the Guides from the ridge down
to Behmaroo village and beyond to the Native Hospital,
in which were 100 men of the 28th Punjaub Infantry, and
between the Hospital and the corner bastion the 67th,
reinforced by two companies of 92d Highlanders from
the reserve, which later sent to the defence of the eastern
face additional contributions of men and guns. 'From
beyond Behmaroo and the eastern trenches and walls,'
writes Mr Hensman, ' came a roar of voices so loud and
menacing that it seemed as if an army fifty thousand
strong was charging down on our thin line of men. Led
by their ghazees, the main body of Afghans hidden in the
villages and orchards on the east side of Sherpur had
rushed out in one dense mob, and were filling the air with
their shouts of " Allah-il-Allah." The roar surged forward as their line advanced, but it was answered by such
a roll of musketry that it was drowned for the moment,
and then merged into the general din which told us that
our men with Martinis and Sniders were holding their
own against the attacking force.' When the first attack
thus graphically described was made the morning was
still so dark and misty that the outlook from the trenches
was restricted, and the order to the troops was to hold
their fire till the assailants should be distinctly visible.
The detachment of the 28th opened fire somewhat prematurely, and presently the Guides holding Behmaroo

and the trenches on the slopes followed the example, and sweeping with their fire the terrain in front of them broke the force of the attack while its leaders were still several hundred yards away. Between the Hospital and the corner bastion the men of the 67th and 92d awaited with impassive discipline the word of permission to begin firing. From out the mist at length emerged dense masses of men, some of whom were brandishing swords and knives, while others loaded and fired while hurrying forward. The order to fire was not given until the leading ghazees were within eighty yards, and the mass of assailants not more distant than 200 yards. Heavily struck then by volley on volley, they recoiled but soon gathered courage to come on again ; and for several hours there was sharp fighting, repeated efforts being made to carry the low eastern wall. So resolute were the Afghans that more than once they reached the abattis, but each time were driven back with heavy loss. About ten o'clock there was a lull and it seemed that the attacking force was owning the frustration of its attempts, but an hour later there was a partial recrudescence of the fighting and the assailants once more came on. The attack, however, was not pushed with much vigour and was soon beaten down, but the Afghans still maintained a threatening attitude and the fire from the defences was ineffectual to dislodge them. The General resolved to take their positions in flank, and with this intent sent out into the open through the gorge in the Behmaroo heights, four field guns escorted by a cavalry regiment. Bending to the right, the guns came into action on the right flank of the Afghans, and the counter-stroke had immediate effect.

The enemy wavered and soon were in full retreat. The Kohistanee contingent, some 5000 strong, cut loose and marched away northward, with obvious recognition that the game was up. The fugitives were scourged with artillery and rifle fire, and Massy led out the cavalry, swept the plain, and drove the lingering Afghans from the slopes of Siah Sung. The false attack on the southern face from the King's Garden and the Mahomed Shereef fort never made any head. Those positions were steadily shelled until late in the afternoon, when they were finally evacuated, and by nightfall all the villages and enclosures between Sherpur and Cabul were entirely deserted. Some of those had been destroyed by sappers from the garrison during the afternoon, in the course of which operation two gallant engineer officers, Captain Dundas and Lieutenant Nugent, were unfortunately killed by the premature explosion of a mine.

Mahomed Jan had been as good as his word ; he had delivered his stroke against Sherpur, and that stroke had utterly failed. With its failure came promptly the collapse of the national rising. Before daybreak of the 24th the formidable combination which had included all the fighting elements of North-Eastern Afghanistan, and under whose banners it was believed that more than 100,000 armed men had mustered, was no more. Not only had it broken up ; it had disappeared. Neither in the city, nor in the adjacent villages, nor on the surrounding heights, was a man to be seen. So hurried had been the Afghan dispersal that the dead lay unburied where they had fallen. His nine days on the defensive had cost General Roberts singularly little in casualties; his losses were eighteen killed and sixty-eight wounded. The enemy's loss from first to last of the rising was reckoned to be not under 3000.

On the 24th the cavalry rode far and fast in pursuit of the fugitives, but they overtook none, such haste had the fleeing Afghans made. On the same day Cabul and the Balla Hissar were reoccupied, and General Hills resumed his functions as military governor of the city. Cabul had the aspect of having undergone a sack at the hands of the enemy ; the bazaars were broken up and deserted and the Hindoo and Kuzzilbash quarters had been relentlessly wrecked. Sir Frederick Roberts lost no time in despatching a column to the Kohistan to punish Meer Butcha by destroying that chief's forts and villages, and to ascertain whether the tribesmen of the district had dispersed to their homes. This was found to be the case, and the column returned after having been out five days. After making a few examples the General issued a proclamation of amnesty, excluding therefrom only five of the principal leaders and fomentors of the recent rising, and stipulating that the tribesmen should send representatives to Sherpur to receive explanations regarding the dispositions contemplated for the government of the country. This policy of conciliation bore good fruit ; and a durbar was held on January 9th, 1880, at which were present about 200 sirdars, chiefs, and headmen from the Kohistan, Logur, and the Ghilzai country. Rewards were presented to those chiefs who had remained friendly ; the General received the salaams of the assembled sirdars and then addressed them in a firm but conciliatory speech.

The country remained still in a disturbed state, but there was little likelihood of a second general rising. General Roberts was resolved, however, to be thoroughly prepared to cope with that contingency should it occur. Sherpur was encircled by a military road, and all cover and obstructions for the space of 1000 yards outside the enciente were swept away. Another road was constructed from Behmaroo village to the Siah Sung heights and yet another from the south-eastern gateway direct to the Balla Hissar, on both of which there were bridges across the Cabul river. Along the northern face of Cabul from Deh Afghan to the Balla Hissar, a road broad enough for guns was made, and another broad road cut through the lower Balla Hissar. Another military road was built through the Cabul gorge to the main Ghuznee and Bamian road in the Chardeh valley. Strong forts were built on the Asmai and Sher Derwaza heights and on the spur above the Balla Hissar, which, well garrisoned and supplied adequately with provisions, water, and ammunition, would enable Cabul as well as Sherpur to be held. The latter was greatly strengthened, the eastern point of the Behmaroo heights being converted into something like a regular fortress. Later, in March, when the Cabul force had increased to a strength of about 11,500 men and twenty-six guns, the command was formed into two divisions, of which the first remained under the Lieutenant-General, the second being commanded by Major-General John Ross. The line of communications was in charge of Major-General Bright, and Brigadier-General Hugh Gough was the cavalry commander in succession to Brigadier-General Massy. On the 2d of May,

Sir Donald Stewart arriving at Cabul from Candahar, took over the chief command in North-Eastern Afghanistan from Sir Frederick Roberts. Sir Donald's march from Candahar, which was an eventful one, is dealt with in the next chapter.

CHAPTER VI

AHMED KHEL

WHILE Sir Frederick Roberts had been fighting hard in North-Eastern Afghanistan, Sir Donald Stewart had been experiencing comparative tranquillity in his Candahar command. As soon as the news reached him of the destruction of Cavagnari's mission he had promptly concentrated his troops, and so early as the third week of September (1879) he was in a position to carry out his orders to create a diversion in aid of Roberts' advance on Cabul by making a demonstration in the direction of Ghuznee and placing a garrison in Khelat-i-Ghilzai. No subsequent movements of importance were undertaken in Southern Afghanistan during the winter, and the province enjoyed almost unbroken quietude. In Herat, however, disturbance was rife. Ayoub Khan, the brother of Yakoub Khan, had returned from exile and made good his footing in Herat, of which formerly he had been conjoint governor with Yakoub. In December he began a hostile advance on Candahar, but a conflict broke out between the Cabul and Herat troops under his command, and he abandoned for the time his projected expedition.

In the end of March Sir Donald Stewart began the march toward Cabul which orders from India had prescribed.

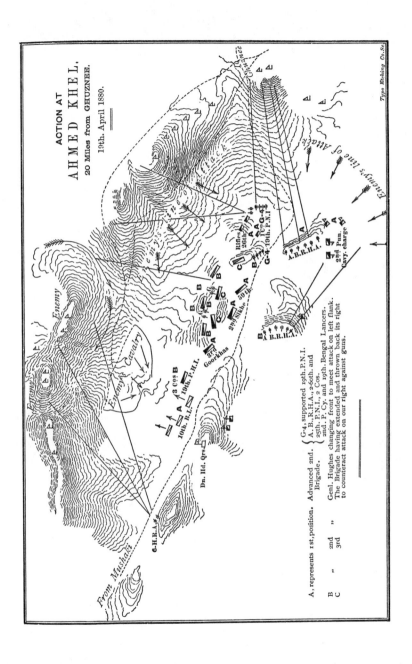

ACTION AT
AHMED KHEL.
20 Miles from GHUZNEE.
19th. April 1880.

Typo Etching Co. Sc.

From Mushaki

Enemy

Enemy's Cavalry

Enemy

Dm. Hd. Qrs.

10th. B.L.

19th. P.N.I.

3 Cos. B

Goorkhas

37th

2nd Sikhs. 59th.

Rifles.

26th.

A.B.R.H.A.

G-4.

19th. P.N.I.

A.B.R.H.A.

2nd Pun.

Cavy. charge

Enemy's line of Attack

To Ghuznee

A, represents 1st. position. Advanced 2nd. }
Brigade. }

{ G-4, supported 19th.P.N.I.
{ A. B. R.H.A., 2-60th. and
{ 25th. P.N.I., 2 Cos.
{ 2nd. P. Cy. and 19th. Bengal Lancers.

B   "   2nd   "   Genl. Hughes changing front to meet attack on left flank.
C   "   3rd   "   The Brigade having extended and thrown back its right
                  to counteract attack on our right against guns.

He left behind him in Candahar the Bombay division of his force under the command of Major-General Primrose, whose line of communication with the Indus valley was to be kept open by Phayre's brigade, and took with him on the northward march the Bengal division, consisting of two infantry brigades and a cavalry brigade. The first infantry brigade was commanded by Brigadier-General Barter, the second by Brigadier-General Hughes, and the cavalry brigade, which divisional headquarters accompanied, by Brigadier-General Palliser. Khelat-i-Ghilzai was reached on 6th April; the Bengal portion of its garrison joined the division and the advance was resumed on the following day. Until Shahjui, the limit of the Candahar province, the march was uneventful; but beyond that place extreme difficulties were experienced in procuring supplies, for the villages were found deserted and the inhabitants had carried off, destroyed, or hidden their stores of grain. The force was embarrassed by a horde of Hazaras, who swarmed in wild irregularity on its flanks, plundering and burning with great vindictiveness, eager to wreak vengeance on their Afghan foes. And it had another although more distant companionship, in the shape of several thousand hostile tribesmen and ghazees, whose fanaticism their moullas had been assiduously inciting, and who marched day by day parallel with the British right flank along the foothills at a distance of about eight miles. Their attitude was threatening but it was not thought wise to meddle with them, since their retreat over the hills could not well be cut off, and since the policy of non-interference would tend to encourage them to venture on a battle. The soundness of this reasoning was soon to be made manifest.

On the night of April 18th the division was encamped at Mushaki, about thirty miles south of Ghuznee. The spies that evening brought in the information that the enemy had resolved on fighting on the following morning, and that the position they intended to take up was the summit of a low spur of the Gul Koh mountain ridge, bounding on the west the valley followed by the road. This spur was said to project in a north-easterly direction toward the Ghuznee river, gradually sinking into the plain. During a great part of its length it flanked and overhung the road, but near where it merged into the plain the road passed over it by a low saddle at a point about six miles beyond Mushaki. At dawn of the 19th the column moved off, Palliser leading the advance, which Sir Donald Stewart accompanied, Hughes commanding the centre, Barter bringing up the rear and protecting the baggage. An hour later the enemy were visible in great strength about three miles in advance, presenting the aspect of a vast body formed up on the spur and on the saddle crossed by the road, and thus threatening Stewart at once in front and on both flanks. The British general at once made his dispositions. His guns were on the road in column of route. The three infantry regiments of Hughes' brigade came up to the left of and in line with the leading battery, the cavalry took ground on the plain on its right, and a reserve was formed consisting of an infantry regiment, two companies sappers and miners, and the General's escort of a troop and two companies. Orders were sent back to Barter to send forward without delay half the infantry of his brigade. In the formation described the force resumed its advance until within striking distance. Then the two batteries came into action on either side of the road ; the horse-battery on the right, the flat ground to its right being covered by the 2d Punjaub Cavalry ; the field-battery on the left. Sir Donald Stewart's proper front thus consisted of the field and horse-batteries with their supports, but since it was apparent that the greatest strength of the enemy was on the higher ground flanking his left, it behoved him to show a front in that direction also, and for this purpose he utilised Hughes' three infantry regiments, of which the 59th was on the right, the 2d Sikhs in the centre, and the 3d Goorkhas on the left. Part of the reserve infantry was sent to make good the interval between the left of the artillery and the right of the infantry.

The guns had no sooner come into action than the enemy in great masses showed themselves on spur and saddle and plain, bent seemingly on an attempt to envelop the position held by the British. 'Suddenly,' writes Hensmen, 'a commotion was observed in the most advanced lines of the opposing army ; the moullas could be seen haranguing the irregular host with frantic energy, the beating of the tom-toms was redoubled, and then as if by magic waves on waves of men—ghazees of the most desperate type—poured down upon the plain, and rushed upon General Stewart's force. The main body of the Afghan army remained upon the hill to watch the ghazees in their reckless onslaught, and take advantage of any success they might gain. The fanaticism of the 3000 or 4000 men who made this desperate charge has perhaps

never been equalled ; they had 500 or 600 yards to cover
before they could come to close quarters, and yet they
made nothing of the distance.   Nearly all were well armed
with tulwars, knives, and pistols.   Some carried rifles and
matchlocks, while a few—and those must have been
resolute fanatics indeed—had simply pikes made of
bayonets, or pieces of sharpened iron fastened on long
shafts.   Their attack broke with greatest violence on our
flanks.   On our left flank the 19th Bengal Lancers were
still moving into position when the ghazees rushed in
among them.   In an instant they were hidden in the cloud
of dust and smoke, and then they galloped toward the right
rear, and struck into the reserve in rear of the Lieutenant-
General and his staff.   All was confusion for a moment ;
the ammunition mules were stampeded, and with the
riderless horses of the lancers killed or wounded in the
mêlée, dashed into the headquarter staff.   The ghazees
had continued their onward rush, and were engaged in
hand-to-hand fighting with our infantry.   Some of them
penetrated to within twenty yards of the knoll on which
the staff were watching the action, and so critical was the
moment that Sir Donald Stewart and every man of his
staff drew their swords and prepared for self-defence.'
The hurried retirement of the lancers had left the left flank
bare.   It was turned by the fierce rush of the fanatics, who
were actually in rear of the leftward infantry regiment
and in the heart of the British position.   The Goorkhas had
been thrown into momentary confusion, but their colonel
promptly formed them into rallying squares, whose fire
mowed down the ghazees and arrested the headlong
vehemence of their turning movement.   But it was not

the British left only which was temporarily compromised by the furious onslaught of the fanatics. Their enveloping charge broke down the defence of the weakly-manned interval between the left of the artillery and the right of the infantry. The detachments holding that interval were forced back, fighting hand-to-hand as the sheer weight of the assault compelled them to give ground; the 59th, in its effort to throw back its right to cover the interval and protect the guns, was thrown into confusion and gave ground; and the guns, their case shot exhausted and the Afghans within a few yards of their muzzles, had to be retired. The onslaught on the right front of the horse-battery was delivered with great determination, but was held at bay and finally crushed by the repeated charges of the 2d Punjaub cavalry.

Every man of the reserves was hurried into the fighting line; the soldiers were steadied by the energetic efforts of their officers and settled down to a steady and continuous fire from their breechloaders; the guns poured their shells into the hostile masses; and the fire of the forty-pounders on the left effectually arrested the attempt of the Afghan horse to move round that flank. The hard-fought combat lasted for an hour; at ten o'clock the 'cease fire' sounded, and the British victory was signal. The enemy was dispersing in full flight, and the cavalry was chasing the fugitives across the plain on the right. How reckless had been the whirlwind charges of the ghazees was evidenced by the extraordinary number of their dead whose corpses strewed the battlefield. In no previous conflict between our troops and the

Afghans had the latter suffered nearly so heavily. More than 1000 dead were counted on the field, and many bodies were carried away; on a moderate computation their total loss must have been between 2000 and 3000, and that in an estimated strength of from 12,000 to 15,000. The casualties of the British force were seventeen killed and 124 wounded, of whom four died of their wounds. The injuries consisted almost wholly of sword slashes and knife stabs received in hand-to-hand encounters. The pursuit was soon recalled, but the Hazaras took up the chase with ardour and in the rancour of vengeance slew and spared not.

Sir Donald Stewart tarried on the field only long enough to bury his dead and have his wounded attended to; and soon after noon his force resumed its march. Ghuznee was reached on the 21st, where there was a halt of three days. It had been reported that the indomitable Mushk-i-Alum was raising the tribesmen of Zurmut and Shilgur to avenge the defeat of Ahmed Khel, and a cavalry reconnaissance made on the 22d had found a gathering of 2000 or 3000 men about the villages of Urzoo and Shalez, six miles south-east of Ghuznee. On the morning of the 23d a strong column commanded by Brigadier-General Palliser moved on the villages, which were found occupied in considerable force. They were too solidly built to be much injured by artillery fire, and the Afghans lay close in the shelter they afforded. Palliser hesitated to commit his infantry to an attack. Sir Donald Stewart having arrived, ordered the infantry to carry the villages without delay, and the affair was soon over, the tribesmen suffering severely from the rifle

fire as they evacuated the villages, and later in the
pursuit made by the cavalry and horse-artillery. On
the following day the march toward Cabul was resumed.

On the 16th April Major-General Ross had been
despatched from Cabul by Sir Frederick Roberts on the
mission of joining hands with Stewart's division. On
the 20th Ross opened heliographic communication
with Sir Donald, and was informed of the latter's victory at Ahmed Khel. But the junction of the two
forces was not accomplished until the 27th; and in the
interval the force commanded by General Ross had
received considerable annoyance at the hands of tribal
levies gathered by local chiefs. The tribesmen interfered
with the roadmaking operations of his sappers in the
vicinity of Sheikabad, and some fighting occurred in very
rugged country on the 23d. Trivial loss was experienced by his command, but the demonstrations of the
tribesmen evinced with what inveterate determination,
notwithstanding so many severe lessons, the Afghans
persisted in their refusal to admit themselves conquered.
Driven away with severe loss on the 25th, those indomitable hillmen and villagers were back again on the following morning on the overhanging ridges; nor were they
dispersed by the 'resources of civilised warfare' until
more of them had paid with their lives the penalty of
their obstinate hostility. On the 28th, at Sheikabad, Sir
Donald Stewart took leave of the division which he had
led from Candahar, and proceeded to Cabul with General
Ross' force to assume the chief command in North-
Eastern Afghanistan. His division turned aside into

the Logur valley, where it remained at until the final concentration about Cabul in anticipation of the evacuation. By the reinforcement brought by Stewart the Cabul field force was increased to a strength of about 18,000 men.

CHAPTER VII

THE AMEER ABDURRAHMAN

THE occupation of Afghanistan by the British troops had been prolonged far beyond the period originally intended by the authorities. But the strain of that occupation was great, and although it had to be maintained until there should be found a ruler strong enough to hold his own after the evacuation, the decision was definitely arrived at to withdraw from the country before the setting in of another winter. Mr Lepel Griffin, a distinguished member of the political department of the Indian Civil Service, reached Cabul on 20th March, his mission being to further the selection and acceptance of a capable ruler to be left in possession. The task was no easy one. There was little promise in any of the Barakzai pretenders who were in Afghanistan, and in the address which Mr Griffin addressed in Durbar to a number of sirdars and chiefs in the middle of April, he preserved a tone at once haughty and enigmatical. One thing he definitely announced, the Viceroy's decision that Yakoub Khan was not to return to Afghanistan. The State was to be dismembered. As to the future of Herat the speaker made no allusion; but the province of Candahar was to be separated from Cabul and placed under an independent

K

Barakzai prince. No decision could for the present be given in regard to the choice of an Ameer to rule over Cabul. The Government desired to nominate an Ameer strong enough to govern his people and steadfast in his friendship to the British; if those qualifications could be secured the Government was willing and anxious to recognise the wish of the Afghan people, and nominate an Ameer of their choice.

But in effect the choice, so far as the English were concerned, had been already virtually made. On the 14th of March Lord Lytton had telegraphed to the Secretary of State advocating the 'early public recognition of Abdurrahman as legitimate heir of Dost Mahomed, and the despatch of a deputation of sirdars, with British concurrence, to offer him the throne, as sole means of saving the country from anarchy'; and the Minister had promptly replied authorising the nomination of Abdurrahman, should he be found 'acceptable to the country and would be contented with Northern Afghanistan.' Abdurrahman had known strange vicissitudes. He was the eldest grandson of the old Dost; his father was Afzul Khan, the elder brother of Shere Ali. After the death of the Dost he had been an exile in Bokhara, but he returned to Balkh, of which province his father had been Governor until removed by Shere Ali, made good his footing there, and having done so advanced on Cabul, taking advantage of Shere Ali's absence at Candahar. The capital opened its gates to him in March 1866; he fought a successful battle with Shere Ali at Sheikabad, occupied Ghuznee, and proclaimed his father Ameer. Those were triumphs, but soon the wheel came round full circle. Afzul had but a short life as Ameer, and Abdurrahman had to retire to Afghan Turkestan. Yakoub, then full of vigour and enterprise, defeated him at Bamian and restored his father Shere Ali to the throne in the winter of 1868. Abdurrahman then once more found himself an exile. In 1870, after much wandering, he reached Tashkend, where General Kaufmann gave him permission to reside, and obtained for him from the Czar a pension of 25,000 roubles per annum. Petrosvky, a Russian writer who professed to be intimate with him during his period of exile, wrote of him that, ' To get square some day with the English and Shere Ali was Abdurrahman's most cherished thought, his dominant, never-failing passion.' His hatred of Shere Ali, his family, and supporters, was intelligible and natural enough, but why he should have entertained a bitter grudge against the English is not very apparent; and there has been no overt manifestation of its existence since he became Ameer. To Mr Eugene Schuyler, who had an interview with him at Tashkend, he expressed his conviction that with £50,000 wherewith to raise and equip an army he could attain his legitimate position as Ameer of Afghanistan. Resolutely bent on an effort to accomplish this purpose, he was living penuriously and saving the greater part of his pension, and he hinted that he might have Russian assistance in the prosecution of his endeavour. The selection of a man of such antecedents and associations as the ruler of a ' buffer ' state in friendly relations with British India was perhaps the greatest leap in the dark on record. Abdurrahman came straight from the position of a Russian pensionary; in moving on Afghanistan he

obeyed Russian instructions ; his Tashkend patrons had
furnished him with a modest equipment of arms and
money, the value of which he undertook to repay if
successful. It is of course possible that those functionaries of a notoriously simple and ingenuous government
started and equipped him in pure friendly good nature,
although they had previously consistently deterred him.
But there was not a circumstance in connection with
Abdurrahman that was not suspicious. Three distinct
hypotheses seem to present themselves in relation to this
selection as our nominee ; that Lord Lytton had extraordinary, almost indeed preternatural foresight and
sagacity ; that he was extremely fortunate in his leap in
the dark ; that he desired to bring to the naked *reductio
ad absurdum* the 'buffer state' policy. When Abdurrahman began his movement is uncertain. So early as
the middle of January it was reported at Sherpur that
he had left Tashkend, and was probably already on the
Afghan side of the Oxus. In a letter of February 17th
Mr Hensman speaks of him as being in Badakshan,
where his wife's kinsmen were in power, and describes
him as having a following of 2000 or 3000 Turcoman
horsemen and possessed according to native report of
twelve lakhs of rupees. On the 17th of March Lord
Lytton telegraphed to the Secretary of State that he
was in possession of 'authentic intelligence that the
Sirdar was in Afghan Turkestan, having lately arrived
there from Badakshan.'

It was regarded of urgent importance to ascertain
definitely the disposition of Abdurrahman, and whether he
was disposed to throw in his lot with the British Govern-

Dawson's Ph. Sc.

The Ameer Abdurrahman.

ment, and accept the position of its nominee in Northern Afghanistan. The agent selected by Mr Griffin to open preliminary negotiations was a certain Mohamed Surwar, Ghilzai, who had been all his life in the confidential service of the Sirdar's family. Surwar was the bearer of a formal and colourless letter by way simply of authentication ; but he also carried full and explicit verbal instructions. He was directed to inform the Sirdar that since he had entered Afghan Turkestan and occupied places there by force of arms, it was essential for him to declare with what object he had come, and whether actuated by friendly or hostile feelings toward the British Government, which for its part had no ill-feeling toward him because of his long residence within the Russian Empire and his notoriously close relations with that power. That the British Government was able to benefit him very largely in comparison with that of Russia ; and that wisdom and self interest alike suggested that he should at once open a friendly correspondence with the British officers in Cabul. That his opportunity was now come, and that the British Government was disposed to treat him with every consideration and to consider most favourably any representations he might make. It had no intention of annexing the country, and only desired to see a strong and friendly chief established at Cabul ; and that consequently the present communication was made solely in Abdurrahman's own interest, and not in that of the British Government. He was desired to send a reply by Surwar, and later to repair to Cabul, where he should be honourably received.

Surwar returned to Cabul on 21st April, bringing a

reply from Abdurrahman to Mr Griffin's letter. The tone of the reply was friendly enough, but somewhat indefinite. In conversation with Surwar as reported by the latter, Abdurrahman was perfectly frank as to his relations with the Russians and his sentiments in regard to them. It had been reported that he had made his escape clandestinely from Tashkend. Had he cared to stand well with us at the expense of truth, it would have been his cue to disclaim all authority or assistance from the Russian Government, to confirm the current story of his escape, and to profess his anxiety to cultivate friendly relations with the British in a spirit of opposition to the power in whose territory he had lived so long virtually as a prisoner. But neither in writing nor in conversation did he make any concealment of his friendliness toward the Russians, a feeling which he clearly regarded as nowise incompatible with friendly relations with the British Government. 'If,' said he to Surwar, 'the English will in sincerity befriend me, I have no wish to hide anything from them'; and he went on to tell how the Russians had forbidden him for years to make any effort to interfere in Afghan affairs. This prohibition stood until information reached Tashkend of the deportation of Yakoub Khan to India. Then it was that General Kaufmann's representative said to him : 'You have always been anxious to return to your country ; the English have removed Yakoub Khan ; the opportunity is favourable ; if you wish you are at liberty to go.' The Russians, continued Abdurrahman, pressed him most strongly to set out on the enterprise which lay before him. They lent him 33,000 rupees, and arms, ammunition, and supplies; he was bound to the Russians by no oath or promise, but simply by feelings of gratitude. ' I should never like,' said he, ' to be obliged to fight them. I have eaten their salt, and was for twelve years dependent on their hospitality.'

Surwar reported Abdurrahman as in fine health and possessed of great energy. He had with him a force of about 3000 men, consisting of four infantry and two cavalry regiments, with twelve guns and some irregulars. He professed his readiness, in preference to conducting negotiations through agents, to go himself to Charikar in the Kohistan with an escort, and there discuss matters with the English officers in person. Surwar testified that the Sirdar had with him in Turkestan no Russian or Russian agent, and this was confirmed through other sources. He had sent forward to ascertain which was the easiest pass across the Hindoo Koosh, but meanwhile he was to remain at Kondooz until he should hear again from Mr Griffin.

While the wary Sirdar waited on events beyond the Hindoo Koosh he was sending letters to the leading chiefs of the Kohistan and the Cabul province, desiring them to be ready to support his cause. That he had an influential party was made clear at a durbar held by Mr Griffin on April 21st, when a considerable gathering of important chiefs united in the request that Abdurrahman's claim to the Ameership should be favourably regarded by the British authorities. In pursuance of the negotiations a mission consisting of three Afghan gentlemen, two of whom belonged to Mr Griffin's political staff, left Cabul on May 2nd carrying to Abdurrahman a letter from Mr

Griffin intimating that it had been decided to withdraw the British army from Afghanistan in the course of a few months, and that the British authorities desired to leave the rulership in capable and friendly hands; that they were therefore willing to transfer the Government to him, recognise him as the head of the State, and afford him facilities and even support in reorganising the Government and establishing himself in the sovereignty. The mission found the attitude of Abdurrahman scarcely so satisfactory as had been reported by Surwar, and its members were virtual prisoners, their tents surrounded by sentries. Abdurrahman's explanation of this rigour of isolation was that he could not otherwise ensure the safety of the envoys; but another construction conveyed to them was that they were kept prisoners that they might not, by mixing with the people, learn of the presence on the right bank of the Oxus of a Russian officer with whom Abdurrahman was said to be in constant communication and on whose advice he acted. Their belief was that Abdurrahman was entirely under Russian influence; that Mr Griffin's letter after it had been read in Durbar in the camp was immediately despatched across the Oxus by means of mounted relays; and that Russian instructions as to a reply had not been received when they left Turkestan to return to Cabul. They expressed their belief that the Sirdar would not accept from British hands Cabul shorn of Candahar. They had urged him to repeat in the letter they were to carry back to Cabul the expression of his willingness to meet the British representative at Charikar which had been contained in his letter sent by Surwar; but he demurred to committing himself even to this slight extent. The letter which he sent by way of reply to the weighty communication Mr Griffin had addressed to him on the part of the Government of India that official characterised as ' frivolous and empty, and only saved by its special courtesy of tone from being an impertinence.'

An Afghan who had sat at Kaufmann's feet, Abdurrahman was not wholly a guileless man ; and the truth probably was that he mistrusted the Greeks of Simla and the gifts they tendered him with so lavish protestation that they were entirely for his own interest. There was very little finesse about the importunity of the British that he should constitute himself their bridge of extrication, so that they might get out of Afghanistan without the dangers and discredit of leaving chaos behind them. But Aburrahaman had come to know himself strong enough to reduce to order that legacy of chaos if it should be left ; and in view of his future relations with his fellow Afghans he was not solicitous to be beholden to the foreigners to any embarrassing extent. He knew, too, the wisdom of 'masterly inactivity' in delicate conditions. And, again, he had no confidence in our pledges. On the 4th of August, the day after the meeting between him and Mr Griffin at Zimma, the latter wrote : ' They (Abdurrahman and his advisers) feared greatly our intention was to rid ourselves of a formidable opponent, and dreaded that if he had come straight into Cabul he would have been arrested, and deported to India.'

A Liberal Government was now in office in England, and was urgent for the speedy evacuation of Afghanistan. Lord Lytton had resigned and had been succeeded as Viceroy by the Marquis of Ripon. Lieutenant-General

Sir Donald Stewart was in chief command at Cabul. A great number of letters from Abdurrahman to chiefs and influential persons throughout Afghanistan were being intercepted, the tone of which was considered objectionable. He was reported to be in close correspondence with Mahomed Jan, who had never ceased to be our bitter enemy. The fact that negotiations were in progress between the British Government and Abdurrahman had become matter of general knowledge throughout the country, and was occasioning disquietude and excitement. So clear were held the evidences of what was termed Abdurrahman's bad faith, but was probably a combination of genuine mistrust, astute passivity, and shrewd playing for his own hand, that it became a serious question with the Indian Government on the arrival of the new Viceroy, whether it was good policy to have anything more to do with him. It was resolved that before breaking off intercourse the suggestion of Sir Donald Stewart and Mr Griffin should be adopted, that a peremptory although still friendly letter, demanding a definite acceptance or refusal of the proffers made, within four days after the receipt, should be sent to Abdurrahman, with a detailed explanation of the arrangements into which we were prepared to enter with regard to him and the future of Afghanistan. A letter was forwarded from Cabul on 14th June, in which Mr Griffin informed the Sirdar that since the British Government admitted no right of interference by foreign powers in Afghanistan, it was plain that the Cabul ruler could have no political relations with any foreign power except the English ; and if any foreign power should attempt to

interfere in Afghanistan, and if such interference should
lead to unprovoked aggression on the Cabul ruler, then
the British Government would be prepared to aid him,
if necessary, to repel it. As regarded limits of the territory, the latter stated that the whole province of Candahar
had been placed under a separate ruler, except Sibi and
Pisheen, which were retained in British possession. Consequently the British Government was unable to enter
into any negotiations on those points, or in respect to
arrangements in regard to the north-western frontier
which were settled by the treaty of Gundamuk. Subject
to those reservations, the British Government was willing
that Abdurrahman should establish over Afghanistan—
including Herat when he should have conquered it—as
complete and extensive authority as was swayed by any
previous Ameer. The British Government would exercise no interference in the internal government of those
territories nor would it demand the acceptance of an
English Resident anywhere within Afghanistan, although
for convenience of ordinary friendly intercourse it might
be agreed upon that a Mahommedan Agent of the British
Government should be stationed at Cabul.

Abdurrahman's reply to this communication was vague
and evasive, and was regarded by Sir Donald Stewart
and Mr Griffin as so unsatisfactory that they represented
to the Government of India, not for the first time, their
conviction of the danger of trusting Abdurrahman, the
imprudence of delaying immediate action, and the necessity of breaking off with him and adopting other means of
establishing a government in Cabul before the impending
evacuation. Lord Ripon, however, considered that 'as

matters stood an arrangement with Abdurrahman offered the most advisable solution, while he doubted whether it would not be found very difficult to enter into any alternative arrangement.' His Excellency's decision was justified by the event. Meanwhile, indeed, Abdurrahman had started on June 28th for the Kohistan. He crossed the Hindoo Koosh and arrived on July 20th at Charikar, where he was welcomed by a deputation of leading chiefs, while the old Mushk-i-Alum, who for some time, thanks to Mr Griffin's influence, had been working in the interests of peace, intimated on behalf of a number of chiefs assembled in Maidan that they were ready to accept as Ameer the nominee of the British Government.

So propitious seemed the situation that it was considered the time had come for formally acknowledging Abdurrahman as the new Ameer, and also for fixing approximately the date of the evacuation of Cabul by the British troops. The ceremony of recognition was enacted in a great durbar tent within the Sherpur cantonment on the afternoon of July 22d. The absence of Abdurrahman, and the notorious cause of that absence, detracted from the intrinsic dignity of the occasion so far as concerned the British participation in it; nor was the balance restored by the presence of three members of his suite whom he had delegated to represent him. A large number of sirdars, chiefs, and maliks were present, some of whom had fought stoutly against us in December. Sir Donald Stewart, who presided, explained to the assembled Afghans that their presence and that of the officers of the British force had been called for in order that the public recognition by the British Government of the Sirdar

Abdurrahman Khan as Ameer of Cabul should be made
known with as much honour as possible. Then Mr
Griffin addressed in Persian a short speech to the
'sirdars, chiefs, and gentlemen' who constituted his
audience. Having announced the recognition of Abdurrahman by 'the Viceroy of India and the Government of
Her Most Gracious Majesty the Queen Empress,' he
proceeded : ' It is to the Government a source of satisfaction that the tribes and chiefs have preferred as Ameer a
distinguished member of the Barakzai family, who is a
renowned soldier, wise, and experienced. His sentiments
towards the British Government are most friendly; and
so long as his rule shows that he is animated by these
sentiments, he cannot fail to receive the support of the
British Government.' Mr Griffin then intimated that the
British armies would shortly withdraw from Afghanistan;
and in his formal farewell there was a certain appropriate
dignity, and a well-earned tribute to the conduct of our
soldiers during their service within the Afghan borders.
' We trust and firmly believe,' said Mr Griffin, 'that your
remembrance of the English will not be unkindly. We
have fought you in the field whenever you have opposed
us ; but your religion has in no way been interfered with ;
the honour of your women has been respected, and every
one has been secure in possession of his property. Whatever has been necessary for the support of the army has
been liberally paid for. Since I came to Cabul I have
been in daily intercourse with you, but I have never
heard an Afghan make a complaint of the conduct of any
soldier, English or native, belonging to Her Majesty's
army.' The durbar was closed by an earnest appeal by

Sir Donald Stewart to all the sirdars and chiefs that they should put aside their private feuds and unite to support the new Ameer.

On August 3d Abdurrahman and Mr Griffin at length met, about sixteen miles north of Cabul. His adherents were still full of excitement and suspicion; but the Ameer himself was calm, cheerful, and dignified. The conference between him and Mr Griffin lasted for three hours and was renewed on the following day. 'He appeared,' wrote Mr Griffin, 'animated by a sincere desire to be on cordial terms with the British Government, and although his expectations were larger than the Government was prepared to satisfy, yet he did not press them with any discourteous insistence, and the result of the interview may be considered on the whole to be highly satisfactory.' The tidings of the Maiwand disaster had reached Sherpur by telegraph, and the Ameer was informed that a necessity might occur for marching a force from Cabul to Candahar. His reply was that the tribes might be hostile, but that if no long halts were made by the way he would have no objections to such a march. In this he showed his astuteness, since the defeat of Ayoub Khan by a British army would obviously save him a contest. So willing to be of service on this matter was he that when the march was decided on he sent influential persons of his party in advance to arrange with the local maliks to have supplies collected for the column. The arrangements made with him were that he was to fall heir to the thirty guns of Shere Ali's manufacture which the out-marching army was to leave in Sherpur, and was to receive 19½ lakhs of rupees

(£190,500) ; ten lakhs of which were given as an earnest
of British friendship, and the balance was money belonging to the Afghan State, which had gone into the commissariat chest and was now restored. At the Ameer's
earnest and repeated request the forts which had been
built around Cabul by the British army, were not
destroyed as had been intended, but were handed over
intact to the new Ameer.

It seemed that Sir Donald Stewart, who was to
evacuate Sherpur on the 11th August, would leave Cabul
without seeing Abdurrahman. But at the last moment
Mr Griffin succeeded in arranging an interview. It was
held early in the morning of the evacuation, in a tent
just outside the Sherpur cantonment, was quite public,
and lasted only for quarter of an hour. Abdurrahman
was frank and cordial. He said that his heart was full
of gratitude to the British, and desired that his best
thanks should be communicated to the Viceroy. At the
close of the interview he shook hands with all 'who
cared to wish him good-bye and good luck,' and sent
his principal officer to accompany the General on his
first day's march, which began immediately after the
parting with Abdurrahman. Sir Donald Stewart's march
down the passes was accomplished without incident,
quite unmolested by the tribes. Small garrisons were
temporarily left in the Khyber posts, and the war-worn
regiments were dispersed through the stations of North-
Western India.

CHAPTER VIII

MAIWAND AND THE GREAT MARCH

WHEN in the early spring of 1880 Sir Donald Stewart quitted Candahar with the Bengal division of his force, he left there the Bombay division, to the command of which General Primrose acceded, General Phayre assuming charge of the communications. The province during the early summer was fairly quiet, but it was known that Ayoub Khan was making hostile preparations at Herat, although the reports as to his intentions and movements were long uncertain and conflicting. Shere Ali Khan, who had been Governor of Candahar during Stewart's residence there, had been nominated hereditary ruler of the province with the title of 'Wali,' when it was determined to separate Candahar from North-Eastern Afghanistan. On June 21st the Wali, who had some days earlier crossed the Helmund and occupied Girishk with his troops, reported that Ayoub was actually on the march toward the Candahar frontier, and asked for the support of a British brigade to enable him to cope with the hostile advance. There was reason to believe that the Wali's troops were disaffected, and that he was in no condition to meet Ayoub's army with any likelihood of success. After Stewart's departure the strength of the British forces at Candahar was dangerously low—only

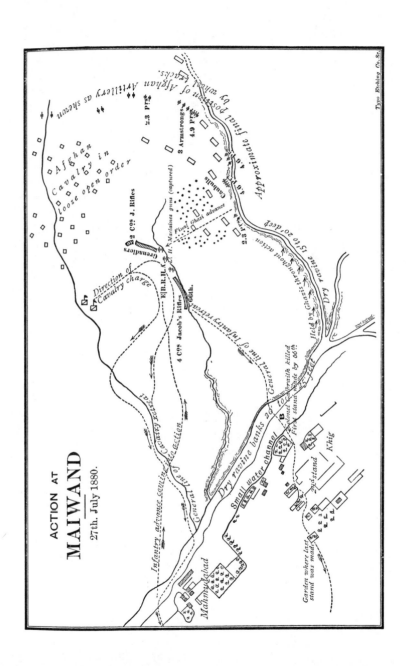

ACTION AT
MAIWAND
27th. July 1880.

Afghan Cavalry in loose open order

Artillery as shown

2.3 P⁻˟

3 Armstrongs

4.9 P⁻˟

Approximate final position of Afghan Artillery by wheel tracks.

4.9⁻˟

4.9⁻˟

Ganbuls

2 C⁰⁵ J. Rifles

E. R. H. Maclaine's guns (captured)

Final Ghazi advance

2.3⁻˟

Direction of Cavalry charge

Grenadiers

E/B. R. H.

66th.

4 C⁰⁵ Jacob's Rifles

General line of Infantry retreat

Held by Ghazis throughout action

Dry ravine 15 to 20 deep

Infantry advance covering Cavalry retreat

General line of action

Dry ravine channel

B

Small water channel

Dry ravine banks 20 to high

Colonel Galbraith killed

Firm stand made by 66th

Mahmudabad

Khig

2ʳᵈ stand

Garden where last stand was made

Typo Etching Co. Sc.

4700 of all ranks; but it was important to thwart
Ayoub's offensive movement, and a brigade consisting of
a troop of horse-artillery, six companies of the 66th, two
Bombay native infantry regiments, and 500 native
troopers, in all about 2300 strong, under the command of
Brigadier-General Burrows, reached the left bank of the
Helmund on July 11th. On the 13th the Wali's infantry,
2000 strong, mutinied *en masse* and marched away up
the right bank of the river, taking with them a battery of
smooth bore guns, a present to Shere Ali Khan from the
British Government. His cavalry did not behave quite so
badly, but, not to go into detail, his army no longer
existed, and Burrows' brigade was the only force in the
field to resist the advance of Ayoub Khan, whose regular
troops were reported to number 4000 cavalry, and from
4000 to 5000 infantry exclusive of the 2000 deserters
from the Wali, with thirty guns and an irregular force of
uncertain strength.

Burrows promptly recaptured from the Wali's infantry
the battery they were carrying off, and punished them
severely. The mutineers had removed or destroyed the
supplies which the Wali had accumulated for the use of
the brigade, and General Burrows therefore could no
longer remain in the vicinity of Girishk. The Helmund
owing to the dry season was passable everywhere, so that
nothing was to be gained by watching the fords. It was
determined to fall back to Khushk-i-Nakhud, a point
distant thirty miles from Girishk and forty-five from
Candahar, where several roads from the Helmund con-
verged and where supplies were plentiful. At and near
Khushk-i-Nakhud the brigade remained from the 16th

until the morning of the 27th July. While waiting and
watching there a despatch from army headquarters at
Simla was communicated to General Burrows from
Candahar, authorising him to attack Ayoub if he thought
himself strong enough to beat him, and informing him
that it was considered of the greatest political importance
that the force from Herat should be dispersed and prevented from moving on toward Ghuznee. Spies brought
in news that Ayoub had reached Girishk, and was dis-
tributing his force along the right bank between that
place and Hydrabad. Cavalry patrols failed to find the
enemy until the 21st, when a detachment was encountered
in the village of Sangbur on the northern road about
midway between the Helmund and Khushk-i-Nakhud.
Next day that village was found more strongly occupied,
and on the 23d a reconnaissance in force came upon a
body of Ayoub's horsemen in the plain below the Garmao
hills, about midway between Sangbur and Maiwand.

Those discoveries were tolerably clear indications of
Ayoub's intention to turn Burrows' position by moving
along the northern road to Maiwand and thence pressing
on through the Maiwand pass, until at Singiri Ayoub's
army should have interposed itself between the brigade
and Candahar. There was certainly nothing impossible
in such an endeavour, since Maiwand is nearer Candahar
than is Khushk-i-Nakhud. Why, in the face of the information at his disposal and of the precautions enjoined
on him to hinder Ayoub from slipping by him toward
Ghuznee through Maiwand and up the Khakrez valley,
General Burrows should have remained so long at Khushk-
i-Nakhud, is not intelligible. He was stirred at length on

the afternoon of the 26th, by the report that 2000 of Yakoub's cavalry and a large body of his ghazees were in possession of Garmao and Maiwand, and were to be promptly followed by Ayoub himself with the main body of his army, his reported intention being to push on through the Maiwand pass and reach the Urgundab valley in rear of the British brigade. Later in the day Colonel St John, the political officer, reported to General Burrows the intelligence which had reached him that the whole of Ayoub's army was at Sangbur; but credence was not given to the information.

The somewhat tardy resolution was taken to march to Maiwand on the morning of the 27th. There was the expectation that the brigade would arrive at that place before the enemy should have occupied it in force, and this point made good there might be the opportunity to drive out of Garmao the body of Yakoub's cavalry reported in possession there. There was a further reason why Maiwand should be promptly occupied ; the brigade had been obtaining its supplies from that village, and there was still a quantity of grain in its vicinity to lose which would be unfortunate. The brigade, now 2600 strong, struck camp on the morning of the 27th. The march to Maiwand was twelve miles long, and an earlier start than 6.30 would have been judicious. The soldiers marched fast, but halts from time to time were necessary to allow the baggage to come up ; the hostile state of the country did not admit of anything being left behind and the column was encumbered by a great quantity of stores and baggage. At Karezah, eight miles from Khushk-i-Nakhud and four miles south-west of Maiwand, information was brought in that the whole of Yakoub's army was close by on the left front of the brigade, and marching toward Maiwand. The spies had previously proved themselves so untrustworthy that small heed was taken of this report; but a little later a cavalry reconnaissance found large bodies of cavalry moving in the direction indicated and inclining away toward Garmao as the brigade advanced. A thick haze made it impossible to discern what force, if any, was being covered by the cavalry. About ten A.M. the advance guard occupied the village of Mundabad, about three miles south-west of Maiwand. West of Mundabad, close to the village, was a broad and deep ravine running north and south. Beyond this ravine was a wide expanse of level and partially cultivated plain across which, almost entirely concealed by the haze, Ayoub's army was marching eastward toward Maiwand village, which covers the western entrance to the pass of the same name. If General Burrows' eye could have penetrated that haze, probably he would have considered it prudent to take up a defensive position, for which Mundabad presented many advantages. But he was firm in the conviction that the enemy's guns were not up, notwithstanding the reports of spies to the contrary; he believed that a favourable opportunity presented itself for taking the initiative, and he resolved to attack with all possible speed.

Lieutenant Maclaine of the Horse-Artillery, a gallant young officer who was soon to meet a melancholy fate, precipitated events in a somewhat reckless fashion. With the two guns he commanded he crossed the ravine, galloped across the plain, and opened fire on a body of

Afghan cavalry which had just come within view. General
Nuttall, commanding the cavalry and horse-artillery, fail-
ing to recall Maclaine, sent forward in support of
him the four remaining guns of the battery. Those
approached to within 800 yards of the two advanced
pieces, and Maclaine was directed to fall back upon the
battery pending the arrival of the brigade, which General
Burrows was now sending forward. It crossed the ravine
near Mundabad, advanced on the plain about a mile in a
north-westerly direction, and then formed up. There
were several changes in the dispositions ; when the engagement became warm about noon the formation was
as follows :—The 66th foot was on the right, its right
flank thrown back to check an attempt made to turn it
by a rush of ghazees springing out of the ravine in the
British front ; on the left of the 66th were four companies
of Jacob's Rifles (30th Native Infantry) and a company
of sappers, the centre was occupied by the horse-artillery
and smooth bore guns, of which latter, however, two had
been moved to the right flank ; on the left of the guns
were the 1st Grenadiers somewhat refused, and on the
extreme left two companies of Jacob's Rifles. The cavalry
was in the rear, engaged in efforts to prevent the Afghans
from taking the British infantry in reverse. The position
was radically faulty, and indeed invited disaster. Both
flanks were *en l'air* in face of an enemy of greatly superior
strength ; almost from the first every rifle was in the
fighting line, and the sole reserve consisted of the two
cavalry regiments. The baggage had followed the brigade
across the ravine and was halted about 1000 yards in rear
of the right, inadequately guarded by cavalry detachments.

For half-an-hour no reply was made to the British shell fire, and an offensive movement at this time might have resulted in success. But presently battery after battery was brought into action by the Afghans, until half-an-hour after noon the fire of thirty guns was concentrated on the brigade. Under cover of this artillery fire the ghazees from the ravine charged forward to within 500 yards of the 66th, but the rifle fire of the British regiment drove them back with heavy loss, and they recoiled as far as the ravine, whence they maintained a desultory fire. The enemy's artillery fire was well sustained and effective; the infantry found some protection from it in lying down, but the artillery and cavalry remained exposed and suffered severely. An artillery duel was maintained for two hours, greatly to the disadvantage of the brigade, which had but twelve guns in action against thirty well-served Afghan pieces. The prostrate infantry had escaped serious punishment, but by two P.M. the cavalry had lost fourteen per cent. of the men in the front line, and 149 horses; the Afghan horsemen had turned both flanks and the brigade was all but surrounded, while a separate attack was being made on the baggage. Heat and want of water were telling heavily on the sepoys, who were further demoralised by the Afghan artillery fire.

A little later the smooth bore guns had to be withdrawn for want of ammunition. This was the signal for a general advance of the Afghans. Their guns were pushed forward with great boldness; their cavalry streamed round the British left; in the right rear were masses of mounted and dismounted irregulars who had seized the villages on the British line of retreat. Swarms of ghazees soon showed themselves threatening the centre and left ; those in front of the 66th were still held in check by the steady volleys fired by that regiment. At sight of the ghazees, and cowed by the heavy artillery fire and the loss of their officers, the two companies of Jacob's Rifles on the left suddenly fell into confusion, and broke into the ranks of the Grenadiers. That regiment had behaved well but it caught the infection of demoralisation, the whole left collapsed, and the sepoys in utter panic, surrounded by and intermingled with the ghazees, rolled in a great wave upon the right. The artillerymen and sappers made a gallant stand, fighting the ghazees hand-to-hand with handspikes and rammers, while the guns poured canister into the advancing masses. Slade reluctantly limbered up and took his four guns out of action ; Maclaine remained in action until the ghazees were at the muzzles of his two guns, which fell into the enemy's hands. The torrent of mingled sepoys and ghazees broke in upon the 66th, and overwhelmed that regiment. The slaughter of the sepoys was appalling—so utterly cowed were they that they scarcely attempted to defend themselves, and allowed themselves without resistance to be dragged out of the ranks and killed. A cavalry charge was ordered in the direction of the captured guns, but it failed and the troopers retired in disorder. The infantry, assailed by hordes of fierce and triumphant ghazees, staggered away to the right, the 66th alone maintaining any show of formation, until the ravine was crossed, when the broken remnants of the sepoy regiments took to flight toward the east and the General's efforts to rally them were wholly unavailing. The 66th with some of the sappers and grenadiers, made a gallant stand round its colours in an enclosure near the village of Khig. There Colonel Galbraith and several of his officers were killed, and the little body of brave men becoming outflanked, continued its retreat, making stand after stand until most were slain. The Afghans pursued for about four miles, but were checked by a detachment of rallied cavalry, and desisted. The fugitives, forming with wounded and baggage a straggling column upwards of six miles long, crossed the waterless desert sixteen miles wide, to Hanz-i-Madat, which was reached about midnight and where water was found. From Asu Khan, where cultivation began, to Kokoran near Candahar, the retreat was harassed by armed villagers and the troops had to fight more or less all the way. Officers and men were killed, Lieutenant Maclaine was taken prisoner, and five of the smooth bore guns had to be abandoned because of the exhaustion of the teams. About midday of the 28th the broken remnants of the brigade reached Candahar. When the casualties were ascertained it became evident how disastrous to the British arms had been the combat of Maiwand. Out of a total of 2476 engaged no fewer than 964 were killed. The wounded numbered 167 ; 331 followers and 201 horses were killed and seven followers and sixty-eight horses wounded. Since Chillianwallah the British arms in Asia had not suffered loss so severe.

The spirit of the Candahar force suffered materially from the Maiwand disaster, and it was held that there was no alternative but to accept the humiliation of a siege within the fortified city. The cantonments were abandoned, the whole force was withdrawn into Candahar, and was detailed for duty on the city walls. The effective garrison on the night of the 28th numbered 4360, including the survivors of the Maiwand brigade. So alert were the Afghans that a cavalry reconnaissance made on the morning of the 29th, found the cantonments plundered and partly burned and the vicinity of Candahar swarming with armed men. The whole Afghan population amounting to about 12,000 persons, were compelled to leave the city, and then the work of placing it in a state of defence was energetically undertaken. Buildings and enclosures affording cover too close to the enceinte were razed, communication along the walls was opened up, and gun platforms were constructed in the more commanding positions. The walls were both high and thick, but they were considerably dilapidated and there were gaps and breaks in the bastions and parapet. The weak places as well as the gates were fronted with abattis, the defects were made good with sandbags, and wire entanglements and other obstructions were laid down outside the walls. While this work was in progress the covering parties were in daily collision with the enemy, and occasional sharp skirmishes occurred.

On the 8th August Ayoub opened fire on the citadel from Picquet hill, an elevation north-westward of the city, and a few days later he brought guns into action from the villages of Deh Khoja and Deh Khati on the east and south. This fire, steadily maintained though it was day after day, had little effect, and the return fire gave good results. It was not easy to invest the city since on the west and north there was no cover for the besiegers, but in Deh Khoja on the east there was ample protection for batteries, and the ground on the south-west was very favourable. Its advantages were improved so skilfully that it was at one time believed there was a European engineer in Ayoub's camp. Deh Khoja was inconveniently near the Cabul gate, and was always full of men. So menacing was the attitude of the Afghans that a sortie was resolved on against the village, which was conducted with resolution but resulted in utter failure. The attempt was made on the morning of the 16th. The cavalry went out to hinder reinforcements from entering the village from the eastward. An infantry force 800 strong commanded by Brigadier-General Brooke and divided into three parties, moved out later covered by a heavy artillery fire from the city walls. The village was reached, but was so full of enemies in occupation of the fortress-like houses that it was found untenable, and the three detachments extricated themselves separately. In the course of the retirement General Brooke and Captain Cruickshank were killed. The casualties were very heavy ; 106 were killed and 117 were wounded.

The tidings of the Maiwand disaster reached Cabul on the 29th July by telegram from Simla. The intention of the military authorities had already been intimated that the Cabul force should evacuate Afghanistan in two separate bodies and by two distinct routes. Sir Donald Stewart was to march one portion by the Khyber route ; the other under Sir Frederick Roberts was to retire by the Kuram valley, which Watson's division had been garrisoning since Roberts had crossed the Shutargurdan in September 1879. But the Maiwand news interfered

with those arrangements.   Stewart and Roberts concurred
in the necessity of retrieving the Maiwand disaster by the
despatch of a division from Cabul.   Roberts promptly
offered to lead that division, and as promptly the offer
was accepted by Stewart.   By arrangement with the
latter Roberts telegraphed to Simla urging that a force
should be despatched from Cabul without delay; and recognising that the authorities might hesitate to send on
this errand troops already under orders to return to India,
he took it on himself to guarantee that none of the soldiers
would demur, providing he was authorised to give the
assurance that after the work in the field was over they
would not be detained in garrison at Candahar.   The
Viceroy's sanction came on the 3d August.   The constitution and equipment of the force were entrusted to the two
generals ; and in reply to questions His Excellency was
informed that Roberts would march on the 8th and
expected to reach Candahar on 2d September.   Sir
Donald Stewart gave his junior full freedom to select the
troops to accompany him, and placed at his disposal the
entire resources of the army in transport and equipment.
It cannot truly be said that it was the *elite* of the Cabul
field force which constituted the column led by Roberts
in his famous march to Candahar.   Of the native infantry
regiments of his own original force which he had mustered
eleven months previously in the Kuram only two followed
him to Candahar, the 5th Goorkhas and 23d Pioneers,
and the second mountain battery adhered to him staunchly,
Of his original white troops the 9th Lancers, as ever, were
ready for the march.   His senior infantry regiment, the
67th, would fain have gone, but the good old corps was

weak from casualties and sickness, and the gallant Knowles denied himself in the interests of his men. The two Highland regiments, the 72d and 92d, had done an infinity of fighting and marching, but both had received strong drafts, were in fine condition, and were not to be hindered from following the chief whom, though not of their northern blood, the stalwart sons of the mist swore by as one man.

Sir Frederick Roberts had already represented that it would be impolitic to require the native regiments to remain absent from India and their homes for a longer period than two years. In the case of many of the regiments that term was closely approached, and the men after prolonged absence and arduous toil needed rest and were longing to rejoin their families. 'It was not,' in the words of General Chapman, 'with eager desire that the honour of marching to Candahar was sought for, and some commanding officers of experience judged rightly the tempers of their men when they represented for the General's consideration the claims of the regiments they commanded to be relieved as soon as possible from field service. . . . The enthusiasm which carried Sir Frederick Roberts' force with exceptional rapidity to Candahar was an after-growth evolved by the enterprise itself, and came as a response to the unfailing spirit which animated the leader himself.' The constitution of the force was made known by the general orders published on 3d August. It consisted of three batteries of artillery commanded by Colonel Alured Johnson; of a cavalry brigade of four regiments commanded by Brigadier - General Hugh Gough; and of an infantry division of three brigades commanded by Major-General John Ross. The first brigade was commanded by Brigadier-General Herbert Macpherson, the second by Brigadier-General T. D. Baker, and the third by Brigadier-General Charles Macgregor. Colonel Chapman, R.A., who had served in the same capacity with Sir Donald Stewart, was now Roberts' chief of staff. The marching out strength of the column was about 10,000 men, of whom 2835 were Europeans. Speed being an object and since the column might have to traverse rough ground, no wheeled artillery or transport accompanied it; the guns were carried on mules, the baggage was severely cut down, the supplies carried were reduced to a minimum, and the transport animals, numbering 8590, consisted of mules, ponies, and donkeys. It was known that the country could supply flour, sheep, and forage.

The time specified for the departure of the force from Sherpur was kept to the day. On the 8th the brigades moved out a short distance into camp, and on the following morning the march begun in earnest. The distance from Cabul to Candahar is about 320 miles, and the march naturally divides itself into three parts; from Cabul to Ghuznee, ninety-eight miles; from Ghuznee to Khelat-i-Ghilzai, one hundred and thirty-four miles; and from Khelat-i-Ghilzai to Candahar, eighty-eight miles. Ghuznee was reached on the seventh day, the daily average being fourteen miles—excellent work for troops unseasoned to long continuous travel, tramping steadily in a temperature of from 84° to 92° in the shade. When possible the force moved on a broad front, the brigades and regiments leading by rotation, and halts were made at specified intervals. The 'rouse' sounded at 2.45 A.M. and the march began at four; the troops were generally in camp by two P.M. and the baggage was usually reported all in by five; but the rearguard had both hard work and long hours. There was no sign of opposition anywhere, not a single load of baggage was left behind, comparatively few men fell out foot-sore, and the troops were steadily increasing in endurance and capacity of rapid and continuous marching.

At Ghuznee there was no rest day, and the steadfast dogged march was resumed on the morning of the 16th. The strain of this day's long tramp of twenty miles to Yergati was severe, but the men rallied gamely, and the General by dint of care and expedient was able to keep up the high pressure. 'The method,' writes General Chapman, 'of such marching as was now put in practice is not easy to describe; it combined the extreme of freedom in movement with carefully regulated halts, and the closest control in every portion of the column; it employed the individual intelligence of each man composing the masses in motion, and called on all for exertion in overcoming the difficulties of the march, in bearing its extraordinary toil, and in aiding the accomplishment of the object in view.' On the 20th a distance of twenty-one miles was covered—the longest day's march made; the effort was distressing owing to the heat and the lack of shade, but it was enforced by the absence of water. There was no relaxation in the rate of marching, and Khelat-i-Ghilzai was reached on the eighth day from Ghuznee, showing a daily average of nearly seventeen miles.

The 24th was a halt day at Khelat-i-Ghilzai, where

Sir Frederick Roberts received a letter from General Primrose in Candahar, describing the sortie made on the village of Deh Khoja and giving details of his situation. It was resolved to evacuate Khelat-i-Ghilzai and take on its garrison with the column, which on the 25th resumed its march to Candahar. On his arrival at Tir Andaz on the following day the General found a letter from Candahar, informing him that at the news of the approach of the Cabul force Ayoub Khan had withdrawn from his investment of Candahar, and had shifted his camp to the village of Mazra in the Urgundab valley, nearly due north of Candahar. On the morning of the 27th General Hugh Gough was sent forward with two cavalry regiments a distance of thirty-four miles to Robat, the main column moving on to Khel Akhund, half way to the former place. Gough was accompanied by Captain Straton the principal signalling officer of the force, who was successful in communicating with Candahar, and in the afternoon Colonel St John, Major Leach, and Major Adam rode out to Robat, bringing the information that Ayoub Khan was engaged in strengthening his position in the Urgundab valley, and apparently had the intention to risk the issue of a battle. On the 28th the whole force was concentrated at Robat; and as it was desirable that the troops should reach Candahar fresh and ready for prompt action, the General decided to make the 29th a rest day and divide the nineteen miles from Robat to Candahar into two short marches.

The long forced march from Cabul may be regarded as having ended at Robat. The distance between those two places, 303 miles, had been covered in twenty days.

It is customary in a long march to allow two rest days in each week, but Roberts had granted his force but a single rest day in the twenty days of its strenuous march. Including this rest day, the average daily march was a fraction over fifteen miles. As a feat of marching by a regular force of 10,000 men encumbered with baggage and followers, this achievement is unique, and it could have been accomplished only by thorough organisation and steady vigorous energy. Sir Frederick Roberts was so fortunate as to encounter no opposition. For this immunity he was indebted mainly to the stern lessons given to the tribesmen by Sir Donald Stewart at Ahmed Khel and Urzoo while that resolute soldier was marching from Candahar to Cabul, and in a measure also to the good offices of the new Ameer. But it must be re-membered that Roberts had no assurance of exemption from hostile efforts to block his path, and that he marched ever ready to fight. It will long be remembered how when Roberts had started on the long swift march, the suspense as to its issue grew and swelled until the strain became intense. The safety of the garrison of Candahar was in grave hazard; the British prestige, impaired by the disaster of Maiwand, was trembling in the balance. The days passed, and there came no news of Roberts and of the 10,000 men with whom the wise, daring little chief had cut loose from any base and struck for his goal through a region of ill repute for fanaticism and bitter hostility. The pessimists among us held him to be rushing on his ruin. But Roberts marched light; he lived on what the country supplied; he gave the tribes-men no time to concentrate against him; and two days

in advance of the time he had set himself he reached
Candahar at the head of a force in full freshness of vigour
and burning with zeal for immediate battle.

While halted at Robat on the 29th Sir Frederick
heard from General Phayre that his division had been
retarded in its march by lack of transport, but that he
hoped to have it assembled at Killa Abdoolla on the 28th,
and would be able to move toward Candahar on the 30th.
But as Killa Abdoolla is distant some eight marches from
Candahar, it was obvious that General Phayre could not
arrive in time to share in the impending battle. On the
morning of the 31st the Cabul force reached Candahar.
Sir Frederick Roberts, who had been suffering from fever
for some days, was able to leave his dhooly and mount
his horse in time to meet General Primrose and his
officers to the east of Deh Khoja. The troops halted and
breakfasted outside the Shikapore gate, while General
Roberts entered the city and paid a visit to the Wali
Shere Ali Khan. On his arrival he assumed command of
the troops in Southern Afghanistan; and he remained
resting in the city while the Cabul force marched to its
selected camping ground near the destroyed cantonments on the north-west of Candahar. A few shots were
fired, but the ground was occupied without opposition.
Baker's brigade was on the right, camped in rear of
Picquet hill, in the centre was Macpherson's brigade
sheltered in its front by Karez hill, and on the left among
orchards and enclosures was Macgregor's brigade, in rear
of which was the cavalry.

CHAPTER IX

THE BATTLE OF CANDAHAR

Although Yakoub Khan had ceased to beleaguer Candahar, he had withdrawn from that fortress but a very short distance, and the position he had taken up was of considerable strength. The Urgundab valley is separated on the north-west from the Candahar plain by a long precipitous spur trending south-west from the mountainous mass forming the eastern boundary of the valley further north. Where the spur quits the main range, due north of the city, the Murcha Pass affords communication between the Candahar plain and the Urgundab valley. The spur, its summit serrated by alternate heights and depressions, is again crossed lower down by an easy pass known as the Babawali Kotul. It is continued beyond this saddle for about a mile, still maintaining its south-westerly trend, never losing its precipitous character, and steeply scarped on its eastern face; and it finally ends in the plain in a steep descent of several hundred feet. The section of it from the Babawali Kotul to its south-western termination is known as the Pir Paimal hill, from a village of that name in the valley near its extremity. Ayoub Khan had made his camp near the village of Mazra, behind the curtain formed by the

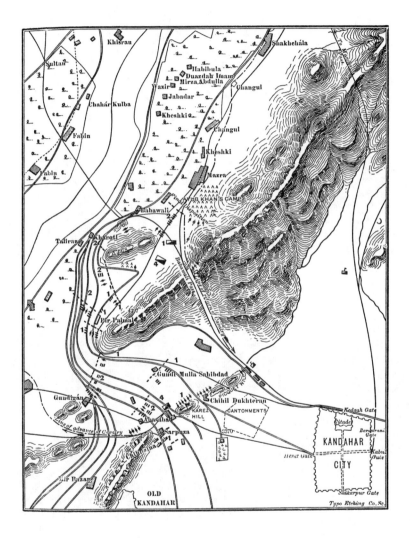

Khisrau

Sultan

Chahár Kulba

Fabin

Fabin

Shakhshála

Habibula
Duazdah Imam
Mirza Abdulla
Wazir
Jabadar
Kheshki
Changul
Changul
Kheshki
Mazra

AYUB KHAN'S CAMP

Babawali

Tahraz
Kharoti

Pir Paimal

Gundi Mulla Sahibdad
Chihil Dukhteran
CANTONMENTS
Gundigan
Karez Hill
Line of advance of Cavalry
Abasabad
Narpuza
Churzina
Pir Bazar

Kedgah Gate
Citadel
Bardurani Gate
KANDAHAR
Herat Gate
Kabul Gate
CITY
Shikarpur Gate

OLD
KANDAHAR

Typo Etching Co. Sc.

spur described, and about a mile higher up in the valley than the point at which the spur is crossed by the road over the Babawali Kotul. He was thus, with that point artificially strengthened and defended by artillery, well protected against a direct attack from the direction of Candahar, and was exposed only to the risk of a turning movement round the extremity of the Pir Paimal hill. Such a movement might be made the reverse of easy. A force advancing to attempt it must do so exposed to fire from the commanding summit of the Pir Paimal; around the base of that elevation there were several plain villages, and an expanse of enclosed orchards and gardens which strongly held were capable of stubborn defence. In the valley behind the Pir Paimal hill there was the lofty detached Kharoti hill, the fire from which would meet in the teeth a force essaying the turning movement; and the interval between the two hills, through which was the access to the Mazra camps, was obstructed by deep irrigation channels whose banks afforded cover for defensive fire, and could be swept by a cross fire from the hills on either flank.

Sir Frederick Roberts at a glance had perceived that a direct attack by the Babawali Kotul must involve very heavy loss, and he resolved on the alternative of turning the Afghan position. A reconnaissance was made on the afternoon of the 31st by General Gough, accompanied by Colonel Chapman. He penetrated to within a short distance of the village of Pir Paimal, where it was ascertained that the enemy were strongly entrenched, and where several guns were unmasked. A great deal of valuable information was obtained before the enemy began to interfere with the leisurely withdrawal. The cavalry suffered little, but the Sikh infantry covering the retirement of the reconnaissance were hard pressed by great masses of Afghan regulars and irregulars. So boldly did the enemy come on that the third and part of the first brigade came into action, and the firing did not cease until the evening. The enemy were clearly in the belief that the reconnaissance was an advance in force which they had been able to check and indeed drive in, and they were opportunely audacious in the misapprehension that they had gained a success. The information brought in decided the General to attack on the following morning; and having matured his dispositions, he explained them personally to the commanding officers in the early morning of September 1st. The plan of attack was perfectly simple. The Babawali Kotul was to be plied with a brisk cannonade and threatened by demonstrations both of cavalry and infantry; while the first and second brigades, with the third in reserve, were to turn the extremity of the Pir Paimal hill, force the enemy's right in the interval between that hill and the Kharoti eminence, take in reverse the Babawali Kotul, and pressing on up the Urgundab valley, carry Ayoub Khan's principal camp at Mazra. The Bombay cavalry brigade was to watch the roads over the Murcha and Babawali Kotuls, supported by infantry and artillery belonging to General Primrose's command, part of which was also detailed for the protection of the city; and to hold the ground from which the Cabul brigades were to advance. General Gough was to take the cavalry of the Cabul column across the Urgundab, so as to reach by a wide circuit the anticipated line of the Afghan retreat.

Soon after nine A.M. the forty-pounders on the right of Picquet hill began a vigorous cannonade of the Babawali Kotul, which was sturdily replied to by the three field-guns the enemy had in battery on that elevation. It had been early apparent that the Ayoub's army was in great heart, and apparently meditating an offensive movement had moved out so far into the plain as to occupy the villages of Mulla Sahibdad opposite the British right, and Gundigan on the left front of the British left. Both villages were right in the fair way of Roberts' intended line of advance; they, the adjacent enclosures, and the interval between the villages were strongly held, and manifestly the first thing to be done was to force the enemy back from those advanced positions. Two batteries opened a heavy shell fire on the Sahibdad village, under cover of which Macpherson advanced his brigade against it, the 2d Goorkhas and 92d Highlanders in his first line. Simultaneously Baker moved out to the assault of Gundigan, clearing the gardens and orchards between him and that village, and keeping touch as he advanced with the first brigade.

The shell fire compelled the Afghan occupants of Sahibdad to lie close, and it was not until they were near the village that Macpherson's two leading regiments encountered much opposition. It was carried at the bayonet point after a very stubborn resistance; the place was full of ghazees who threw their lives away recklessly, and continued to fire on the British soldiers from houses and cellars after the streets had been cleared. The 92d lost several men, but the Afghans were severely punished; it was reported that 200 were killed in this village alone.

While a detachment remained to clear out the village, the brigade under a heavy fire from the slopes and crest of the Pir Paimal hill moved on in the direction of that hill's south-western extremity, the progress of the troops impeded by obstacles in the shape of dry water-cuts, orchards, and walled enclosures, every yard of which was infested by enemies and had to be made good by steady fighting.

While Macpherson was advancing on Sahibdad, Baker's brigade had been pushing on through complicated lanes and walled enclosures toward the village of Gundigan. The opposition experienced was very resolute. The Afghans held their ground behind loopholed walls which had to be carried by storm, and they did not hesitate to take the offensive by making vigorous counter-rushes. Baker's two leading regiments were the 72d and the 2d Sikhs. The left wing of the former supported by the 5th Goorkhas, the old and tried comrades of the 72d, assailed and took the village. Its right wing fought its way through the orchards between it and Sahibdad, in the course of which work it came under a severe enfilading fire from a loopholed wall which the Sikhs on the right were attempting to turn. Captain Frome and several men had been struck down and the hot fire had staggered the Highlanders, when their chief, Colonel Brownlow, came up on foot. That gallant soldier gave the word for a rush, but immediately fell mortally wounded. After much hard fighting Baker's brigade got forward into opener country, but was then exposed to the fire of an Afghan battery near the extremity of the Pir Paimal spur, and to the attacks of great bodies of ghazees, which were withstood stoutly by the Sikhs and driven off by a bayonet attack delivered by the Highlanders.

The two brigades had accomplished the first part of their task. They were now in alignment with each other ; and the work before them was to accomplish the turning movement round the steep extremity of the Pir Paimal ridge. Macpherson's brigade, hugging the face of the elevation, brought up the left shoulder and having accomplished the turning movement, swept up the valley and carried the village of Pir Paimal by a series of rushes. Here, however, Major White commanding the advance of the 92d, found himself confronted by great masses of the enemy, who appeared determined to make a resolute stand about their guns which were in position south-west of the Babawali Kotul. Reinforcements were observed hurrying up from Ayoub's standing camp at Mazra, and the Afghan guns on the Kotul had been reversed so that their fire should enfilade the British advance. Discerning that in such circumstances prompt action was imperative, Macpherson determined to storm the position without waiting for reinforcements. The 92d under Major White led the way, covered by the fire of a field battery and supported by the 5th Goorkhas and the 23d Pioneers. Springing out of a watercourse at the challenge of their leader, the Highlanders rushed across the open ground. The Afghans, sheltered by high banks, fired steadily and well ; their riflemen from the Pir Paimal slopes poured in a sharp cross fire; their guns were well served. But the Scottish soldiers were not to be denied. Their losses were severe, but they took the guns at the point of the bayonet, and valiantly supported by the Goorkhas and pioneers, shattered and dispersed the mass of Afghans, which was reckoned to have numbered some 8000 men. No chance was given the enemy to rally. They were headed off from the Pir Paimal slopes by Macpherson. Baker hustled them out of cover in the watercourses in the basin on the left, and while one stream of fugitives poured away across the river, another rolled backward into and through Ayoub's camp at Mazra.

While Macpherson had effected his turning movement close under the ridge, Baker's troops on the left had to make a wider sweep before bringing up the left shoulder and wheeling into the hollow between the Pir Paimal and the Kharoti hill. They swept out of their path what opposition they encountered, and moved up the centre of the hollow, where their commander halted them until Macpherson's brigade on the right, having accomplished its more arduous work, should come up and restore the alignment. Baker had sent Colonel Money with a half battalion away to the left to take possession of the Kharoti hill, where he found and captured three Afghan guns. Pressing toward the northern end of the hill, Money to his surprise found himself in full view of Ayoub's camp, which was then full of men and in rear of which a line of cavalry was drawn up. Money was too weak to attack alone and sent to General Baker for reinforcements which, however, could not be spared him, and the gallant Money had perforce to remain looking on while the advance of Macpherson and Baker caused the evacuation of Ayoub's camp and the flight of his cavalry and infantry toward the Urgundab. But the discovery and capture of five more Afghan cannon near Babawali village was some consolation for the enforced inaction.

Considerable numbers of Ayoub's troops had earlier pushed through the Babawali Pass, and moved down toward the right front of General Burrows' Bombay brigade in position about Picquet hill. Having assured himself that Burrows was able to hold his own, Sir Frederick Roberts ordered Macgregor to move the third brigade forward toward Pir Paimal village, whither he himself rode. On his arrival there he found that the first and second brigades were already quite a mile in advance. The battle really had already been won but there being no open view to the front General Ross, who commanded the whole infantry division, had no means of discerning this result ; and anticipating the likelihood that Ayoub's camp at Mazra would have to be taken by storm, he halted the brigades to replenish ammunition. This delay gave opportunity for the entire evacuation of the Afghan camp, which when reached without any further opposition and entered at one P.M. was found to be deserted. The tents had been left standing ; ' all the rude equipage of a half barbarous army had been abandoned —the meat in the cooking pots, the bread half kneaded in the earthen vessels, the bazaar with its *ghee* pots, dried fruits, flour, and corn.' Ayoub's great marquee had been precipitately abandoned, and the fine carpets covering its floor were left. But in the hurry of their flight the Afghans had found time to illustrate their barbarity by murdering their prisoner Lieutenant Maclaine, whose body was found near Ayoub's tent with the throat cut.

To this deed Ayoub does not seem to have been privy. The sepoys who were prisoners with Maclaine testified that Ayoub fled about eleven o'clock, leaving the prisoners in charge of the guard with no instructions beyond a verbal order that they were not to be killed. It was more than an hour later when the guard ordered the unfortunate officer out of his tent and took his life.

The victory was complete and Ayoub's army was in full rout. Unfortunately no cavalry were in hand for a pursuit from the Mazra camp. The scheme for intercepting the fugitive Afghans by sending the cavalry brigade on a wide movement across the Urgundab, and striking the line of their probable retreat toward the Khakrez valley, may have been ingenious in conception, but in practice did not have the desired effect. But Ayoub had been decisively beaten. He had lost the whole of his artillery numbering thirty-two pieces, his camp, an immense quantity of ammunition, about 1000 men killed; his army was dispersed, and he himself was a fugitive with a mere handful along with him of the army of 12,000 men whom he had commanded in the morning.

The battle of Candahar was an effective finale to the latest of our Afghan wars, and it is in this sense that it is chiefly memorable. The gallant men who participated in the winning of it must have been the first to smile at the epithets of 'glorious' and 'brilliant' which were lavished on the victory. In truth, if it had not been a victory our arms would have sustained a grave discredit. The soldiers of Roberts and Stewart had been accustomed to fight and to conquer against heavy numerical odds, which were fairly balanced by their discipline and the superiority of their armament. But in the battle of Candahar the numerical disparity was non-existent, and Ayoub had immensely the disadvantage as regarded trained strength. His force according to the reckoning ascertained by the British general, amounted all told to 12,800 men. The strength of the British force, not including the detail of Bombay troops garrisoning Candahar, was over 12,000. But this army 12,000 strong, consisted entirely of disciplined soldiers of whom over one-fifth were Europeans. The accepted analysis of Ayoub's army shows it to have consisted of 4000 regular infantry, 800 regular cavalry, 5000 tribal irregular infantry of whom an indefinite proportion was no doubt ghazees, and 3000 irregular horsemen. In artillery strength the two forces were nearly equal. When it is remembered that Charasiah was won by some 2500 soldiers of whom only about 800 were Europeans, contending against 10,000 Afghans in an exceptionally strong position and well provided with artillery, Sir Frederick Roberts' wise decision to make assurance doubly sure in dealing with Ayoub at Candahar stands out very strikingly. Perforce in his battles around Cabul he had taken risks, but because those adventures had for the most part been successful he was not the man to weaken the certainty of an all-important issue by refraining from putting into the field every soldier at his disposal. And he was wisely cautious in his tactics. That he was strong enough to make a direct attack by storming the Babawali Kotul and the Pir Paimal hill was clear in the light of previous experience. But if there was more 'brilliancy' in a direct attack, there was certain

to be heavier loss than would be incurred in the less
dashing turning movement, and Sir Frederick with the
true spirit of a commander chose the more artistic and less
bloody method of earning his victory. It did not cost
him dear. His casualties of the day were thirty-six
killed including three officers, and 218 wounded among
whom were nine officers.

The battle of Candahar brought to a close the latest
of our Afghan wars. Sir Frederick Roberts quitted
Candahar on the 9th September, and marched to Quetta
with part of his division. On the 15th October, at Sibi,
he resigned his command, and taking sick leave to
England sailed from Bombay on the 30th October.
His year of hard and successful service in Afghanistan
greatly enhanced his reputation as a prompt, skilful, and
enterprising soldier.

The Pisheen and Sibi valleys are the sole tangible
results remaining to us of the two campaigns in Afghanistan sketched in the second part of this volume—campaigns which cost the lives of many gallant men slain in
action or dead of disease, and involved the expenditure
of about twenty millions sterling. Lord Beaconsfield's
vaunted 'scientific frontier,' condemned by a consensus
of the best military opinions, was rejected by the Liberal
Government which had recently acceded to power, whose
decision was that both the Khyber Pass and the Kuram
valley should be abandoned. On this subject Sir
Frederick Roberts wrote with great shrewdness : 'We
have nothing to fear from Afghanistan, and the best
thing to do is to leave it as much as possible to itself.

It may not be very flattering to our *amour propre*, but I feel sure I am right when I say that the less the Afghans see of us the less they will dislike us. Should Russia in future years attempt to conquer Afghanistan, or invade India through it, we should have a better chance of attaching the Afghans to our interest if we avoid all interference with them in the meantime.' During the winter of 1880-1 the Khyber and the Kuram were evacuated by the British troops, the charge of keeping open and quiet the former being entrusted to tribal levies paid by the Indian Government.

So far, then, as regarded the north-western frontier, the *status quo ante* had been fallen back upon. But there was a keen difference of opinion in regard to the disposition of the salient angle furnished by Candahar. Throughout the British occupation and the negotiations with Abdurrahman, the annexation of Candahar had been consistently repudiated. The intention on our part announced was to separate it from Cabul, and to place it under the independent rule of a Barakzai prince. Such a prince had actually been appointed in Shere Ali Khan, and although that incompetent Sirdar was wise enough to abdicate a position for which he was not strong enough, this action did not relieve us from our pledges against annexation. Nevertheless many distinguished men whose opinions were abstractly entitled to weight, were strongly in favour of our retention of Candahar. Among those were the late Lord Napier of Magdala, Sir Henry Rawlinson, Sir Edward Hamley, Sir Donald Stewart, and Sir Frederick Roberts. Among the authorities opposed to the occupation of Candahar were such men as the late

Lord Lawrence and General Charles Gordon, Sir Robert Montgomery, Lord Wolseley, Sir Henry Norman, Sir John Adye, and Sir Archibald Alison.

While the professional experts differed and while the 'Candahar debates' in Parliament were vehement and prolonged, the issue, assuming that fidelity to pledges was still regarded as a national virtue, was perfectly clear and simple. In the frank words of Sir Lepel Griffin: 'We could not have remained in Candahar without a breach of faith.' And he added with unanswerable force: 'Our withdrawal was in direct accordance with the reiterated and solemn professions which I had been instructed to make, and the assurances of the Government of India to the chiefs and people of Cabul. . . . The wisdom of the policy of retiring from Candahar may be a fair matter for argument, but it was one on which both Governments were agreed. I am convinced that withdrawal, after our public assurances, was the only practicable policy.'

Lord Ripon acted on his instructions 'to keep in view the paramount importance of effecting a withdrawal from Candahar on the earliest suitable occasion.' The abdication of the Wali Shere Ali Khan cleared the air to some extent. A British garrison under the command of General Hume wintered in Candahar. Ayoub Khan was a competitor for the rulership of the southern province, but he received no encouragement, and after some negotiation the Ameer Abdurrahman was informed that Candahar was reincorporated with the kingdom of Afghanistan, and it was intimated to him that the capital would be given over to the Governor, accompanied by a suitable military force, whom he should send. On the 1st of April an Afghan force entered Candahar, followed presently by Mahomed Hassan Khan, the Governor nominated by the Ameer. General Hume soon after marched out, and after halting for a time in the Pishcen valley to watch the course of events in Candahar, he continued his march toward India. The restless Ayoub did not tamely submit to the arrangement which gave Candahar to Abdurrahman. Spite of many arduous difficulties, spite of lack of money and of mutinous troops, he set out toward Candahar in July 1881. Mahomed Hassan marched against him from Candahar, and a battle was fought at Maiwand on the anniversary of the defeat of General Burrows on the same field. Ayoub was the conqueror, and he straightway took possession of the capital and was for the time ruler of the province. But Abdurrahman, subsidised with English money and English arms, hurried from Cabul, encountered Ayoub outside the walls of Candahar, and inflicted on him a decisive defeat. His flight to Herat was followed up, he sustained a second reverse there, and took refuge in Persia. Abdurrahman's tenure of the Cabul sovereignty had been at first extremely precarious; but he proved a man at once strong, resolute, and politic. In little more than a year after his accession he was ruler of Shere Ali's Afghanistan; Candahar and Herat had both come to him, and that without very serious exertion. He continues to reign quietly, steadfastly, and firmly; and there never has been any serious friction between him and the Government of India, whose wise policy is a studied abstinence from interference in the internal affairs of the Afghan kingdom,

INDEX

——o——

THE END.